Praise for *Web Copy That Sells*

"When it comes to writing the words on your website that make people pull out their credit cards and buy whatever you're selling, Maria Veloso is an absolute genius. But what's truly amazing is her singular skill in simplifying the craft of writing web copy that sells into a discipline that's both learnable and infinitely easy."

—Thomas Myer, Freelance Technical Copywriter, www.myerman.com

"I am just blown away by the way Maria Veloso takes complicated copywriting techniques, such as applying psychological tactics, and explains them so that I, a copywriting newbie, can easily understand them. And not only understand them conceptually, but understand how to use them and feel comfortable using them in my writing. Maria is nothing short of a copywriting genius, and *Web Copy That Sells* is the most outstanding book for learning how to sell on the web."

—Tim Warren, Dallas, Texas, CEO of GreatMarketingStuff.com

"I have a pretty thorough grounding in offline copywriting, but I've found the methods and techniques described in your book quite mind-boggling. They go beyond common practice and embrace a practicality that makes the whole discipline very comfortable. Much of what you've introduced is applicable to offline work as well. I thank you for expanding my vision of how this craft can be practiced and for opening my mind to developing a much broader array of tools to use."

—Bruce Midgett, Owner, MBP Custom Publishers, Missoula, Montana

"Maria, I cannot even begin to tell you how much I'm enjoying myself writing copy the way you've taught it in your book! I just love it—and whenever I write copy for anyone, they're always blown away by the results! And I've just barely gotten started. I actually look forward to getting out of bed every single day to write this way. I'm so grateful that I found your book! This has changed my life—and at a time when I was stagnating after doing non-stop traditional marketing for over 20 years. So glad I found your book—so glad, so glad . . ."

—Susan B. Loebl, Web Copywriting Specialist, www.webcopywriting.us

"Maria, you have definitely revolutionized the proper techniques for writing web copy that sells! Your book is absolutely the most astonishing and easy-to-follow guide for business owners who want to take their business 10 steps forward and start making a name for themselves in the online world. Thank you, Maria. You're absolutely amazing!"

—Carlos Garcia, Publisher, *Wealthy Secrets* newsletter, London, Ontario, Canada

"*Web Copy That Sells* truly delivers on its promise of changing people's minds and accelerating their decision to buy. Maria Veloso's Neuro-Affective Principle is the most psychologically persuasive blueprint for writing copy I've ever come across, both online and offline. The first time I read a copy piece that employed the formula, I found it so enticing and irresistible that I was ready to buy even before knowing the price and obtaining the rest of the details. This book is essential for anyone who actually wants to make money online, whether as a copywriter or as someone seeking to boost website responses. It's definitely a book I plan to keep on my desk so that I can refer to it often."

—Diane Eble, Author of 11 books, Professional Book Publishing Coach/Consultant, and Copywriter, WordsToProfit.com

"*Web Copy That Sells* is the gold standard of web copywriting—the Rolls-Royce among the array of books and courses that teach the craft of writing copy specifically for the Internet. The Trifecta Neuro-Affective Principle that Maria Veloso teaches in this book is a compelling way to change prospects' minds in favor of your product or service, cause them to subconsciously 'feel right' about your offer, and cause them to look no further than your product or service to fulfill their needs. This formula alone is worth more than the book's weight in gold! The distillation of the formula into what Maria calls 'cyber bites' creates an extraordinary concentration of power in web copy and online marketing communications that produces extraordinary results. This book is a far cry from the sleazy, snake-oil-vendor type of salesmanship that is so prevalent on the Web—and is infinitely more irresistible. Internet buyers have no power to resist buying whatever is being sold using Maria's techniques! I personally believe Maria is, hands down, the best copywriter in the world, but what's even more impressive is her ability to teach the craft of web copywriting in a way that is simple enough for just about anyone to learn. The sophisticated and elegant, yet powerful, style of web copywriting she presents in this book is truly a testament to the doctrine that 'advertising is truth well told.'"

—Elin Bullmann, www.TheWriteEffect.com, Bend, Oregon

"Maria Veloso's book, *Web Copy That Sells,* is a godsend. It is the best thing I have read regarding writing for the Web because it specifically discusses the unique culture, mind-set, and psychology of the Internet population, and presents an easy-to-follow five-step formula for getting people to buy what you're selling on your website. I have bought lots of books for my extensive copywriting library and none come close to Maria's book."

—Eugene Pepper, La Canada, California

"*Web Copy That Sells* changed the way I thought about my online business and gave me all the tools and the proper direction that I needed to write my own web copy. As a result, I now have a thriving online business, and I successfully sell my products and services on the Internet using the copywriting skills I learned."

—Connie Ragen Green, www.EbookWritingandMarketingSecrets.com

"Maria Veloso's copywriting book is simply *incredible*! I got a copy of *Web Copy That Sells* in the mail, and it's the most amazing book on copywriting I have ever seen. Maria breaks it down into a simple process so easy that anyone can follow it. I always thought of myself as a gifted writer, but by following the steps in her well-laid-out book, I was able to take my writing to the next level. I love the power of words; I feel like this book has helped me unleash a whole new palette to paint with. The words that resulted were simple, compelling, and powerful. I'm so thankful for this incredible book!"

—Kristie Tamsevicius, Work at Home Expert, www.KristieT.com

"Maria Veloso is a fantastic teacher! In her book, *Web Copy That Sells*, she presents ideas clearly and powerfully, and they pull the reader along painlessly—just like her web copy does! I initially took this attitude: 'Okay, let's see if Maria can really get me salivating for her book!' Sure enough, after only three paragraphs, I was ready to purchase! A person would have to be 'brain-dead' to *not* feel the power of the kind of copy she teaches."

—Lloyd Standish, www.AnemiaAnswer.com, Cornville, Arizona

"Maria Veloso's book, *Web Copy That Sells*, provides the unique skills and techniques that enable a copywriter or anyone who writes online copy to flat-out sell like never before. These techniques are so powerful and dynamic it's hard to believe. I've read all the books on online copywriting but *Web Copy That Sells* is, by far, the very best to date. I recommend this book to anyone who really wants to make their site sell or needs to understand how to write e-mail and get it through the spam filters as well as get it read. This book covers it all. Maria Veloso has done a great job and provided a valuable service. I highly recommend this powerful book to all copywriters and anyone who needs to write copy for the Web."

—Susanna K.Hutcheson, Executive Creative Director,
Power Communications LLC, www.powerwriting.com

"I've been in the direct marketing field for countless years and have made a lot of money at it. I've also done a massive amount of reading and research on the subject of copy-writing, but Maria Veloso's book, *Web Copy That Sells,* stands out as one of the most memorable high points. It is superbly contructed—with zero fluff and puff. And it brings literally everything that's important about selling online together in one place. One standout worth its own mention is this: Never before has 'NLP for marketers' been introduced so well into a direct-response copy flow and made so accessible. As a Brit, I'm usually averse to obvious Yankisms—but this book really is 'awesome!' Well, well done."

—Chris Pay, United Kingdom

"This book is a *must-have*. I'm a good writer . . . but before I read this book, I didn't have a clue how to write web copy. I didn't really know how to get people to *read my whole website* and *buy*. I became so frustrated when I would look at my site stats. I noticed that people would go to my website, but they would only *stay for a few seconds* max. I did some research and I came across *Web Copy That Sells*. Since using the tips and sugges-tions that Maria talks about . . . I have seen a *complete turnaround* in how long people stay on my site. I am also able to *close more sales* for first-time visitors. This book is amazing!"

—Rachel Johnson, Website Owner and Copywriter, Miami, Florida

"I've read Hopkins, Caples, Collier, Sugarman, Schwab, Schwartz, Ogilvy, Bencivenga, Halbert, Carlton, Roy Williams, and many, many more-but Maria Veloso's book, *Web Copy That Sells,* is the best marketing book I've ever read."

—Chris Moreno, Kennebunkport, Maine

"*Web Copy That Sells* is far and away the best volume I've seen on writing for the Web. I'm already putting the techniques I learned from it into practice, and plan to read the book more than once."

—Peter Losh, Internet and E-Commerce Manager, FarStone Technology, Inc.

"Maria, I've just purchased your book, *Web Copy That Sells,* and started reading it. All I can say is . . . totally *amazing*! I have barely scratched the surface, yet I cannot believe the simplicity with which you break down the most important aspects of web copywriting! I am loving it . . . and must confess . . . you have lit the writer's fire in me once again! A while back, I enrolled in an expensive copywriting course offered by a prestigious writers' institute. Now that I have read your book, I can honestly say that course doesn't hold a candle to the advice you offer in *Web Copy That Sells*. Your unique 'mentoring' tone conveys an understanding of how human nature reacts, as a reader and writer of web copy. Your book is a refreshing change for the up-and-coming Internet entrepreneur who wants to master this make-or-break business tool. Thanks for giving me the advantage of making a connection with a 'true' voice in my education of web copywriting! *Web Copy That Sells* will enable my efforts at web copywriting . . . an attainable triumph!"

—Lourdes Torres, CEO and Founder, www.LatinoClicks.com,
North Smithfield, Rhode Island

"I read Maria's book, not once, not twice—but three times over the past three months. That's because each time I would immerse myself in her proven web copywriting concepts and formulas, something inevitably would happen. My online sales increased! That's why her powerful book is extremely difficult to put down. Especially when you start considering what can happen when you *apply her unique concepts* to your promotional articles, free reports, newsletters, online ads, autoresponder e-mails, or website copy."

—Tony Ostian, Certified Master of Web Copywriting, The Web Copy Guy

"*Web Copy That Sells* has certainly helped to usher in a whole new era for copywriting. That's why it's not just copywriting any more, it's *web copywriting*! The web copywriting process has been thoroughly tested and proven on the Internet. It works, and Maria shows you why and how! In her own convincing writing style she pours on an abundance of easy-to-understand concepts, strategies, and techniques and then supports all her claims. She literally walks you through the entire writing process effortlessly. Her knowledge is not only straightforward; her writing style is captivating, too. If you're looking for the "Sacred Book" on Web Copywriting. You've come to the right place!"

—Marshall A. Ronco, Web Copywriter, www.marcocopy.com

WEB COPY THAT SELLS

Second Edition

WEB COPY THAT SELLS

Second Edition

The Revolutionary Formula for Creating Killer Copy That Grabs Their Attention and Compels Them to Buy

Maria Veloso

⋅AMACOM

American Management Association

New York · Atlanta · Brussels · Chicago · Mexico City · San Francisco
Shanghai · Tokyo · Toronto · Washington, D. C.

Special discounts on bulk quantities of AMACOM books are available to corporations, professional associations, and other organizations. For details, contact Special Sales Department, AMACOM, a division of American Management Association, 1601 Broadway, New York, NY 10019. Tel.: 212–903–8316. Fax: 212–903–8083. Web site: www.amacombooks.org

This publication is designed to provide accurate and authoritative information in regard to the subject matter covered. It is sold with the understanding that the publisher is not engaged in rendering legal, accounting, or other professional service. If legal advice or other expert assistance is required, the services of a competent professional person should be sought.

Library of Congress Cataloging-in-Publication Data

Veloso, Maria.
   Web copy that sells : the revolutionary formula for creating killer copy that grabs their attention and compels them to buy / Maria Veloso—2nd ed.
      p.   cm.
   Includes index.
   ISBN 978-0-8144-1304-3
   1. Electronic commerce.   2. Web sites—Design.   3. Internet marketing.   4. Internet advertising.   I. Title.
HF5548.32.V45 2009
658.8'72—dc22

2008042436

Printing number
10 9 8 7 6 5 4 3 2 1

To laugh often and love much;
to win the respect of intelligent persons and the affection of children;
to earn the approbation of honest citizens and endure the betrayal of false friends;
to appreciate beauty;
to find the best in others;
to give of one's self;
to leave the world a bit better, whether by a healthy child,
a garden patch or a redeemed social condition;
to have played and laughed with enthusiasm and sung with exultation;
to know even one life has breathed easier because you have lived
—this is to have succeeded.

—Ralph Waldo Emerson

Contents

Foreword

On July 23, 2000, I received an e-mail with the following subject line:

> Subject: Mark, here are the Top 10 Reasons Why You Need to Have Me Working for You

I get hundreds of e-mails a day—but the subject line of this e-mail stopped me dead in my tracks. The e-mail was from a woman named Maria Veloso. Her e-mail began as follows:

> Dear Mark,
>
> Have you ever wished you could "clone" yourself so that all the ideas you have "in development" can materialize with lightning speed?

Then, the e-mail went on to give ten compelling reasons why Maria would be an asset to my company, Aesop Marketing Corporation.

I was sufficiently intrigued by her e-mail that I phoned her and told her that I might have a position for which she would qualify. However, I gave her this word of warning:

"It's the most miserable job you could possibly have in my company."

When I told her it was the job of a copywriter, she was puzzled. "Why do you think that's such a miserable job, Mark?" she asked.

"Because you'll be writing copy for me," I said. I told her I'd be extremely difficult to please because I had excruciatingly high standards. I also told her that because I had always done my own copywriting and never trusted anyone to write on my behalf, I'd constantly be cracking the whip on anyone who had the misfortune of becoming my copywriter.

Without skipping a beat, she said, "I'm up to the challenge, Mark."

I shook my head, feeling sorry that this woman didn't know what she was getting herself into. I agreed to interview her soon thereafter. She showed me her copywriting samples, and it was easy to tell that she was skilled in writing copy for the offline markets. But I wondered how well she could learn how to write web copy.

That's when she told me she's been a big fan of my unique approach to online copywriting for years—and that she had bought several products and services from my company over the years on the strength of the copy I wrote. She was eager to learn my style of copywriting and reiterated that she wanted to become my copywriting clone.

"Okay," I said. "You're hired!"

At the time, my company (Aesop) was already a multimillion-dollar enterprise and was enjoying international fame in Internet marketing circles because of the unconventional, nonconformist marketing campaigns we were running.

When I gave Maria her first copywriting assignment, I could tell she was eager to prove her skill as a copywriter. Three days later, when she handed me the copy she had written, I told her flat out that it wasn't the way I wanted copy at Aesop to be written. She definitely had great copywriting skills, but they were tailored for the offline world—not the web.

I thought my rebuff would discourage her, but she was undaunted. She was determined to learn the right way of writing web copy. Thus began my mentorship of Maria Veloso. I began to teach her the little-known mechanics and art of writing for the Internet buying public. She took copious notes and was a quick study. In as little as a few weeks' time, I saw her web copywriting begin to show promise.

In October 2000, two months after she started working for me, she handed me a six-page copy piece that pulled in *$18,000 in two days.* That was when I was convinced she was a *killer copywriter.* But that wasn't the end of her copywriting education. Not by a long shot.

Over the following months and years, I continued to conduct the most ambitious (and expensive) market testing ever attempted in Internet marketing. I hired an entire staff of programmers, statisticians, and analysts, whose only job was to test every conceivable element of the copy we produced at Aesop—from headlines to price points, offers, guarantees, formats, involvement devices, e-mail subject lines, lead-ins, and so on. You name it—I had my research staff test it, take the raw data, and convert it into usable form.

People called me "The Fanatic of Online Market Testing," but I rather enjoyed having that reputation. It was my attempt to identify those seemingly marginal elements of web copy and online marketing communications that made a significant difference in our sales figures. Because Aesop had amassed a database of millions of names, consisting of customers, subscribers, and prospects, we had the luxury of conducting huge marketing tests, wherein our test samples were as large as 20,000 names apiece—a number that was larger than most other companies' entire mailing lists. As a result, we produced the most scientifically validated—and conclusive—results ever obtained.

For 15 months, Maria had a ringside seat and witnessed the blow-by-blow action being churned out by my marketing statisticians and analysts. She was privy to some of the most priceless pieces of marketing intelligence ever assembled.

She saw, for instance that many of the concepts that I had introduced to Internet marketing, such as the Zeigarnik effect, cognitive dissonance, the linear path, and so on (see Chapter 5), had a dramatic effect on click-through rates and sales conversions. She saw the full-scale findings of what has become known as my *Confidential Internet Intelligence Manuscript,* which my marketing staff had assembled at a cost of over $237,000—a manuscript that revealed e-mail marketing strategies that work (see Chapter 7), among other things.

Having had the benefit of all this, Maria's copywriting had nowhere to go but up. Being armed with as much web copywriting ammunition as any of the copywriting greats alive, she took the ball and ran with it. She's one of the very few copywriters in the world who "get" web copywriting. I am deeply gratified to have been instrumental in her becoming one of the top copywriting professionals in the industry today.

That said, it is also flattering to see that Maria has taken many of the concepts I pioneered and tested, and distilled them into the book you now have in your hands. If you're tempted to take the concepts she presents on these pages for granted, I'm here to tell you that you're walking past a gold mine. If the results of my extensive marketing research are any indication, I can say, without a doubt, that the information in this book is well-founded and accurate.

Some of the information in this book is indescribably powerful. I encourage you to use it ethically to take your online sales—or your copywriting career if you're a copywriter—to the highest level.

Mark Joyner
#1 Best-Selling Author of
MindControlMarketing.com,
The Irresistible Offer
and others

Acknowledgment

This book would not have been possible if it weren't for the valuable lessons I learned from my mentor and friend, Mark Joyner. I owe a debt of gratitude to him for more things than I could possibly sum up here.

Mark was the first person I had ever seen use the editorial style of direct-response copywriting online. His approach to copywriting, where he wrapped his sales pitch in the cushions of an editorial piece, has become the copywriting model that I employ almost exclusively. It was Mark who taught me that writing sales copy for the web is distinctly different from writing sales copy for the offline (brick-and-mortar) world. Mark also taught me the significance of the prospect's frame of mind when it comes to selling (and it became the basis of my book *Frame-of-Mind Marketing: How to Convert Your Online Prospects into Customers*). Mark also introduced me to many of the psychological devices that I use in writing web copy, which have produced the signature model of web copywriting with which I'm identified today.

▶ *The Zeigarnik effect.* Although this principle has become widely used among marketers in recent years, Mark was the pioneer at successfully applying it to web copy and Internet marketing—along with the "linear path" methodology, which is part of his "Source of the Nile" theory.

▶ *Cognitive dissonance.* To my knowledge, this concept had never been mentioned in a marketing book prior to Mark's inclusion of it in his marketing course titled 1001 Killer Internet Marketing Tactics. Although other marketers may have previously used the cognitive dissonance technique, as well as the Zeigarnik effect, no one has ever identified the tandem concepts in relation to business and marketing or established their scientific validity the way Mark has.

Finally, the bulk of the e-mail strategies I discuss in Chapter 4 are owed in no small part to the research spearheaded by Mark at Aesop. For these reasons and more, I consider him the honorary coauthor of this book.

My goal is to bring what I've learned to you.

Maria Veloso
November 2008

Introduction to Second Edition

I cannot teach anybody anything,
I can only make them think.
—Socrates

The subtitle of this second edition of *Web Copy That Sells* is *The Revolutionary Formula for Creating Killer Copy That Grabs Their Attention and Compels Them to Buy.* The formula refers to the same one referred to in the first edition—a five-step blueprint or a template that anyone could easily use to create web copy that has a high likelihood of selling. But as with most formulas that do succeed at facilitating and simplifying the process of accomplishing a specific task, the end result may not always be as successful.

For instance, major motion picture studios have a formula that they follow when releasing a movie to the public. An entire marketing machinery consisting of movie trailer showings, publicity appearances by the stars of the movie, advertising, a glittering movie premiere, and a host of other promotional activities are put into motion months in advance of the movie's release. The formula makes the movie likely to become a box office hit. However, if the movie turns out to be not as popular with the moviegoing public as the studio executives had anticipated, box office sales will be disappointing.

Likewise, when someone uses the five-step formula for writing killer copy, the resulting copy and the sales it generates sometimes prove disappointing. That's because the effectiveness of a sales proposition depends on several variables, not the least of which is the marketer's (or copywriter's) ability to decide how to distill an entire sales proposition into the formula's framework. Decisions need to be made, and oftentimes the decisions a marketer or copywriter makes highlight a weaker point and ignore the most salient attributes of the product or service. Web copy that is built on such a poor foundation, therefore, has very little chance of selling, even when it follows the formula.

In this second edition, I've presented the remedy to all but eliminate the disappointing results that might come from the use of the formula. While the five-step formula remains the blueprint for writing web copy, I'm also presenting a heretofore unpublicized principle that I call the Trifecta Neuro-Affective Principle™. When utilized in any selling situation either on or off the web, this principle changes your prospects' minds in favor of your product or service and accelerates their decision to buy what you're selling.

In the context of the formula, the Trifecta Neuro-Affective Principle eliminates the need for you to make decisions about which points of your sales proposition to include or exclude because the principal triggers are predetermined for you. Proper implementation of the principle virtually guarantees successful results from the use of the formula and also dramatically shortens the need for superfluous words and long-scrolling copy that characterized early forms of copy on the web.

This comes at such an opportune time because the current landscape of Web 2.0 tends to favor short, succinct, digestible bites of copy, for which I coined the term *cyber bite*. Cyber bites have the power not only to create a sales-advancing impact on people but also potentially to become *memes* (a term coined by Richard Dawkins in 1976, derived from the words *mime* and *mimic,* representing cultural ideas that are passed from one individual to another in a manner analogous to the propagation of biological genes) that get transmitted verbally and virally, thereby creating significant buzz for any product or service.

The expanded material in this second edition makes this book not just for online marketers and copywriters but for anyone who sells anything—either on or off the web.

 Web copy refers to the words on a website, in an e-mail, or in other online marketing communications that cause prospects to do what you want them to do—pick up the phone, register, subscribe, or buy your product or service.

The World Wide Web is no longer in its infancy and the age of Web 2.0 is already upon us, yet I find that most people who do business on the Internet are still in the dark as far as selling on the web is concerned. The fact is, most companies, business enterprises, and entrepreneurs who are selling products and services on the Internet are still conducting marketing and sales operations online the way they do business in the brick-and-mortar world. They're still taking marketing principles that work well in the offline world and trying to force them to work on the web. And they still don't realize that many principles that are effective in print, on the radio, on billboards, in direct mail, and via other types of offline advertising simply do not translate well on the web. In fact, they can even kill sales.

Most of all, they still make the common mistake that most website owners, Internet entrepreneurs, and online companies make: *They drive traffic to their website before making sure they have web copy that sells.*

Words are the true currency of the web. The single most important ingredient in a commercial website is web copy. Words make the sale, and no amount of cool graphics, interactive bells and whistles, cutting-edge design, or sophisticated e-commerce infrastructure could ever compare to the selling ability of compelling web copy.

Because selling on the web is text driven, nothing happens until someone writes the words that get people to click, sign up, read, register, order, subscribe, or buy whatever you're selling. According to a four-year study, conducted by Stanford University and the Poynter

Institute for Media Studies and published in 2000, of the habits of Internet news readers on normally scrolling screens, "the first thing people look at on a webpage tends to be text." The Poynter Institute's more recent EyeTrack '07 study conducted in July 2007, which had 600 participants from 18 to 60 years old, corroborates the same.

I've sold everything from books to software to stock-picking services, franchises, self-improvement programs, career development products, handcrafted gifts and art pieces, consumable products, membership clubs, weight loss products, tax-saving programs, seminars, consulting services, and more on the web, and in the process I've learned that both the five-step blueprint, and the other principles and devices revealed in this book can help any website owner take a casual website visitor and turn that surfer into a prospect and, subsequently, into a customer—all through the sheer power of words.

Jakob Nielsen, one of the top usability engineers for the web and author of *Designing Web Usability* (Peachpit Press, 1999) and other books, wrote:

> Words are usually the main moneymakers on a website. Better writing is probably the single most important improvement you can make to your site.

For this reason, if you have a website (or plan to create one) that sells a product or service, you need to hire a web copywriter—or learn the craft of web copywriting yourself. This brings me to the reason for this book. When I wrote the first edition in 2004, I was motivated by the fact that every time I surfed the Internet I came across countless websites that were so poorly written that I couldn't imagine them generating a single sale. Some of those websites offered excellent products and services, but they utilized weak web copy that didn't do justice to the products and services. Several years have passed since the publication of that first edition, and I'm dumbfounded that most companies and individuals doing business on the web still haven't discovered how to use the power of words to sell effectively via their websites. It's a shame, because the web provides an incredible channel for marketing virtually anything to anybody in any part of the world.

Adding to the challenge facing website owners and Internet entrepreneurs is the fact that there is a scarcity of web copywriting specialists equipped to take on the unique challenge of web communication and online selling. This situation is unlikely to change in the foreseeable future because even with the increasing numbers of professional writers transitioning into web copywriting, the numbers of e-commerce websites that need professional web copywriting are increasing at an even faster pace. Consequently, even if you're a website owner, Internet entrepreneur, or online company that could find good web copywriters and could afford to pay their standard rates of $125 to $235 per hour, chances are that the good ones would be too busy to take on your project.

My solution—and my reason for writing this book—is to teach you the principles of web copywriting so you can write web copy yourself. Whether you are a businessperson writing your own copy or a writer entering the business or transitioning from other kinds of advertising copywriting, my goal is to teach you how to take your writing skills and apply them to web writing. Writing web copy that converts prospects into customers is a discipline all its own. It's a highly specialized genre of writing that combines marketing wherewithal with a deep understanding of the Internet's unique culture, mind-set, psychology, and language.

Additionally, this revised edition redefines web copy in the context of the continually evolving commercial landscape of the Internet and establishes updated rules for communicating successfully in what is being called Web 2.0—the second generation of web-based communities and applications, including but not limited to the following forms of online communications:

▶ Audio
▶ Video (such as YouTube, Yahoo! Video, and iFilm)

▶ Social networks (such as MySpace, Facebook, and LinkedIn)

▶ Blogs

▶ Viral communications

Furthermore, this new edition includes copywriting principles *not only* for direct-response types of websites (which was the central focus of the first edition) but also for corporations, advertising agencies, business-to-business markets, catalog-style businesses, and newbies who want to grow their online businesses with killer web copy. With Internet advertising revenues exceeding $21 billion in 2007 (source: Internet Advertising Bureau), due emphasis has also been given to strategies for writing short-form ads.

What most online businesspeople and some professional copywriters don't realize is that web copywriting is distinctly different from any other kind of advertising copywriting and offline marketing communications. It is also quite different from writing content for the web. Of course, it also bears some similarities to all of these. Additionally, web copy encompasses more than just words in cyberspace. It's a way of communicating on the web that takes into account the ever-changing lifestyles and preferences of the Internet buying population. Sometimes that includes the use of graphic depictions of words to better communicate ideas and change people's minds in favor of your product or service (see Chapter 6). The trends that are in a constant state of flux necessitate continuing education on how people are willing to consume marketing messages, as will be shown in the discussion of the YouTube revolution in Chapter 11.

In this second edition, it is also my objective to provide the newest strategies, techniques, devices, and tools for writing copy in a market that has become immune and unresponsive to the marketing strategies that were effective four or more years ago. Most of the general web copywriting rules that I presented in the first edition have remained the same, but the delivery and execution have changed with the times.

Who needs this book? You do, if you are

▶ An Internet marketer, entrepreneur, or website owner who sells (or plans to sell) a product or service online via your own e-commerce website

▶ A marketing professional who is in charge of your company's online sales operations (an advertising, marketing, or brand manager)

▶ An advertising professional who plans, approves, or executes Internet marketing campaigns or writes advertising copy on behalf of clients

▶ A writer who is tired of being underpaid and barely earning a living—and who wants to transition to the lucrative specialty of web copywriting

▶ A webmaster who wants to learn the skill of web copywriting in order to expand the services you provide your clients

▶ An aspiring online entrepreneur who is seeking the most cost-efficient way to start a successful online business using a simple web copywriting formula

▶ Someone with moderate-to-good writing skills who wants to become a highly paid professional writer in one of the hottest, most in-demand fields in today's marketplace

Whether or not you aspire to become a professional web copywriter, you can apply the principles presented in this book to any website, incorporate them into your marketing communications (e-mail, online advertising, newsletters, online video, audio, etc.), and generate measurably increased sales and profits.

Although the web copywriting principles I present herein are largely derived from direct-response types of web copy, they can be adapted to virtually all copywriting applications on the web. Whether your goal is to write web copy for branding purposes, generate leads, build a mailing list, generate more sales, obtain repeat

customers, ensure customer satisfaction, or improve customer retention, you will benefit from the principles revealed in this book
because they will sharpen the edges of your marketing messages,
making them more effective.

I've been writing advertising copy since 1977 and specializing in
web copywriting since 1996, and this gives me a broader perspective
of the craft than most people have. Yet I "stand on the shoulders of
giants," learning from those who came before me—masters of influence like Robert Cialdini and marketing legends like Rosser Reeves,
Victor Schwab, Robert Collier, and Eugene Schwartz—whose powerful concepts I've battle-tested and fine-tuned for the web.

WHAT THIS BOOK WILL DO FOR YOU ▼

When I encountered the World Wide Web in 1996, I already had 19
years of copywriting experience under my belt, but I soon discovered that writing copy for the web was a highly specialized craft.
There was a multitude of things to learn—and unlearn. It's my goal
to teach you the things I've learned and help you avoid some of the
errors I made.

As you go through the book, here are some of the lessons and
tools you'll find:

- ▶ Chapter 1 introduces you to the three fundamental rules for
  writing web copy that appeals to the unique predisposition
  of the Internet population, and reveals a technique that will
  give you the mind-set of a killer web copywriter in five hours
  or less.

- ▶ Chapter 2 discusses the five simple questions (about your
  product or service) that, when answered, make your web
  copy practically write itself.

- ▶ Chapter 3 reveals the formula for measuring the selling
  quotient of your copy, showing you how to evaluate your

copy's selling ability and how to get an immediate boost in your response rate.

▶ In Chapter 4 you'll discover the amazing power of e-mail marketing, how to write attention-grabbing e-mail copy, and new ways of rising above the overcrowded e-mail jungle.

▶ The most powerful psychological principles underlying web copy that sells are explored in Chapter 5, which offers devices, strategies, tactics, and tips that can make any web-site sizzle with sales activity.

▶ Chapter 6 reveals the Trifecta Neuro-Affective Principle, which features the three principal triggers that you need to employ to change your prospects' minds in favor of your product or service, and to accelerate their decision to buy.

▶ The most important involvement devices that dramatically increase the "stickiness" of your website—and make website visitors more likely to buy what you're selling—are discussed in Chapter 7.

▶ In Chapter 8, I show you how to write compelling online ads, newsletters (or e-zines), autoresponder messages, and other marketing communications that can propel your online business to uncharted heights.

▶ Chapter 9 shows you how to write killer copy for the lucra-tive business-to-business (B2B) market.

▶ Chapter 10 provides the essential guidelines for creating a two- to three-minute online video that gets high Google rankings and generates sales, while offering a glimpse of how to craft effective marketing messages and gain visibil-ity, sales, and even fame by learning the social dynamics of Web 2.0 such as video-sharing sites, blogs, social network-ing sites, and podcast directories.

▶ After you've learned the craft of web copywriting, Chapter 11 reveals the four-step foolproof secret to success in all your copywriting endeavors and the latest breakthrough methods for driving traffic to your website.

You simply can't model successful websites and expect to succeed on the web. You need to model the *process* through which the success is attained, not the outcome of that process. For this reason, we examine the steps, the psychology, and the philosophies that are considered in writing successful web copy rather than modeling the web copy itself and trying to adapt it where it isn't appropriate. Instead of simply presenting blueprints or power words and phrases, I'll demonstrate how to acquire the mind-set with which to view websites, e-mail, and all other marketing communications so that you, too, can write web copy that sells.

Very few people truly understand the complexities of communicating on the Internet. However, by the time you finish reading this book, you'll know more about web copywriting than 99 percent of the population. More important, you will be able to parlay that specialized knowledge into a six-figure income in the field of web copywriting or dramatically increase the sales of your website.

1

Getting Started:
The Dynamics of
Web Selling

Don't worry that you'll take a shot and you'll miss.
The fact is, you'll miss every shot you don't take.
—Anonymous

In the advertising world, the words employed to communicate a sales message in an advertisement or commercial are called *advertising copy,* and the people who write these words are known as *copywriters.* (This term should not be confused with *copyright,* which is a legal mechanism that protects your ownership of what you write.)

Similarly, *web copy* refers to the words employed to communicate a sales message on the web, and the people who write these words are *web copywriters.* Although distinctly different in tone from advertising copy, web copy has the same objectives—that is, to generate leads, customers, sales, and, consequently, profits for a website. (Web copy also should not be confused with web content, which consists of words written for the web for the purpose of informing, communicating, entertaining, or edifying the reader, not necessarily communicating a sales or marketing message.)

Web copywriting is one of the most exciting crafts and professions I know of. I often equate it with alchemy, but whereas alchemy is the science that turns base metals into gold, web copywriting turns words into money seemingly out of thin air. Think about it. The Internet is the only place where anyone can truly market every day for little or no money and have the chance at making a fortune. Personally, I have seen many companies and entrepreneurs do it—even on a shoestring budget.

Whatever your writing skills are, don't worry! Practically anyone with moderate to good writing skills can learn how to write web copy. One of the best copywriters in the offline world, Joe Sugarman, almost flunked English in high school. One of his copywriting students, a grapefruit farmer who had never written sales copy, made millions of dollars over the years using sales copy he wrote to sell grapefruit by mail.

Before any discussion of web copywriting is attempted, it is necessary to consider a few facts and figures about the Web in order to have a clear concept of the online marketing environment in which one needs to operate.

▶ As of July 2008, there were approximately 175.4 million websites (according to a Netcraft Web Server Survey)!

▶ The average Internet surfer who uses a search engine visits 25 websites among the displayed search results in three to four minutes. Therefore, the average duration of stay on each website is approximately eight seconds, including the click and load time.

▶ An estimated 39 trillion pieces of e-mail are sent out each year, of which 80 percent are spam mails.

Why would the staggering number of websites and e-mails be of any concern to you when doing business on the Web—especially since all those other websites are not necessarily your competitors? Here's why: On the Internet, you're competing for a piece of the Internet surfers' online time, and you're also competing for *mind share*. In a cyberuniverse characterized by information overwhelm, every company, individual, or entity that has any kind of Internet presence competes for your prospects' online time and mind share and is therefore your competitor, for all intents and purposes.

With the aforementioned facts in mind, we can now lay the foundation for communicating successfully on the web.

THREE FUNDAMENTAL RULES FOR WRITING WEB COPY THAT SELLS

It amuses me that whenever I run a successful campaign with great web copy, I find a few dozen copycats mimicking certain parts of my work. Invariably, however, they merely copy the words but fail to duplicate the *strategy* or *tactic* behind the words, which is what really makes the copy effective. The writing strategy I employ in every web copy piece that I write is founded on three relatively simple rules.

Rule 1: Don't Make Your Website Look Like an Ad

Depending on which source you believe, the average person is exposed to anywhere between 1,500 (*Media Literacy Report* published by UNICEF) and 5,000 (Charles Pappas, Yahoo! *Internet Life* columnist) advertising messages per day from TV, billboards, radio, the Internet, and practically everywhere we turn. That's an average of 3,250 advertisements per day. Therefore, the last thing we want to see when we land on a website is yet another ad. Additionally, since most of us have been inundated with ads for most of our lives, we have developed instinctive mechanisms to tune out commercial messages.

Yet many online businesses seem to go out of their way to make their websites look like ads, billboards, or other commercial media. Don't fall into this trap, because if you do, you'll turn away potential customers. Your website should provide the solid information that your prospect is looking for, and whenever possible it should have an editorial feel to it. Above all, it should be free of hype. Why? Because people usually go online to find information. Few people log on saying, "I can't wait to see ads, and I can't wait to buy stuff!" No, that usually doesn't happen.

People go online to find information. That's why they call it the information superhighway. Even if they are shopping for something—say a DVD player or an antiaging skin care product—they are generally seeking information, not advertising, about those products. There is a myth that the Internet is an advertising medium or one big shopping channel. It's *not*.

Here's the first distinction between offline advertising copy and effective web copy. Web copy needs to provide good information that appeals to the target audience; that is, ideally, it must not look or feel like a sales pitch.

Editorial-Style Web Headlines

Don't Buy a DVD Player Unless It Meets These 5 Criteria

How a Simple Formula Has Been Scientifically Proven to Cure Cancer and Virtually All Diseases
[Courtesy of OneMinuteCureForAllDiseases.com]

How to Sell Your Home Fast at Top Dollar—Even in a Soft Real Estate Market

Can Streaming Audio Really Double Your Website Sales? A recent Internet research study says you can.

What You Don't Know About Foreclosure Could Cost You Much More Than Just Your Home
[Courtesy of SurviveYourForeclosure.com]

Where does the selling come in? It comes from expertly crafted copy that tilts the website visitor's favor toward your product or service. In other words, avoid blatant sales pitches; instead, provide irresistible information that slides smoothly into a sales pitch for your product.

Why? Because people online do not want to be sold to. A study conducted by web usability experts John Morkes and Jakob Nielsen (reported in a paper titled *Concise, Scannable and Objective: How to Write for the Web*) showed that web users "detest anything that seems like marketing fluff or overly hyped language ('marketese') and prefer factual information." If web visitors ever do get sold on something, they want to be finessed, not bombarded by blatant advertising.

It bears repeating that your sales pitch should not sound like an ad, but rather it should read like an editorial, testimonial, advice, case study, or endorsement. If you want an example of this kind of writing in the brick-and-mortar (meaning *offline*) world, think *advertorial* (editorial-style ads) or press release. In the offline world, editorial-style ads boost readership significantly over standard-looking ads. David Ogilvy, legendary advertising man, wrote in his book *Ogilvy on Advertising* (Knopf, 1985), "There is no law which says that advertisements have to look like advertisements. If you make them *look* like *editorial pages,* you will attract more readers. *Roughly six times* as many people read the average article as the average advertisement [emphasis mine]. Very few advertisements are read by more than one reader in twenty." In fact, in a split-run test conducted in *Reader's Digest,* an editorial-style ad boosted response by 80 percent over the standard ad layout.

Naturally, not every website can employ the editorial-style approach to web copywriting. It may not be feasible for catalog-style websites, for instance, to use editorial articles for each one of their products, especially if they carry hundreds of products. However, the informational guideline can still be adapted when crafting headlines and catalog descriptions. Here are a few examples:

A year of exposure to the sun is like a week at the beach without sunscreen.
(This editorial-style headline was used by a skin care company to advertise a product that provides sun protection.)

Replacing Sour Cream and Mayonnaise in Your Creamy Dressing and Dip Recipes Cuts Down as Much as 1800 Calories. But You Can't Do That With Just Any Yogurt.
(This editorial-style headline was used by a yogurt company.)

Losing One Pound of Weight Takes 4 Pounds of Pressure Off Your Knees.
(This headline was used by the makers of a pain relief medicine.)

Notice that in each of the preceding examples the headline provides information that is not only interesting but also speaks to the needs of the product's target audience. An interesting phenomenon happens when you give information that is useful to your prospect. He or she is likely to feel at the subconscious level that in order to get the benefit alluded to in the headline (i.e., protection from the sun, weight loss, or pain relief), only your product will do the job. The yogurt company brought that idea home with the line "But You Can't Do That With Just Any Yogurt"; however, the other two conveyed the same idea.

When I worked as the director of creative web writing at Aesop Marketing Corporation, Mark Joyner commissioned extensive in-house marketing research to test the effectiveness of every imaginable element of our web copy and other online marketing communications. To give you an idea of the magnitude of the research, Aesop's database consisted of millions of Internet entrepreneurs, and we frequently tested copy elements on samples of 20,000 names for each testing variable. The sales results I witnessed at Aesop made clear to me the effectiveness of the editorial style of copywriting. In the tests in which I've been involved, editorial-style web copy outpulled sales letter–style Web copy

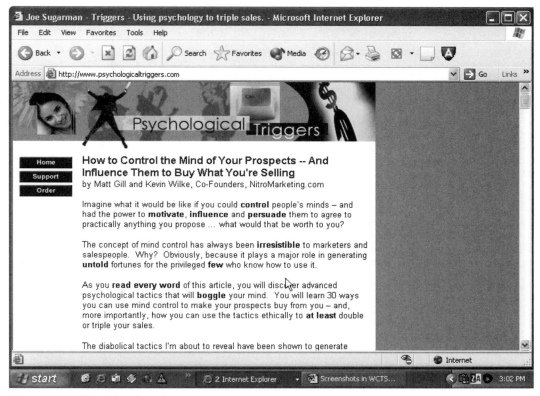

Figure 1.1 Editorial-style web copy.

every single time. Remember, people generally tune out ads, but they tune in to editorial information. (See Figure 1.1.)

Rule 2: Stop Readers Dead in Their Tracks

Online business owners spend a lot of time and money trying to get traffic to their websites. Building web traffic is very important, but it won't mean a thing unless you do one thing first. That is, create compelling web copy that will stop them dead in their tracks and get them to do what you want them to do when they get there.

Back in April 2004, when the first edition of this book went to press, Google had 36 million websites indexed, but as of July 2008, just four years later, that number had multiplied by a factor of almost five to 175.4 million websites, all clamoring for attention! It's no wonder, then, that in order for words to wield their magical power on the web, they have to be tailored specifically for the information-flooded Internet public, among whom attention span is a rare commodity.

 FACT: If your website is little more than an online brochure, it's not only a very weak selling tool, but it has very little chance of selling anything in the crowded Internet marketplace. (See Figure 1.2.)

"Breakthroughs Journal" is a good example of a website that stops visitors dead in their tracks. The headline incites curiosity ("Does Coral Calcium Really Reverse Aging, Extend Your Life Span, and Cure Degenerative Diseases like Cancer?"), and the subheadline ("5 Facts You Must Know Before It's Too Late") injects emotion, drama, and a sense of urgency. Its copy, written in the editorial style, follows through by giving readers a sense that they're reading a news item, not an advertisement.

Rule 3: Capture E-Mail Addresses

For a website to succeed, it must have effective direct-response web copy that induces action from a single exposure. Just think. What's the point in getting someone to come to your website if the site visit doesn't generate a response such as picking up the phone and calling your business, subscribing to your newsletter, signing up for your mailing list, or buying your product or service?

Generating a response means more than impressing web visitors with cool graphics or technology or getting them to bookmark your site. What's the point in having cutting-edge web design, eye-popping graphics, and a sophisticated e-commerce infrastructure if you are unable to entice your visitors long enough for them to do what you want them to do?

Figure 1.2 Attention-grabbing website.

If you are selling something on your website, chances are that less than 5 percent of your site's visitors will ever buy your product. Conversion rates vary with each industry, but the typical healthy rate for online stores is 0.5 percent (.005) to 1.5 percent (.015), according to the *Bock Newsletter* on Yahoo! Store (issue 32). "Conversion rates of 2 percent to 5 percent are fairly typical today," according to a report entitled *Getting Clicks with Casual Customers* at CNET News. Even the best marketers with the most successful websites seldom convert more than 5 percent of their web visitors into customers.

What happens to the 95 percent of your web visitors who came and went? For most websites, nothing. Those prospects are gone for good, never to return. That's why it is absolutely essential for your

"How to Pay Less for Almost Everything"
The world's best *bargain hunters* and haggle hounds reveal their **secrets** for easily finding the *lowest prices* on things you buy everyday. Once you learn these simple, but **ingenious** strategies for getting more and spending less, it's like having given yourself a **20% (or more) pay raise** -- tax-free!

Send for this **FREE report** today. Simply fill in your name and address in the form below -- and this **valuable** report will be sent to your e-mail box automatically *within minutes*!

[Your contact information will be handled with the *strictest confidence*, and will never be sold or shared with third parties.]

☐	**Send me my FREE report now.**
Email address:	
First Name:	
Last Name:	

Add Address

Figure 1.3 Exit pop-up opt-in offer.

website to have an opt-in mechanism. The chances are slim that people will buy from you the first time they visit your website. After all, they don't even know you. Rather than lose them, ask for something that is easier and less intimidating than pulling out a credit card—ask them to give you their e-mail address. It's a simple, nonthreatening way to initiate a relationship.

Trust, as we all know, is an important issue in e-commerce, and finding ways to build trust in an online environment is a continuing challenge for Internet businesses. On the web, people buy from people they like and trust. They like people who provide them with information they need, who are not overly aggressive in trying to market their products, and who are easy to do business with. They trust people who deliver on the promises they make, who take time to develop a relationship with them, who provide good customer service, and who have an articulated privacy policy to which they strictly adhere. Capturing contact information is the first step in developing rapport with prospective customers and in building a relationship that will foster online sales—now and in the future. (See Figure 1.3.)

An opt-in offer, such as "How to Pay Less . . ." is one way to capture a visitor's e-mail address. (See Chapter 2 for a complete discussion of opt-in mechanisms.)

THE FIRST LOOK

What is the most important element of a website? The first screen (or the first eyeful) is the prime selling space of your website, and what you put in it makes or breaks its success. Do not confuse the first screen with the first page, which is often referred to as the home page or the landing page of a website. The first screen is only part of the page that appears on the screen when you land on a website; it's the screen you see before you scroll down or sideways. In a print newspaper, its counterpart is the information above the fold, which draws maximum readership.

Often, the first screen is the first, last, and only thing people see on a website before they click away. For this reason, don't make the mistake many companies do of putting a large logo or your company name in gigantic letters on that screen. Some companies do this for branding purposes, but in most cases the company name and logo don't have to take up half of the first screen. Your logo doesn't need to be large—it's not a selling feature. While it may stroke your ego, it won't increase your sales. An oversized logo wastes valuable selling space.

Conversely, a headline *must* be included in the first screen. It is the most important component of a webpage. Consider how pointless it would be for a newspaper to have no headline. A website without a headline is just as pointless, yet it's remarkable how many websites fail to put a headline in this prime selling space.

In my years of surfing the web, I've observed that the majority of commercial websites that do have headlines have weak, uninteresting ones, and, as a result, they are missing a critical opportunity to attract and retain website visitors.

On my Web Copywriting University website, I used the headline "So You Want a Website That Sells?" followed by the subheadline "Here are surefire strategies no one is telling you about." (See Figure 1.4.) This headline calls out to a target audience: those who want a website that sells. A headline that calls out to a specific target audience is one way to capture the attention of the web visitor. Contrariwise, when you call out to everyone, you often call out to no one.

I started the body copy with the following question: "Why do some online businesses make money so easily on the web—while you try everything possible and get barely enough customers, sales and profits?" I do this because when you ask a question, the brain is compelled to answer it. Readers are more likely to believe an idea that their brain seems to have come up with on its own than an idea that is presented from outside.

Never underestimate the power of your reader's imagination. Compare the impact of the following two examples (one a question and one a statement):

1. What if there was a way you could convert 15 percent, 25 percent—even 50 percent or more—of your website visitors into customers; how much more money would you earn as a result?

2. Your business can convert 15 percent, 25 percent—even 50 percent or more—of your website visitors into customers and earn a lot of money.

Notice that the statement makes a claim that a reader may or may not believe. Contrast that with the question, which introduces the possibility of an ideal scenario and allows the brain to draw its own conclusions and paint its own pictures.

Figure 1.4 Targeted headline captures attention.

I like to use "What if . . ." questions or "Imagine what would happen if . . ." or "Think back . . ." That way, you let your readers envision the scene for themselves. According to Robert Collier, publisher and author of several books, most notable of which is *The Robert Collier Letter Book* (Robert Collier Publications, 2000), which many consider the bible for writing sales letters, "The reader colors that mental picture with his own imagination, which is more potent than all the brushes of all the world's artists." The things that people imagine about your product or service often exceed the reality.

Notice that I featured a powerful testimonial very early in the web copy. Why? This puts a blanket of credibility on the rest of the copy. Therefore, everything the visitor reads from that point on is influenced by that glowing testimonial, which makes it more believable.

WEB COPY DOs AND DON'Ts ▼

Do strive to write in a conversational style. The more friendly and approachable, the better.

Do use contractions. When people talk, they frequently use contractions. It's intimate, and it increases readership. Use "I've" instead of "I have," "it's" instead of "it is," "we'll" instead of "we will."

Do use common colloquialisms. When you use colloquialisms, you draw your reader closer because you appear more familiar, more friendly, more up close and personal instead of distant and at arm's length.

Use colloquialisms that are understandable to most people who have a reasonable familiarity with the English language. Some colloquialisms that have found their way into mainstream online communications include:

dough	money
laid-back	calm, relaxed
make waves	cause trouble
bent out of shape	become upset
broke	having little or no money
come up for air	take a break
cool	great
twenty grand	$20,000 (fifty grand for $50,000, a hundred grand for $100,000, etc.)
keep your cool	remain calm
blown away	greatly impressed, amazed, surprised
megabucks	a lot of money
blow a fuse	lose your temper
bummed	depressed
con	deceive
has deep pockets	has a good source of money

glitzy	fancy
honcho	boss
get a kick out of	enjoy

Avoid using colloquialisms that might cause misunderstandings. Because the Internet is international, some colloquialisms such as "table a proposal" (postpone the discussion) or "the presentation bombed" (the presentation was a complete failure), which are generally understood by most Americans, may mean something completely different to non-Americans. You should also avoid using regional or locally based colloquialisms and slang, as they frequently are misunderstood by Americans from other parts of the country as well as non-Americans.

Don't use corporate jargon (also called corporatespeak), as it may communicate very little to anyone outside a particular industry.

Consider the following two examples written for a fictitious online business called My Web Store:

1. My Web Store is an e-commerce solutions provider committed to helping people leverage the power of technology to create value-added, win-win cyberspaces that impact global retail markets.

2. My Web Store is a first-of-its-kind form of e-commerce that enables anyone to open a 24/7 online store in as little as five minutes—for just $1 a day.

Which statement are web visitors more likely understand? The second, of course. The first employs highfalutin jargon instead of clear, straightforward words and phrases that people can understand. Even if you read it several times, you'd still be wondering what it's trying to say. Corporatespeak such as this constitutes a blatant failure to communicate effectively. Contrast that with example 2, which immediately communicates a clear benefit, singularity, ease, and economy—everything a prospective customer wants to know.

In direct-response marketing, if no one understands what you're saying, no one will buy what you're selling. Therefore, avoid corporatespeak and opt for clear, uncomplicated language.

Do use strategically placed testimonials. Testimonials are a powerful sales tool, whether you're selling online or offline. To apply testimonials successfully when selling online, they need to be positioned strategically throughout the website. An ideal place to position a powerful testimonial is very early on the webpage, preferably in the first or second screen. In that position, the testimonial puts a blanket of credibility on the rest of the copy. (See Figure 1.5.)

RingingCedars.com, a website offering a series of books that has sold over 10 million copies without the benefit of advertising, uses dynamically generated testimonials on its website header, actually displaying a different testimonial every time any webpage on the website is refreshed or reloaded. Web visitors are therefore presented with ever-changing testimonials every time they visit the website or click through to other webpages within the website.

It's also important to sprinkle testimonials strategically throughout your web copy, especially in areas where they reinforce your selling arguments. Testimonials are also particularly useful in your order form, right before you ask for the order (before your call to action), and in your order confirmation e-mail (to reinforce the sale).

Don't try to impress your readers with your fancy vocabulary. Effective copywriting isn't about making grandiose claims. It is about communicating in a way that people can easily understand.

Don't be pompous. Let the testimonials make you look good. People online don't like marketese or bragging, boastful language.

READING ON THE WEB ▼

How do people read on the web? According to Jakob Nielsen, author of *Homepage Usability: 50 Websites Deconstructed* (Pearson, 2001) and holder of 71 patents relating to making the Internet easier to use, "They don't."

Figure 1.5 Powerful testimonial from PC Magazine *in the first screen.*

Yes, you read that correctly. People don't read online. They *scan.*

Nielsen, together with John Morkes, director of the Human-Computer Interaction Group at Trilogy Software and, like Nielsen, a usability expert, conducted several scientific studies about reading and writing on the web. They discovered that people read webpages very differently than printed pages. In 1997, they reported that the majority (79 percent) skim webpages quickly (stopping only when something interesting catches their eye); only 16 percent read everything word for word. This corroborates the more recent tests conducted by the Poynter Institute for Media Studies in July 2007; using eye-tracking equipment on 600 participants from 18 to 60 years old, these tests found that most readers are indeed scanners.

This is very important to those of us who write web copy or sell on the web. It indicates that writing successful web copy means writing scannable web copy.

Five Ways to Write Scannable Copy
1. Use bulleted lists to summarize content.
2. Highlight (by using **bold** or *italic* fonts or by <u>underlining</u>) selected keywords to help scanners move through your web copy.
3. Write meaningful subheads.
4. Present one idea per paragraph.
5. Use the inverted pyramid style of writing; that is, present key points and conclusions first, followed by less important information and background material.

Exercise: Using your scroll bar, scan through a website. Is the copy inviting to read? Does it incorporate elements that make it scannable and engaging—or does it have huge blocks of text that discourage you from reading further? How many times does something in your copy catch your eye and cause you to read something of interest? Make your copy more scannable by applying the five suggested techniques.

Bonus idea: Use text boxes to feature interesting anecdotes, stories, testimonials, and case histories, and to further break up your web copy into readable, bite-size chunks.

Think about how you read a sales letter that comes in the mail. It's three-dimensional, and it exists in a spatial realm, whereas a webpage is two-dimensional—it's in a flat realm. Whether you realize it or not, you write in a manner suitable for the printed page, not the web, because that's the medium you are accustomed to. There are big differences.

Imagine you have a multiple-page sales letter in your hands. You can view an entire page in one glance, you can shuffle through or skim through the pages quickly, you can go straight to the order form or the last page to read the P.S. (the P.S. is the second-most-read part of a sales letter because people can get to it in a second). Now look at a webpage—you see only one screen, which is just a fraction of a page, at a time. You don't have the luxury of shuffling through the pages. The best you can do is use the scroll bar or a mouse click to go from page to page.

Do you see why you can't simply take offline copywriting principles and apply them to the web?

WORDS TELL, EMOTION SELLS
▼

People's emotions are the primary motivating factors for buying. People buy on emotion and justify their purchases with logic. Both on and off the web, a strong copy platform is built on proven emotional drivers such as anger, exclusivity, fear, greed, guilt, and salvation, to name a few.

Take a look at the first screen of the 24 Techniques for Closing the Sale website (Figure 1.6). Notice that good web copy starts with a dramatic promise.

> *Headline:* These Ain't Your Granddaddy's Closing Techniques, Boy!
>
> *Subheadline:* These are 24 of the most ruthless tactics—kept under wraps for years—that can turn even your most hard-nosed prospects into cash-generating customers.

The purpose of the headline—and to a certain extent the subheadline—is to offer compelling information, solve a problem, take away pain, help someone achieve a goal, and fulfill a desire. Conversational language that sounds the way people do helps crank up the emotional volume.

The language used on this website carries the emotional intensity of the headline through to its opening paragraph:

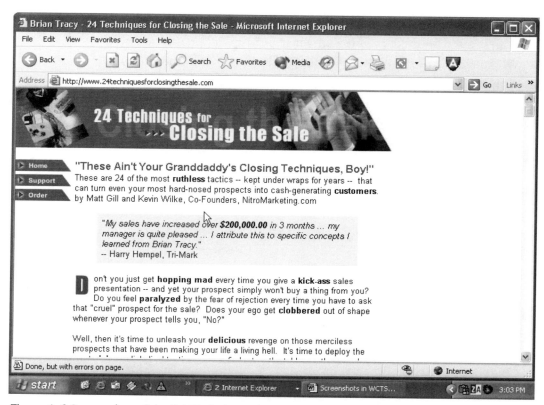

Figure 1.6 Screen shot of the 24 Techniques for Closing the Sale website.

Don't you just get **hopping mad** every time you give a **kick-ass** sales presentation—and yet your prospect simply won't buy a thing from you? Do you feel **paralyzed** by the fear of rejection every time you have to ask that "cruel" prospect for the sale? Does your ego get **clobbered** out of shape whenever your prospect tells you, "No?"

The copy leads the target audience (salespeople) through the excruciating agony of the traditional sales process, a process with which they are all too familiar. It builds the selling proposition on the reader's emotions so that the reader feels the pain and begins to beg for the benefits promised in the headline and subheadline.

Consider the following headlines that I recently found on websites:

How to Stop Your Divorce
Even When Your Spouse Wants Out of Your Marriage

What Will You Do When Creditors Try to Seize Your Assets to Collect on Debts You Owe Them?
Is Your Personal Property at Risk?

Both headlines appeal to the reader's fear of loss—one of the greatest motivators. The fact is, people generally go to greater lengths to keep from losing what they have than to gain something of the same (or greater) value. The old sales adage "Fear of loss is greater than the desire for gain" is as true online as it is in offline selling situations.

I recently saw a pop-up ad that shocked the living daylights out of me. The pop-up looked like an Instant Message box and had a shadowy image of a man as the inset picture, with the caption "Mr. Hacker." Underneath the picture were these words:

I read your e-mails.
I pay with your credit card number.
I transfer money from your account to mine.

I felt the blood drain from my face and my body went cold all over as I read and reread the words. The shock finally wore off when I realized that it was an advertisement for an antispyware program—and I would have bought the program if I hadn't already had one on my computer. That's an excellent, albeit extreme, use of the fear-of-loss motivator.

HOW TO BECOME A GREAT WEB COPYWRITER IN FIVE HOURS OR LESS
▼

Perhaps you've heard of the concept of modeling success. If you want to achieve success at anything, the fastest way to do it is by modeling the strategies of those who are already successful at it. That way, you take something complex and synthesize it into its essence so you can use it immediately.

You've probably heard of real estate agents going into selling mode by constantly repeating to themselves, "I'm going to sell this house." Annette Bening did this so well in her portrayal of a Realtor in the movie *American Beauty*. Successful real estate agents start off with the mind-set that the sale is already made. Model the strategy that successful people use to be successful.

In web copywriting, the best way to model success is to select a website that you admire greatly and that you know has produced tons of sales for its owner. Start copying it by hand. *Write the entire sales letter out in your own handwriting*. Write it out two or three times over the next week. Depending on how fast you write, this will take roughly five hours—less if you write quickly or if the sales letter you choose is short.

This takes a lot of discipline, not to mention time, but I assure you, it is worth the effort. You will not know the value of this until you do it. It's positively eye-opening. I learned this technique from Ted Nicholas, a renowned direct marketer, copywriter, and author of several books, including *Magic Words That Bring You Riche$* (Nicholas Direct, 1998).

Once you write this sales letter over and over again, you will start internalizing the wording, the phraseology, the rhythm, even the mind-set of the person who wrote the copy. Your brain assimilates it, and you practically step into the mind of the writer. This is by far the best modeling exercise I've found for accelerating web copywriting skills.

Next time you sit down to write web copy, the wording, the phrasing, and even part of the writer's thought process will have become a part of you, and you will find that it becomes much easier to sit down and begin flowing right into a winning sales piece.

2

A Simple Blueprint for Writing Killer Web Copy

Internalize the Golden Rule of sales that says, "All things being equal, people will do business with, and refer business to, those people they know, like, and trust."
—Bob Burg

Before you write one word of copy, you must first

▶ Know your *objective*
▶ Know your *target audience*
▶ Know the *product or service*

Your objective: What are you trying to accomplish? What response are you trying to obtain? Your objective might not be to make a sale, but rather to get your reader to send for free information or to get your reader to sign up for your mailing list. Or your objective might be to sell your product or service.

Your target audience: The more you know about your target audience, the easier it is to convince them that they need your product or service. The more specific your knowledge of your target audience is, the better. Let's say you are selling a book on weight loss. Your target audience is overweight people, but you might fine-tune that to target overweight people whose jobs revolve around computer work and who have no time to work out, let alone go to the gym. This is the target audience of a website called WeightLossTricksThatWork.com. (See Figure 2.1.)

Your product or service: After identifying the audience to whom you are writing, it's essential to know the product or service about which you're writing. Immerse yourself in it. The five Ws of journalism are a handy tool to use for this: What? Why? Where? When?

Figure 2.1 This targeted headline calls out to a specific audience.

Who? and the bonus How? Before you begin writing, ask yourself:

> What is the product or service? What is it made of?
>
> Why was it invented or developed?
>
> Where did it originate?
>
> When was it discovered?
>
> Who invented or discovered it?
>
> How is it made?

Learn everything you can about your product or service. Uncover the benefits of owning your product or using your service. Only after you identify your objective, familiarize yourself with your target audience, and know your product or service thoroughly is it time to start writing.

CREATING THE BLUEPRINT: FIVE SIMPLE QUESTIONS YOU MUST ASK ▼

I've distilled the entire web copywriting process into five easy steps that make the task of writing web copy as easy as pie—and as enjoyable. Each step in the blueprint takes the form of a question. Once you answer each of the five questions about any product or service, you'll have the blueprint, a miniversion of your web copy. Note: As you are answering these five questions, *don't get creative*. Just answer factually. We'll get creative later.

Question 1: What Is the Problem?

Most sales, both online and offline, are based primarily on solving a problem. Having identified your target audience, your job now is to identify the problem that your target audience has that can be solved by your product or service. In copywriting terms these are known as the *three Ps*—pain, problem, or predicament.

This is where you play doctor. You diagnose the problem. The people in your target audience may not even know they have a problem, so it is your job to make them recognize it. Many web copywriters and marketers shove the solution down their viewers' throats before their readers recognize that there is a problem. That's like a doctor prescribing medicine before you feel sick.

There's another aspect to it as well. Once your audience understands that they have a problem, you have to let them know that *you* understand their problem. There's an old saying that goes something like this: "People don't care how much you know until they know how much you care."

> **Step 1:** *Write down your target audience's problem.* A few sentences will do. Your reader must be able to say, "Hey, she really understands my problem," or "He reads me like a book," or "She knows me so well it's as though she's been eavesdropping on my conversations or reading my mail." That's why I keep emphasizing that before you write a word of copy, you have to know your audience.

Question 2: Why Hasn't the Problem Been Solved?

Extending the doctor metaphor, this is where you further identify the history of the problem, predicament, or pain and look into the previous remedies or solutions that have been attempted but failed. As you progress through all five steps of this blueprint, you'll begin to see how the answer(s) to this question serves to build your audience's anticipation about a new solution you're about to reveal.

> **Step 2:** *Write down the reason(s) why the problem continues, persists, or lingers.* How is it that they haven't solved their problem, and why are they still stuck in the rut? Again, a few factual sentences will do.

Question 3: What Is Possible?

In coaching, this is called *possibility thinking.* This is where you set the stage for what life could be like and what could happen when your audience's problem, pain, or predicament is eliminated. You must go beyond stating the obvious. "The pain in your lower back will disappear" is not enough. You must draw a picture of what is possible now that the pain is gone. "You will be able to engage in activities [specify activities] you were unable to engage in because of your back pain," or "You can accomplish all your goals and dreams because the pain is no longer there to stop you." This is the dramatic promise.

> Step 3: *Write down what's possible.* Paint a picture of the way things will be when your prospect's problems are solved. Again, a few sentences will do.

Question 4: What Is Different Now?

How will things change for your prospects? This is where you explain who you are and how your product or service can help them, as well as what's different about your product or service that will eliminate their problem. This is where your unique selling proposition (USP) comes in. A USP is something that sets you, your product or service, or your business apart from every other competitor in a favorable way. It's the competitive advantage that you proclaim to your prospects, customers, or clients.

> Step 4: *Write a few sentences about what differentiates your product/service.* Present just the substance—not the details.

Question 5: What Should You Do Now?

If you answered the first four questions and established your objective, you know what the answer to this question is. You simply tell your viewers to do what you started out wanting them to do—that is, to sign up, pick up the phone, register, opt in, or buy the product or service you're selling.

> Step 5: *State clearly what you want your prospect to do.* This is the call to action.

There you have it. Once you have answered the five questions, you have the blueprint for building your web copy. You now have the structure; all you have to do is decorate it. The fact is, with this blueprint alone, you can make some sales.

The Anatomy of the Blueprint

Recently, I had the opportunity to observe a business acquaintance named Ralph, a personal development coach, generate leads for his services during a Chamber of Commerce networking event. I noticed how successfully he was able to interest several people in his coaching services in such a small amount of time, so I took a closer look at how he could accomplish this with just a few words to each prospect. It didn't take long to realize that his sales pitch was nothing more than skillfully weaving the five steps of the blueprint into casual conversation. His conversations went something like this:

> PROSPECT: What kind of work do you do, Ralph?
>
> RALPH: I'm a personal development coach.
>
> PROSPECT: Hmmm . . . what exactly is that?
>
> RALPH: Let me ask you a question: Are there three things you'd like to accomplish in your life right now that for some reason or other you haven't been able to accomplish yet?
>
> PROSPECT: Sure. I think I can think of more than three things.
>
> RALPH: Why do you think you haven't been able to accomplish them?
>
> PROSPECT: [*Answers vary from person to person. They range from "I haven't focused enough attention on accomplishing them" to "I*

have an unsupportive boss/spouse/family" to "I can't seem to
find the time or energy to devote to them" to "I'm stuck in a rut
and I'm still trying to figure my way out of it," and so on.]

RALPH: What if you were able to eliminate [*here, Ralph*
reiterates the challenge the prospect mentioned for not
accomplishing his or her goals]; how would your life change?

PROSPECT: [*Again, answers to this question vary from person to*
person. "Why, I'd be able to spend more time with my family,
and that would make me happy," or "I'd be able to work less and
earn more," or "I'd have the money to buy a house/send my kids
to college/go on more vacations," etc.]

RALPH: What if I told you I have a unique approach to help
you take care of [*again, Ralph names the prospect's problem*],
which will help get you from where you are now to where
you want to be—not in a few years, but within the next
60 to 90 days? Would you be interested in a 15-minute
free consultation to find out how I can do that for you?

PROSPECT: Sure, why not?

At this point, Ralph takes his business card out of his pocket and
asks what day and time would suit the prospect for the free consultation. When the prospect answers, Ralph writes the appointment on
the card and hands the card to the prospect, telling the prospect to
call him at the appointed date and time. He then turns the card over
and points to a diagram on the back.

RALPH: Right before you call me, I'd like you to do something
fun. I'd like you to do this quick exercise here, tell me what
your answer is when you call me, and I'll explain what your
answer means.

PROSPECT [*looking at the card*]: Okay, you got it. I'll call you
then.

Do you see what Ralph did? He managed to get a prospect interested in his services in a matter of one or two minutes, and he

generated a lead that might eventually turn into a client, which, of course, was his objective.

Let's examine the conversation more closely to see how it relates to our blueprint. When prospects ask Ralph about his work, Ralph uses it as an opportunity to identify their problems (step 1). Instead of making an educated guess about what their problem(s) might be, he makes the prospects identify their problems by asking them to think of the top three things they have yet to accomplish. Then he asks why they haven't been able to accomplish them (step 2), and the prospects give specific reasons. Ralph next asks the what-if question; that is, he makes prospects imagine how life would be different if the problem(s) were eliminated (step 3). After his prospects answer the question, Ralph mentions his unique approach to helping them take care of the problem(s) so they can get from where they are in life to where they want to be in the next 60 to 90 days (step 4). This is followed up with an offer of a free 15-minute phone consultation at an appointed date and time (step 5). The fun exercise on the back of the card is a device Ralph employs to make sure prospects call him and to minimize no-shows.

Ralph's networking sales pitch is one small example of just how powerful the blueprint is. When you are able to successfully identify your prospect's problem and explain why the problem hasn't been solved, what's possible, what's different now, and what the prospect should do now, you have the basis of a successful sales pitch in a nutshell. Although the blueprint works exceedingly well on the Internet, where web buyers' attention is difficult to capture, it can be applied to almost any situation that requires a direct response, both online or offline—from an "elevator speech" to a full-scale sales presentation.

Are you beginning to see how powerful the blueprint is? Do you think you can answer these five questions for any product or service you want to sell? If you answered yes, you're already a web copywriter.

Outstanding web copy starts with the five-step blueprint. Now let's examine how a website started out as a blueprint, was fleshed out into six pages of web copy that sold several hundred thousand dollars' worth of a product in a few months, and continues to sell to this day. The product is a $27 e-book that shows Internet entrepreneurs how to get free money from the government to start, grow, or expand their Internet businesses. The author is Matthew Lesko, who has written more than 70 books (including two *New York Times* bestsellers) showing everyday people how to get grants and free money from U.S. government sources. Before we look at the web copy, we'll take a look at the five-step blueprint upon which the copy was built:

Step 1. *What's the problem?* Internet entrepreneurs like you need money to start, grow, or expand your business.

Step 2. *Why hasn't the problem been solved?* Loans and financing for Internet businesses are hard to come by or qualify for. Free money programs, such as government grants, are neither advertised nor generally publicized—therefore, very few people know about them. The few who are aware of them lack the specialized knowledge of how to successfully obtain the free money.

Step 3. *What's possible?* Now you can get as much money as you need for your Internet business—and you don't have to pay it back.

Step 4. *What's different now?* The real trick is in knowing how to ask for the money. Matthew Lesko has developed a completely legal and ingenious secret formula that works every time. He discovered the secret formula because for the past 25 years he has specialized in uncovering obscure government programs that most ordinary citizens know nothing about.

Step 5. *What should you do now?* Get the e-book that shows you step-by-step how to get the free money to which you're entitled.

That's it! End of blueprint.

Now take a look at the website at www.FreeStuffForEntrepreneursOnTheInternet.com, shown in Figure 2.2.

Figure 2.2 A fleshed-out version of the blueprint.

Every piece of web copy that I've written follows the same sequence and development set forth in the blueprint. Years of copywriting have made me instinctively structure my sales copy in that logical sequence. It wasn't always that way. When I first started writing copy, I would force-feed my brain with all manner of clever, innovative ways to craft my sales proposition—and usually ended up with volumes of words, research, and web copy that I later had to spend hours (sometimes days) chiseling down to a lean, mean selling machine. In other words, I was doing everything backward.

Then I devised this blueprint that made web copywriting a breeze. It is a loose adaptation of an executive summary template developed by my colleague and friend Alex Mandossian, a web traffic conversion specialist, marketing consultant, and copywriter. I realized that if I started with this blueprint and fleshed it out only as necessary, I came up with the same quality web copy that I'd been producing for years, but, using the blueprint, I slashed as much as 80 percent off the time it took to write copy.

When you model success, you need to model the strategy, not the result (meaning you don't mimic someone else's writing style; you simply use the technique). The blueprint is one of the most important strategies that I can teach you. In my opinion, if you follow it, it's almost impossible to experience writer's block—and you won't have to put on the "writer's hat," so to speak. You won't struggle to be creative or clever or amusing or profound. You just write down the facts. Later, during the fleshing-out phase, you make those facts come alive.

This five-step blueprint is the "formula" originally introduced in the first edition of this book. It facilitates the process of writing web copy. The Trifecta Neuro-Affective Principle (see Chapter 6), which is being presented for the first time in this edition, works in tandem with this blueprint and often makes this blueprint write itself. If you prefer to write short copy as opposed to the long copy often associated with direct-response types of websites, go directly to Chapter 6 now. But if you prefer to write long, fully fleshed-out copy, read on.

PUTTING THE BLUEPRINT TO WORK: FIVE EASY STEPS TO MAKING YOUR WEB COPY SELL ▼

Let's suppose you've written down the five steps of the blueprint: You've identified the problem, you've described what's possible, you've established why the problem hasn't been solved, you've established what's changed, and you've suggested what action should be taken. What have you got? Is this your web copy? Obviously not, but it is the heart and soul—the framework—for writing web copy.

Some people will buy simply based on your answers to those five questions, but to get *most* people to buy, you must flesh out the blueprint until it becomes a virtual salesperson who sells for you day and night, 24/7, weekends and holidays, 365 days a year, without a vacation or sick leave.

You have created your blueprint. How do you build your house? As with the blueprint, there are five steps you need to take to flesh it out and make readers respond.

Step 1: Inject Emotion

I don't care how wonderful your vocabulary or how excellent your grammar is, if your words lack emotion, you won't sell a thing unless you can appeal to an emotion. Remember, *people buy on emotion and justify with logic.*

There are many ways to inject emotion. Here are a few examples:

▶ Does it frustrate you that your business is making only a small fraction of its profit potential?

▶ Don't you just get hopping mad every time you give a kick-ass sales presentation and your prospect *still* won't buy a thing from you?

▶ Do you suffer from feelings of isolation or of being left behind—and worry that you're doomed to a lonely, unmarried life?

▶ Does your impending foreclosure make you feel like a failure, like the world is closing in on you—and so overwhelmed and depressed that you wish you were dead?

Injecting Emotion into What's Possible

▶ Can you imagine what your life would be like if all your debts were paid and you had triple-A credit?

▶ How would you like it if your business earned a five-figure income every month—even while the economy is on a downswing?

▶ What would it mean if you were the featured guest of popular radio and TV shows? Imagine thousands—potentially millions—of people hearing your story.

Figure 2.3 illustrates a device I call the *emotional scenario*. It paints a vivid picture of what it would be like for the reader to experience your product or service.

It's seven o'clock Monday morning. You're not really looking forward to another **grueling** week of selling, so you turn on your computer. While you **sip your morning coffee,** you watch Brian Tracy on RealVideo giving you 24 Techniques for Closing the Sale in 63 minutes flat.

It's now 8:03 A.M., and you're feeling **unstoppable** and positively **empowered** because Brian Tracy has just given you a personal coaching session that got you **charged up** with everything you need **to get those sales.**

The next moment, you're out the door. You talk to your first prospect, and moments later you make your first sale with the **greatest of ease.** Feeling **high** on your victory, you go on to your next prospect, and, again within moments, you've got another sale in your pocket. No sweat! This goes on all day long, and you **surprisingly** find yourself smiling all the time. Gone are the stress and fear that you used to have—and in their place is a deep-seated confidence that you can **win over** any prospect you speak to. It's never been this easy!

Then, toward the end of the day, you pick up the phone to set up your future appointments. Every single prospect you call says yes, they'd be happy to see you or talk to you this week.

You think to yourself, "If only every day could be like this . . . why, I might just earn a **six-figure income** this year."

Could this really happen to you? Don't be surprised if it does.

Figure 2.3

An emotional scenario such as this one accomplishes several things:

- ▶ It connects your reader to your product or service on an *emotional* level. Emotion sells.
- ▶ It assumes that the sale is already made.
- ▶ It allows the reader to take ownership of the product and have a *virtual experience* of it with excellent results.

Oftentimes, what you're really selling is the *emotional experience,* sometimes even more so than the product or service itself. This is explained in more detail in the section entitled "The Cyrano Effect" (see Chapter 5).

Step 2: Add Bullet Points, Bonuses, Guarantee, and Close

The formula for writing bullets is first to state the benefit and then follow up by painting a picture of how your viewer's life will change when he or she gets that benefit or by elevating the desirability of that benefit by injecting emotion, drama, or intrigue. Bullets need to be powerful and tight.

Mouthwatering Bullets

Here are examples of great bullets (the first is an example of injecting emotion, drama, or intrigue; the second paints a picture):

- ▶ Our revolutionary tutoring technology improves your child's math skills at least two grade levels higher than his or her present grade level. Imagine how confident your child will be when he finally realizes that math is easy—and how proud it will make you!
- ▶ How a self-made millionaire invented this irresistible tactic. It virtually eliminates the need to close the sale because the sale will close itself for you—like a ripe apple dropping out of a tree into your hand.

I learned how to write bullets by studying and writing out by hand the bullets of great copywriters. You can do the same.

Bonuses

It is a widely accepted belief in direct marketing that significantly more sales are generated by an offer that includes a free bonus or gift. Although there aren't scientific studies that support this belief, it stands to reason that receiving attractive incentives creates a significantly greater desire to purchase the core product. It is not uncommon for people to buy a product primarily because of the freebies they get by buying it. "Gifts with purchase" have become a staple at cosmetics counters everywhere because they significantly encourage impulse buying. Obviously, the bonus or gift must be desirable to the target audience and must relate in some way to the product or service being offered. If it has a dollar value worth noting, you should also mention that.

Free bonuses or gifts are particularly powerful when attached to a deadline for ordering, because the deadline injects urgency. You need to set a deadline to compel the reader to respond immediately instead of putting off the buying decision. That's where a dynamic date script is helpful. This is a small script that advances the deadline date displayed on your webpage every day. When people read your web copy, it looks something like this:

> When you order the Memory Foam mattress pad by Friday, June 20, 2008, you will also receive two (2) Memory Foam pillows absolutely free. These pillows are sold separately for $89.00 apiece, but they're yours *free* when you purchase a Memory Foam mattress now.

The day and date advance by one every day, automatically updating your deadline. Dynamic date scripts are widely available for free from various script sources on the web. You simply decide how many days into the future you'd like your prospect to act on your offer, and any web developer or programmer (or anyone who's familiar with html) can simply insert that into the script and install the code into your webpage.

Guarantees

Often, the sale is made with the promise of a money-back guarantee. This is where you eliminate the risk to the buyer and remove any remaining obstacles to making a sale.

The Close

Just because you have presented your offer doesn't mean your prospect will buy what you've offered. You have to close the sale. It's no different from visiting a store and looking at a product you are interested in buying; even after all your questions have been answered, until a salesperson closes the sale with a question like "How would you like to pay for that?" the sale isn't made unless you happen to be a highly motivated buyer, determined to buy that item then and there.

Before you ever ask for that order, it's essential that the prospect be primed for the close. The sequence of presenting copy elements (and hot buttons) is crucial. Unlike a store, where the price is out there for the buyer to see, in your web copy you must wait until the end to reveal the price and ordering instructions. This puts your reader in the proper frame of mind to buy, because by the time you present the price you have laid out all the benefits and information your prospect needs. This is another way to keep the editorial feel of your web copy and not reveal your sales pitch too soon.

This is one of the reasons I generally do not put an order button on the left navigation bar of websites over which I have total control. If I've gone to a lot of trouble to make my web copy look like an editorial, I don't want to ruin that by putting an order button on the first screen, thereby removing all doubt that the editorial is actually an ad in disguise.

Another reason is that many web visitors click on the order button even before reading the web copy because they want to know what they are getting themselves into and whether or not they want what you're offering. If they click before they read, the order page then determines whether visitors read your web copy or not. It defeats the purpose of your copy, which is to use its power to get readers happily involved with your product or service.

In addition, an order button allows people to make a judgment about the price before knowing the details of your offer. If I had an order button on my Web Copywriting University website, for instance, and you clicked on it and found that my audio course costs $297, would you read my web copy? The bottom line is, few people are predisposed to spend that much money until they understand the value of what they are getting for that investment.

One of the major mistakes website owners make is that they fail to close the sale. They go to great lengths to get people to visit their websites, and they do everything possible to make a compelling selling argument about their product or service, but at the last moment, when the prospect is just about ready to buy, they drop the ball and fail to ask for the order. Internet marketers who are reluctant to ask for the order are usually among the unsuccessful ones. For any offer to be successful, you must be clear and explicit when you ask for the order. Include every detail, even those that seem obvious to you. Make it easy for the prospect to buy.

What Does It Take to Close a Sale?

Online or offline, simply asking for the order does *not* close the sale. "Click here to order" or a similar phrase does *not* constitute a close. As a rule, web visitors click on the order button only after you have done the necessary steps to close the sale. If you haven't given enough information, you haven't closed the sale. Period.

Closing the sale starts on the home page—usually as early as the first or second screen. Those of you who have sold offline know that clinching the sale often takes several trial closes leading up to the final close. Just like a real-life salesperson, your website should contain trial closes. If you look at the website shown in Figure 2.4, you'll see that I used eight closes to sell the software program.

You must always remember that people's *buying decision times vary.* Some people are ready to buy after they have found a benefit or

---

8 Trial Closes (and 1 Final Close) Were Used to Sell *Sculptor 3*

Note: Underlined words are text links that lead to the order page.

1) I've shown you how *Sculptor 3* uses computerization to literally immerse you in 7 of the top manifesting technologies simultaneously—and materialize your desires faster than you ever thought possible. Now, it's time for you to <u>act on this</u>.

2) Well, the good news is that you can own *Sculptor 3* for less than $100! Yes, that's right. Valuable as it is, *Sculptor 3* can be yours for a one-time investment of just $97 (USD). If you're in a hurry and can't wait to get started, click here to <u>experience *Sculptor 3* now</u>.

3) <u>Get started</u> creating your ideal life now.

4) So you have nothing to lose when you <u>give it a try</u> today. Within minutes, you will get download instructions, and you can start enjoying the benefits of *Sculptor 3* immediately.

5) To give you an even better value on your *Sculptor 3* investment, you'll also get 7 FREE gifts valued at $127 when you order <u>right now</u>.

6) Remember, I can't guarantee that you'll receive the 7 FREE gifts above unless you order *Sculptor 3* right now.

7) With *Sculptor 3*, you don't have to learn anything. Instead, it can do all the work for you—making it easy to apply manifesting principles to your life and helping you get what you want the easy and effective way. <u>Get started now</u>.

8) Imagine ... in as little as a few days or weeks, you could be manifesting the life you've always dreamed of. Imagine being totally debt-free, enjoying improved health ... happy and loving relationships ... your dream house ... all because you decided to say "YES" today.

9) Final Close:

Click to ORDER Via Our SECURE SERVER!

Figure 2.4 Several attempts to close the sale are necessary for successful web selling (www.affirmware.com.au).

two, and some aren't ready to buy until they've read every word on the website. For this reason, you have to catch them at every point at which they're likely to buy.

Step 3: Add Credibility-Building Elements

If you've immersed yourself in your product or service, you have probably uncovered testimonials, interesting stories or case studies, significant facts, quotes, or statistics related to your product or service. If for some reason you haven't, you can do speedy research on the web to fill in the gaps.

Again, for examples of these all you have to do is take a look at my web copywriting samples—particularly the ones enclosed in text boxes. See the stories that pull people in, the testimonials that support and strengthen the selling proposition, the interesting stories that both inform and whet my readers' appetites for what I have to offer, and so on. For specific examples, go to www.HowDoIGetHim Back.com, www.PsychologicalTriggers.com, or www.FreeStuffFor EntrepreneursOnTheInternet.com.

Step 4: Add Psychological Devices and Involvement Devices

These are such important and complex topics that I'll be devoting all of Chapters 5, 6, and 7 to them. Among the topics we examine are the following:

- ► Persuasion devices that get people to commit to the sale such as using your readers' desire to appear consistent to themselves and others, testimonials from satisfied customers, or even your readers' emotional satisfaction, investment, and involvement in your service or product

- ► Psychological devices such as cliffhangers to excite your readers' sense of anticipation to get them to read every word of your copy

- ► Hypnotic commands that bypass your readers' conscious minds and overcome resistance, and how to embed them into your copy

- ► Specific words that make your web copy much more believable to your readers

Step 5: Replace Rational Words with Emotional Words

You probably have heard the concept of right-brain and left-brain functions: The left hemisphere of the brain is the rational, logical, organized, analytic, linear, critical side; the right hemisphere is the creative, emotional, intuitive side, the realm of the imagination. Since people buy on emotion, the more you appeal to the right side of the brain, the more you'll sell. You do this by using emotional words, not intellectual, rational, bland, and boring words. Here are a few examples:

Use the phrase *find out* instead of the word *learn*.

Instead of saying *accolade* use *applause*.

Use *rich* instead of *wealthy*.

Say *worried* instead of *concerned*.

Instead of saying *The following are . . .* , say *Here are . . .*

Try this: Take a look at the list of left-brain and right-brain words in Figure 2.5. Next, look at the web copy you've written, identify any left-brain (or rational) words, and replace those left-brain words with the right-brain (or emotional) words. How can I make it simpler than that?

Paul Galloway, an Internet programmer, created a neat little Common Gateway Interface (CGI) script to automatically replace all instances of left-brain (rational) words on any website with right-brain (emotional) words. A CGI script is a small program that takes data from a web server and does something with it; in this case, it replaces certain words from one database (rational words) with corresponding words from another database (emotional words).

If you go to www.paulgalloway.com/cgi-bin/emotional_words.cgi and type in the URL of your website, it will show your website with all the rational words displayed in red, followed by the suggested emotional words you might want to replace them with.

Take a look, too, at Figure 2.6, which gives a list of web words and phrases that sell.

Tip: Replace the word *if* with *when* whenever you are describing what people will get from you. This is part of assuming that the sale is made.

Left-Brain (Rational) Words/Phrases	Right-Brain (Emotional) Words/Phrases	Left-Brain (Rational) Words/Phrases	Right-Brain (Emotional) Words/Phrases
accelerate	speed up	intelligent	bright
accolade	applause	I regret	I'm sorry
additionally	here's more/there's more	jesting	joking
aid	help	large	big
allow	let	learn	find out
anticipate	expect	manufacture	make
astute	smart	notion	idea
at an end	over	nude	naked
attractive	good looking	observed	seen
avid	eager	obstinate	stubborn
beneficial	good for	omit	leave out
challenge	dare	perceive	see
circular	round	perhaps	maybe
combat	fight	peril	danger
completed	finished	perspiration	sweat
concerned	worried	pleased	happy
concerning	about	preserve	save
construct	build	prevent	stop
courageous	brave	purchase	buy
demise	death	propitious	favorable
difficult	tough/hard	receive	get
diminutive	small	requested	ask for
disclose	reveal/explain	reply	answer
donate	give	select	pick/choose
elderly	old	soiled	dirty
facilitate	ease	stomach	belly
famished	hungry	strike	hit
fatigued	tired	subsequent to	since
fearful	afraid	sufficient	enough
following is/are	here's/here are	superior	better
for	because	tardy	late
fortunate	lucky	terminate	end
futile	hopeless	tidings	news
gratification	enjoyment	utilize	use
hasten	hurry	wealthy	rich
huge	giant	youthful	young
humorous	funny		
ill	sick		
immediately	right now		
inform	tell		

Figure 2.5 Left-brain versus right-brain expressions.

acclaimed, amazingly simple, announcing, appetizing, astonishing, automatically
booming, breakthrough
cash in, critical
discover, does the trick
easy-to-follow, enhanced, electrifying, exciting, exclusive, exponential
fantastic, fascinating, first, free
generous, good-as-gold, guaranteed
how-to
improved, incredible, initial, introducing
limited offer, love
handy, high-voltage, honest-to-goodness
immaculate, in-depth, ingenious, innovative, instantly, intensity, invaluable,
     irresistible
legendary
megawatt, mouthwatering
never been easier, new, no-holds-barred
one-stop shopping, outstanding, overwhelming
phenomenal, pioneer, powerful, proven techniques
rack up profits, rejuvenating, renewed, renowned, reproducible, revealed,
     revolutionary
satisfying, secrets, serene, shocking, skilled, special, spectacular, startling,
     step-by-step, successful, super
tactic, tempting, time-sensitive, trailblazing, trick
ultimate, unbeatable, unforgettable, uninhibited, unique, unlimited, urgent
within minutes, wonderful
you

Figure 2.6 Web words and phrases that sell.

REINFORCING THE FRAMEWORK: A SUMMARY ▼

First, *identify* your objective and your target audience; then get to
know your product or service thoroughly.

Second, *create* your blueprint by answering the following five questions:

1. What's the problem?
2. Why hasn't the problem been solved?
3. What's possible?
4. What's different now?
5. What should you do now?

Third, *flesh out* your web copy by taking the blueprint and

1. Injecting emotion into it
2. Adding bullet points, bonuses, the guarantee, and the close
3. Adding credibility-building elements such as testimonials, interesting stories or case studies, significant facts, quotes, or statistics
4. Adding psychological and involvement devices
5. Replacing all rational words with emotional words

3

Crafting Your Copy

*You can have everything in life you want if you will just help
enough other people get what they want.*
—Zig Ziglar

Now that you know how to create a blueprint for writing web copy
and understand how to use the five simple steps for fleshing out the
body copy, it's time to put your copy together and add some important touches—the keys to making your web copy sell.

CONSTRUCTING YOUR WEB COPY

The purpose of web copy—and it can't be said too often—is to generate leads, customers, sales, and, consequently, profits for a website.

Its objective is to compel the online prospect to respond in some way or take action of some kind. It tells the audience to do something specific during or at the end of the presentation of the marketing message.

The AIDA Principle

The four fundamentals of writing good copy are summed up in the time-honored AIDA principle:

A	Capture the audience's *attention*.
I	Get the audience's *interest*.
D	Build *desire* for your offer.
A	Induce *action*.

Benefits and Features

Features are the attributes, properties, or characteristics of your product or service. Benefits, on the other hand, are what you can do, what you can have, or what you can be because of those features. Consumers buy benefits—and not features. This is one of the most important lessons you can learn in writing copy. For example, people don't buy a power drill for its impressive specs; rather, they buy the holes that the power drill makes.

When writing copy that sells, therefore, keep your eye firmly on the benefits. The best way to distinguish benefits from features is with the following exercise: Begin by stating the feature. Then follow it up with the sentence "What that means to you is . . ." or the phrase ". . . which means that you can . . ."

> *Feature:* Your *Windows Mobile* phone gives you the mobile version of Microsoft Office . . .
>
> *Benefit:* . . . which means that even when you're on the road, you can open and edit Word and Excel documents and view PowerPoint documents.

Feature: Your *Windows Mobile* phone comes with Outlook Mobile.

Benefit: What that means to you is that while you're on the move, you can catch up on your e-mail, manage your calendar, and update your contacts with the familiar Outlook features you know from your PC.

The Unique Selling Proposition

One of the cornerstones of writing sales-pulling copy is the unique selling proposition (USP), the thing that sets you, your product/service, or your business apart from every other competitor in a favorable way. It's the competitive advantage that you proclaim to your prospects, customers, or clients.

Some of the best-known and most recognizable USPs are these:

Avis: *"We're number two. We try harder."*

FedEx: *"When it absolutely, positively has to be there overnight."*

Domino's Pizza: *"Fresh, hot pizza in 30 minutes or less."*

Apple iPhone 3G: *"Twice the speed, half the price."*

Secret® Deodorant: *"Strong enough for a man. But made for a woman."*

Altoids: *"Curiously strong mints."*

M&M's: *"The milk chocolate that melts in your mouth, not in your hand."*

Wonder Bread: *"Wonder Bread Helps Build Strong Bodies 12 Ways."*

More than just slogans, these USPs convey the idea that no other company, product, or service compares with theirs.

Amazon.com proclaims itself "Earth's Biggest Bookstore," a claim that has been accepted without question by the media, both online and offline. Its USP implies that it has the best selection of books—in essence, "if you can't find it here, you can't find it anywhere"—thereby distinguishing Amazon from all other bookstores. Although Amazon.com is indeed the largest online-only bookstore in the world, Barnes & Noble is "the world's largest bookseller," if you include both on- and offline markets. Amazon.com has managed to blur that distinction by achieving top-of-mind positioning with its USP.

A USP positions your offering as being different from, and consequently more valuable than, your competitors' offerings. It distinguishes your product or service from everyone else's, and in a world that's flooded with products and services of every kind, creating a strong USP is absolutely imperative. Not only does a strong USP give your reader a specific and compelling reason to buy from you instead of your competitors, it establishes the direction of copywriting and is the undercurrent of all marketing efforts as well.

There are online companies whose USPs are clearly conveyed by their domain names. Lowestfare.com (which claims to provide the lowest airfares in the air travel industry) and SurviveYourForeclosure.com (which claims to help people confront their foreclosures head-on and win) are examples of these. So is OneMinuteCureForAllDiseases.com, whose name says it all.

One way to develop a USP is by starting with the words "Unlike most of its competitors . . . ," then filling in the blanks about what differentiates you or your product offering from those of others. For example:

> **Unlike most other fat-burning products, ABC Product makes you lose up to 5 pounds of pure body fat per week—without the use of stimulants that may be harmful to your health.**

Another way to develop a USP is to highlight a feature or benefit that only your product or service contains or features.

Serious Magic, a software company, sells a product called Visual Communicator. Its USP is that it enables people with no technical experience to create with ease—in minutes and without any video editing—video presentations for websites, DVDs, and PowerPoint that have the professional look of a TV newscast. The specificity of the USP ("people with no technical experience," "professional look of a TV newscast in minutes," and "without any video editing") is compelling and serves to differentiate the product from other programs offering video creation capabilities.

The possibilities for crafting a USP are endless. The key is to adopt a USP that fills a void in the marketplace that you or your product can genuinely fill. Remember, too, that a USP can even be used as a headline or as an underlying theme or branding mechanism for all copywriting.

MAKING AN IMPRESSION: THE FIRST PARAGRAPH ▼

The first paragraph is crucial because it is where readers are likely to stop reading if you don't provide them with sufficient reason to continue. Ideally, it should immediately demonstrate that there are desirable rewards for reading on.

There's no need to be lengthy or elaborate. Often, short, punchy, easy-to-read sentences suffice as long as they hold the viewer's attention. One device that some leading copywriters use is to ask a question that will grip the readers' interest and compel them to continue reading.

THE OFFER YOU CAN'T REFUSE ▼

The offer is the very heart of your copy. It is the reason the copy is being written. When writing copy for offline consumption, once you have captured the attention of your readers you need to present your offer as soon as possible to let them know what you are selling and what kind of deal you'll be making. When writing web copy for direct-response offers, that's not necessarily the case. Particularly when writing editorial-style web copy, you must be careful not to uncover your hidden selling too soon. If you do, you will remove all doubt that your editorial is actually an ad in disguise.

Whether you are writing copy for on- or offline use, your offer needs to be clear, concise, and above all *irresistible*. For example:

> Own this deluxe set of knives that never need sharpening for just $19.95—and you'll never buy another set of knives again. It comes with a lifetime replacement guarantee. In the unlikely event that any of these knives should break—we will replace any or all of them free of charge—forever.

Your offer must align with your target audience's desires and needs and, as you know, it must appeal to their emotions.

What motivates people to buy? In his book *Who Am I? The 16 Basic Desires That Motivate Our Actions and Define Our Personalities* (Tarcher/Putnam, 2000), Steven Reiss, a professor of psychology and psychiatry at Ohio State University, describes his theory of human motivation. Reiss, who spent five years conducting studies involving 6,000 people, discovered that 16 desires—power, independence, curiosity, acceptance, order, saving, honor, idealism, social contact, family, status, vengeance, romance, eating, physical exercise, and tranquility—motivate all human behavior. Other studies add the desire to belong, security, integrity, consistency, ownership, exclusivity, safety, admiration, and acknowledgment. All of these complex human desires can be grouped into two basic human needs: the desire to gain pleasure and the desire to avoid pain.

Since copywriting ultimately is about fulfilling human desires and needs, the more successful you are at representing your product or service in a way that plays to those desires and needs, the more successful your sales copy will be. When articulating the offer, your primary viewpoint should always be that of your readers. In other words, you need to focus entirely on your readers. One of the best ways to pull your readers into your copy is by weaving the words *you, your,* and *yourself* throughout. This gets your readers involved in what you are saying and makes them feel as though you are writing to them.

Your offer must summarize the key benefits and advantages of the product or service you're selling. This is effectively done through bullet points—to make the copy more readable and inviting. The following are examples of bullet points for a software program aimed at novel writers:

▶ Walks you, step-by-step, through the process of writing your story—it's like having a personal writing mentor and tutor interactively showing you how to write a great novel.

▶ Simplifies the process of developing a solidly constructed plot and outline for your novel—the plot generator gives you instant access to thousands of suggested plots from virtually all kinds of stories.

▶ Enables you to create rich, dynamic characters with the easy-to-use character developer.

▶ Allows you to instantly find answers to specific questions and get targeted advice for resolving problems while you write.

▶ Provides suggestions for overcoming 100 stumbling blocks that frequently face beginning novelists.

▶ Includes a troubleshooter function that takes you from your writing problem to its remedy with a click of the mouse.

TESTIMONIALS: EFFORTLESS SELLING
▼

Testimonials add *credibility* because they are the actual words of real people, not actors or spokespeople. They can be quite disarming because your readers are able to identify with other people's experiences with your product or service.

No one knew the power of testimonials as well as W. Clement Stone, the late philanthropist and author, who founded the Combined Insurance Company of America in 1919 and was one of the richest men in America during his lifetime. In 1930, Stone had over 1,000 agents selling insurance for him all over the United States. He was known to have a simple way of training his agents. He instructed them to go into people's homes but discouraged them from making any sales pitch. Stone told them they didn't need to go through the song-and-dance routine that other insurance agents went through of trying to appeal to people's fear of dying and leaving their loved ones behind without any money. Instead, Stone sent each agent out in the field with a three-ring binder filled with about 200 pages of testimonials from satisfied insurance clients. The agent was instructed to flip through the binder, showing his prospective client a few pages of testimonials. Afterward, he would try to close the sale, and if the prospect wasn't ready to sign with his service yet, he would flip through a few more pages of testimonials, try to close the sale again, and repeat the process. Invariably, by the time the agent got to page 25 (or sooner), the prospect was sold. With this simple sales technique, agents were able to close new insurance policy sales like clockwork, and as a result Combined Insurance Company of America grew into a billion-dollar company.

Everyone knows that life insurance is a hard sell because you're selling an intangible concept. So why did the testimonials work so well in closing insurance sales? Because of what Robert Cialdini, author of *Influence: The Psychology of Persuasion* (Collins Business, 2006), calls *social proof,* a psychological phenomenon that occurs in social situations when people are uncertain how to behave and therefore assume that other people possess more knowledge about the situation than they do. They deem the behavior of others appropriate or better informed and, consequently, do what those others have done. Insurance prospects, being unsure of which decision to take, defer to the perceived wisdom of the people who had bought the insurance policies before them and, consequently, buy the insurance policy themselves.

If testimonials work so well in effortlessly advancing the sale of life insurance, doesn't it stand to reason that they would effortlessly advance online sales as well? We don't have to look too far to know that the answer to this question is yes. Just take a look at all the blogs, forums, and social networking sites where people congregate to obtain other people's opinions about products or services they're considering buying. When you feature testimonials on your website, you save prospects the trouble of having to ask for other people's opinions of your product or service elsewhere. The majority of people base their buying decision on the strength of testimonials alone.

I can cite several instances when testimonials have caused me to buy without as much as a second thought, but the one that is most illustrative of the power of social proof is an e-mail newsletter I received recently. The newsletter sender reported that he was a member of a mastermind group consisting of 45 seasoned Internet marketers. Each month, they had a teleconference during which each member was given five minutes to share any tips, tactics, techniques, or strategies that made the biggest financial impact on their business with the least amount of effort. In that month's call, he reported that one particular tactic was named the fastest cash generator by 21 of the members. He also mentioned that at one point in the teleconference, five members talked about it consecutively. Essentially, the tactic they were talking about was a piece of software that deploys a virtual chat screen whenever a visitor leaves your website without buying your product or service. That chat screen turns nonbuying website visitors into customers in a matter of minutes—and has the potential of increasing a website's sales by up to 40 percent. A link to the software website was provided, and within minutes I had clicked the order button and paid $197 to get my hands on it.

I had decided I was going to buy the software, sight unseen, even before I arrived at the software website. In fact, it took me less than ten seconds to make a buying decision. It wasn't the promise of a 40 percent increase in website sales that enticed me. I'm quite immune to exaggerated promises made by advertisers, and I'm not one who gets sold very easily. When I analyzed the reason I bought, it could have only been because I figured that if 21 seasoned Internet marketers were impressed by the results they got from this piece of software—enough to report it at the mastermind teleconference—there must be something about the software that's of high value. That's social proof at its best.

There's a software developer I met who created a piece of software that automated the process of gathering the keywords and ad descriptions of the most frequently clicked Google AdWords ads. During the beta test phase of software development, he gave away the software for free to his intended audience just so they could try it out and give him feedback on it. He received dozens of enthusiastic comments about the software from the beta testers. A month before the software was available for sale, before he even had web copy written for his website, he posted all the comments of the beta testers on his website's home page to replace the standard "Site Under Construction" page that was there. There wasn't even a form that captured the contact information of website visitors. All he offered at the bottom of the webpage was his e-mail address for those who wanted more information. By the time he actually launched the product, he had received 351 advance orders from people who didn't even bother asking how much the software cost! This software developer had implemented a variation of the W. Clement Stone method of selling—without even knowing it.

Another website that successfully employs the W. Clement Stone approach is one that sells a dog book titled *Your Dog's Love Letter* (see http://www.DogsLoveLetter.com). The web copy consists of only one short paragraph, the slogan "It's not just a book—it's an emotional experience!" followed by a litany of testimonials from people who support the slogan's claim.

The power of testimonials cannot be overemphasized, and yet many companies that do business online regard them as an afterthought. In spite of the fact that testimonials have become so commonplace and you see them overused or misused in some instances, their power for advancing sales, particularly online where trust is a big issue, is undeniable. In my experience, a website that has one powerful testimonial positioned strategically in the web copy or even the headline can single-handedly sell ten times more than an identical website without that testimonial.

You can obtain testimonials by simply asking customers for them when you fulfill orders or by calling or e-mailing customers and asking for their comments. What was their experience with your product or service: Did they enjoy it? Are they glad they purchased it? When you get positive comments, ask permission to use them in your ad, and don't forget to get a signed release.

The best testimonials are the ones that are *specific* and, preferably, *quantifiable*.

> With the ABC weight loss program, I lost 10 pounds in 9 days without dieting.
>
> I earned 5 times my salary in my spare time by following the ABC trading system.

If your product or service is new, or you don't yet have enough customers who can provide you with testimonials, give away your product or service for free to members of your target audience in exchange for their feedback. Another way to inject the power of social proof into your web copy when you haven't obtained testimonials yet is to use case studies whenever they are available or appropriate for the product or service you're selling.

I have a client, a therapist by profession, who wrote a relationship book that helps women get their ex-boyfriends back. When he came to me to have his web copy written, he had countless stories to tell about women whom he had helped rekindle their relationships. However, due to the sensitive nature of relationship issues, very few of those who had success stories to tell wanted to go on record with a public testimonial that the whole world could see. I asked my client to provide me with case studies based on the success stories his readers told him. Here is a sample case study that I included in the web copy:

The Break-Up That Led to a Happily-Ever-After
This is an actual case study. Names have been changed for privacy reasons.

A client named Charlene came to consult with me last year. She had been dating a man named Martin for six months. Charlene was 43 and had four children. The relationship was going beautifully for a few months, when, out of the blue, Martin told her that he wasn't ready to get married—so he stopped seeing her.

She felt devastated, and when she came to my office for counseling, she broke into tears often as she told me her story. I showed her the **proven game plan** for getting Martin back that I describe in *How Do I Get Him Back*—and she began to implement it. At first, nothing happened and she thought the plan wasn't working—but she stuck to the plan anyway. Seven months later, Martin proposed to her—and three months thereafter they were married.

If you were to ask Martin what caused his change of heart, he would never be able to tell. But Charlene and I know that "the plan" had everything to do with it!

A case study such as the one presented here can be as powerful as, if not more powerful than, a testimonial. That's because, unlike testimonials that usually just state the end results, case studies *tell a story*. A good story captures your prospects' attention and helps to create a bond between your prospects and you. Case studies also present another opportunity to engage the emotions of your readers and cause them to identify with your subject's pain, problem, or predicament—and vicariously experience triumph in the solution you offer. With a case study, you can also elevate the perceived value of your product in your own words, as compared to a testimonial, where you're limited to using the actual words of your customer, whether those sentiments are well articulated or not. Furthermore, a case study tends to appear more factual and objective than a testimonial, as there is a general sense of objectivity conveyed.

TALKING ABOUT MONEY: HOW TO INTRODUCE THE PRICE

First and most important, you must never introduce the price until you've stated the offer. If you do, the majority of your readers might click away before ever learning the more salient points of your offer. Second, when you do introduce the price, equate it with a ridiculously minor purchase or reduce it to a daily cost.

The Minor-Purchase Technique

Here's how the minor-purchase technique was used to introduce the price of a book about how to write news releases:

> Bottom line is, for a few bucks more than the price of a movie for two with popcorn, you can get your hands on the secrets that would mean truckloads of hot leads, sales that would make your head spin, a surge of cash flowing into your business, and first-rate recognition for you and your product that money just can't buy.

Here's how the same technique was used to equate the price of a health book to a minor purchase:

> Your investment in *The One-Minute Cure: The Secret to Healing Virtually All Diseases* is less than the price you'd pay for a single flu shot at a doctor's office (which costs $35 to $45 these days)—but the priceless knowledge you'll gain from it can

protect you and your family not just from the flu, but from virtually all diseases!

The Daily-Cost Technique

Here's how the price was introduced for a shopping cart service that costs $29 per month:

> For just $1 a day, you can now automate your . . .
> - ▶ order processing
> - ▶ e-mail marketing
> - ▶ ad tracking
> - ▶ credit card processing
> - ▶ recurring billing
> - ▶ affiliate program
> - ▶ digital delivery of your electronic products
>
> . . . and all other e-commerce activities your website requires.

This tactic, known as *equating,* can also be used when you are conveying a time frame in your web copy. For example, "In the time it takes you to brew a cup of coffee, you're done with your marketing for the day."

KEEP ON SELLING: WRITING THE ORDER FORM ▼

When I worked as director for creative web writing at Aesop Marketing Corporation, Mark Joyner designed an order form that increased orders by more than 30 percent. Ever since Mark revealed this information in his report *Confidential Internet Intelligence Manuscript,* it's been used successfully by online marketers all over the world. I often use the proven format shown in Figure 3.1.

❑   Yes! I want the *Promotional Products Distributorship Program* delivered to me immediately, and to learn how to grab my share of the $18 billion promotional products industry in as little as 1 week. I understand that I will also receive the following bonuses worth $1300!

· *A $100 discount off the regular $995 price of the Distributorship Program. (Therefore, my price is only $895.)*

· *A 15-minute telephone consultation with Joe McVoy personally (an $87.50 value)—absolutely FREE—to help me get off to a great start in the industry*

· *Unlimited e-mail consultation for 2 full months (60 days). ($350 value)*

· *Annual directory updates—FREE promotional product manufacturer directories ($770 value)*

· *A FREE copy of Promotional Marketing Magazine, a valuable resource of product information for distributors. Plus information on how to get this magazine sent to you automatically every month at absolutely no charge.*

I understand that my order is absolutely risk-free. If, after one year, I have not earned at least 5 times my investment—that is, $4,475—by implementing any of the powerful money-making tactics found in the Distributor Program, I can return it for a 100% refund.

I authorize Promotional Products Consulting, LLC to charge my credit card the amount of $895.00 (+ applicable shipping charges; UPS Ground is only $47.25, UPS 2nd Day is $127.00. Alaska/Hawaii 2nd Day is $139.50).

Here's what Joe Ferraro of Universal Showdown Marketing says: "I've had a screenprinting business for 10 years. I added a promotional products profit center to my business by simply following exactly what Joe McVoy taught me to do in his Distributor Program—which had all the factory sources I needed. In only 7 months, I've started earning a 6-figure income. I've decided to close down my screenprinting business to concentrate on my lucrative promotional products business full-time."

Click here to proceed to the secure order form.

Figure 3.1 Order form that increases orders and minimizes shopping cart abondonment.

The order form features the following components:

▶ Check box—an involvement device that compels prospects to agree to the sale the moment they click on the check box

▶ Summary of offer, bonuses, and guarantee

▶ Price

▶ Assurance of secure ordering (and whenever applicable, mentioning the level of security the order transaction will undergo—for example, "This site is protected by Secure Sockets Layer (SSL), which offers the highest level of encryption security possible for your order.")

▶ How the product or service will be delivered—and when

▶ Testimonial as reinforcement of purchase

THE MONEY-BACK GUARANTEE: A DEAL MAKER
▼

Frequently, the sale is clinched on the promise of a money-back guarantee. This is where you eliminate the buyer risk, thus removing any remaining obstacles standing in the way of the sale.

Simply stating "Money-back guarantee" is an ineffective use of a guarantee, however. You have to craft the guarantee as compellingly as possible so as not to waste this prime opportunity for closing the sale. A common template for creating a guarantee is as follows:

> Do this [*whatever you're asking them to do*], and if you don't [*achieve the result you're claiming they'll get*], then simply give us a call, and we will cheerfully refund your entire purchase price.

For example:

> Take the ABC system for a test drive. If you don't triple your sales in 60 days, then return it for a full refund.

By removing the risk, you make it easier for the prospect to say yes. It is a well-documented fact in direct marketing that the number of people who will take you up on a compelling offer significantly outnumber those who will ask for a refund.

> **Try the Memory Foam mattress pad *now*, risk-free.** If it doesn't give you the most restful sleep you've ever had, or if, for any reason, you're not completely satisfied with it, just let us know within 30 days and we will issue a no-hassle refund, and even send you a Merchandise Return Label so that you

can send the mattress pad back to us at no cost to you—we'll pay for the shipping. In the unlikely event that you would be less than **thrilled** with your new Memory Foam mattress pad, should you decide to request a refund, the 2 Memory Foam pillows are yours to keep and enjoy as our gift just for taking us up on this offer.

A strong guarantee conveys conviction, which has the power to persuade your prospect. It is sometimes possible to construct a guarantee that is so compelling that it could be the reason why someone chooses your product or service over your competitors'. In fact, your guarantee could be so powerful that you might also consider using it as your headline:

> Drive This New Pontiac for 30 Days—and If It's Not the Greatest Car You've Ever Had, We'll Buy It Back

> Drop 5 Strokes on Your Golf Game Today—*Guaranteed*

THE CLOSE: SIGNING ON THE DOTTED LINE ▼

Legendary marketer and copywriter Vic Schwab, who authored the classic *How to Write a Good Advertisement: A Short Course in Copywriting* (Wilshire, 1985), said, "Delay is the enemy of a sale." In writing web copy, your close needs to remove all obstacles that stand in the way of the reader taking action on the offer. The way to do it is by first making the offer and then injecting a sense of urgency in taking action on the offer.

Injecting urgency simply means giving the reader a reason to act now. You can employ one or more of the following:

▶ A free gift/bonus or a discount or reduced price if the reader responds on or before a certain date in the near future. Sweeten the deal, and whet the appetite. Sometimes the bonus can be so compelling that, like the guarantee, it can even be the headline.

▶ A time limit on an offer.

▶ A limited supply.

▶ A notification that prices are going up soon.

The close should also emphasize what the reader gains by responding quickly or loses by delaying action.

The Call to Action

The *call to action* (CTA) is part of the close. Here, you must tell your readers *exactly* what to do. Some marketers miss this important step. Even if it's obvious to you what readers ought to do next, you must direct them to do it. Always use action verbs in the CTA:

Click on the Download button to start your 30-day free trial.

Check the box to select your preference, and then click on the secure online form to proceed with your order.

Simply type your name and e-mail address in the form below, and the free report will be in your e-mail in-box within minutes.

Click on the link below to start generating eBay profits now.

Type in your e-mail address, then click on Go to lock in your position.

GET A CALLING CARD: THE OPT-IN MECHANISM
▼

We all know that most visitors to websites don't become buyers on their first visit—maybe not even on the first several visits. What you need to do is find out how to reach them again.

The best way to do this is with an opt-in mechanism (a tool to get a reader to agree to accept your e-mailed information and correspondence). Remember, the odds are against people buying something the first time they visit your website. After all, they don't even know you. Therefore, you must develop an irresistible—and easy—way for your visitors, at minimum, to give you their e-mail addresses before they go.

In my opinion, crafting your opt-in offer is infinitely more important than crafting the offer for the product itself. That's because you can get as much as 90 percent of your business from those with whom you build e-mail relationships. This is the usual objective, but I advise you not to be shortsighted and focus only on selling but also on building relationships.

Another version of the opt-in offer that has become popular in recent years is the *name squeeze page,* also known as the *squeeze page.* A squeeze page is a landing page that offers access to content, a free report, secret passwords, or other information in exchange for the website visitor's e-mail address and sometimes additional information. I have never liked the term *name squeeze* because it carries the connotation that one is extracting information from an unwilling prospect through force or coercion, and it reduces the person to a name that is to be processed in some manner. I prefer to call them *lead capture* or *registration* pages.

By whatever name, many people frown on this marketing practice because, in most cases, it requires website visitors to give up their contact information before being given access to the website's main pages. With the amount of spam circulating, people are wary about giving their e-mail addresses away, especially to some unfamiliar marketer who will most likely bombard them with a series of unwanted e-mails. What ends up happening, in many cases, is that in order to get access to the information being offered, website visitors resort to giving false names and e-mail addresses. Easily, a double-digit percentage of people will give false information just to get past the registration form and get access to the information.

Although, in essence, a name squeeze page does the same thing an opt-in offer on a website does, it's the timing of the offer that differs. An opt-in offer is usually delivered after website visitors have had access to the information on the website's main page and they have some kind of indication of what the website is about or who's behind it. Therefore, the opt-in offer doesn't come across as overly intrusive. The name squeeze page, on the other hand, is often a landing page that provides no information and yet asks website visitors for their contact information before they're willing to give it. This is no different from a man walking up to a woman he's never met and asking for her name and phone number, with the promise that he'll deliver some goodies at her doorstep.

Even Google tends to frown on websites that have little else on the site but the squeeze page and offers the following guideline: "Try to provide information without requiring users to register. Or, provide a preview of what users will get by registering." (See Figure 3.2.)

Having stated the drawbacks, the advantage of a name squeeze page is that from a marketer's point of view, it may be the best way to capture the contact information of as many of their prospects as possible, albeit reluctant prospects in some cases.

To reduce the number of false opt-ins, you can seek the assistance of a programmer to install Ajax, which is a group of interrelated web development techniques that are used to increase the responsiveness to and interactivity of web pages. Ajax and other, related Web 2.0 technologies enable you to enforce the completeness and accuracy with which website visitors fill out the form. While they type, the registration form checks for e-mail validity, password strength, and other essential information.

An infinitely more engaging, irresistible, and minimally intrusive way to present a squeeze page is through the use of an interactive webpage (see Figure 3.3) that any good programmer can create. When using interactivity such as that shown in Figure 3.3, your squeeze page would still offer the requisite free information, but in addition it would present an offer of a customized blueprint that you prewrote for your particular audience. Your programmer can help you configure the webpage for a wide variety of applications. The

"The Cancer Cure That Works"
This is the Video the Pharmaceutical Industry Doesn't Want You to Watch"

Watch this life-changing video now before it's banned forever.
viewers as of Friday, October 24, 2008.

After you watch this 5-minute video, scroll down to get the FULL STORY.

► Discover the remarkable, **scientifically proven** natural therapy that creates an environment within the body where **cancer and other diseases cannot thrive** -- and enables the body to **cure itself of disease**;

► Learn why this healing method -- called **"the world's greatest healing miracle of all time"** by health practitioners -- may render all cancer drugs, chemotherapy, radiation and other cancer treatments obsolete; and

► Find out how this safe, inexpensive and powerful healing method has been administered by an estimated **15,000 European doctors, naturopaths and homeopaths** to more than 10 million patients in the past 70 years to successfully treat cancer and many other diseases -- and how you can use it, too.

Get the FULL STORY for FREE. Just fill out the form ➡
and the groundbreaking information will be e-mailed to you within minutes.

Here's wishing you a life filled with vibrant health and freedom from cancer!

Madison Cavanaugh

Get the FULL STORY of the scientifically proven cancer cure that most people will never know

The One-Minute Cure for Cancer

Simply enter your **First Name** and **primary email address** below, then click the *"YES, Send Me the FULL STORY!"* button. The link, which will give you FREE access to this groundbreaking information, will be sent to your inbox immediately...

Name:
Email:

YES, Send Me the FULL STORY!

We take your privacy very seriously, and we HATE spam as much as you do. Your Email address will never be shared with anyone else.

Figure 3.2 This registration page provides content in the form of a short video. The video provides a preview of what users will get once they register.

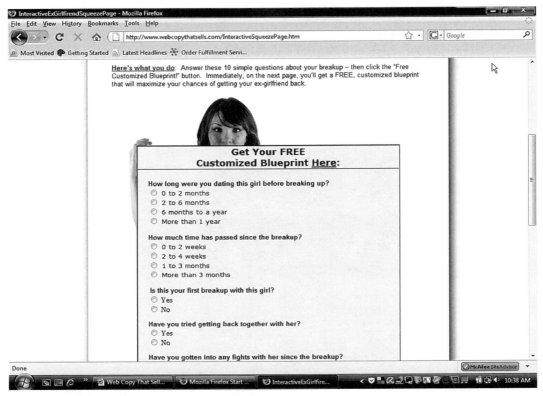

Figure 3.3 Registration page with customization.

interactive website in Figure 3.3, which was created by Mohit Saxena (InnovatorsWeb.com) at a price of only $70, was designed for an entrepreneur who sells a relationship book for men. Go to the website http://www.webcopythatsells.com/InteractiveSqueezePage.htm and fill out the multiple-choice form to see it in action.

When website visitors fill out the form and submit the information, a sales page appears, giving customized information based on the information the website visitors provided. This provides instant gratification to the website visitors, and they begin to feel that their needs are understood, that it's as though someone read their minds. Therefore, they'll be likely to click on the link at the bottom of the page that will take them to the sales page in the proper frame of mind. This mechanism combines the functions of both a name squeeze page and an involvement device, and it goes a long way toward building the rapport and trust that pave the way to the sale.

HOW TO CONSTRUCT A RIVETING HEADLINE
▼

According to David Ogilvy, founder of the Ogilvy & Mather advertising agency and author of *Confessions of an Advertising Man* (rev. ed., Atheneum, 1988) and *Ogilvy on Advertising* (Wiley, 1983), "On the average, five times as many people read the headlines as read the body copy. It follows that, unless your headline sells your product, you have wasted 90 percent of your money."

Here's a plan for crafting never-fail headlines:

Step 1. Write 30 to 50 headlines before you decide on the one you're going to use.

Step 2. Step back from the headline for a day and read it again with a fresh perspective.

Step 3. Ask yourself, "How can this headline be better?" "Is this the best possible headline for my objective, my target audience, and my product or service?"

Most important, don't take shortcuts when crafting the headline. If you write a weak one, you will have failed, because no matter how good the rest of the piece is, no one will ever read it, and, consequently, no one will buy what you're selling. Remember, the most important element of a website is the first screen, and the most important element of the first screen is the headline. Therefore, you must give it the attention it deserves.

The headline is the most important component of any direct-response ad, whether it's a printed sales letter or an advertorial on your website. If you don't stop readers dead in their tracks with your headline, you don't stand a chance of making a sale.

The sales-producing ability of your website is directly proportional to the number of people who read what's on it. That is, the more people who read your web copy, the more sales it will generate. Therefore, the headline must grab the reader's attention, since its primary purpose is to induce people to start reading the copy.

John Caples, the advertising industry's advocate of rigorously tested, measured, and verifiable advertising effectiveness, said in his book *Tested Advertising Methods* (Prentice Hall, 1998), "In a print ad, 75 percent of the buying decisions are made at the headline alone." I'm speculating that online that percentage might be a bit less—perhaps 60 to 65 percent. After factoring in the attention deficit, information overwhelm, and general skepticism so prevalent on the web, 60 to 65 percent is still significant enough that you should take the subject of headlines more seriously than any other aspect of web copy.

What's in a Headline?

Your headline should convey a benefit of interest to your target audience. It must answer the reader's unspoken question, "What's in it for me?" As we've learned, there are two basic approaches to answering that question, and each stems from one of two basic human needs: (1) to gain pleasure or (2) to avoid pain.

You can appeal to the human need to gain pleasure by pointing out how the readers can attain or accomplish something by using your product or service. More particularly, your headline can demonstrate how your product or service will meet your readers' needs or solve their problems. Here are some classic examples of headlines with appeals based on pleasure:

> The Secret to Making People Like You
>
> Make over Your Body Exactly the Way You Want in Just 6 Weeks
>
> Make Anyone Do Anything You Mentally Command—With Your Mind Alone!

How to Win Friends and Influence People

Why Some Consultants Earn $100,000 to $250,000 per Year
While Most Struggle Just to Get By

Play Guitar in Seven Days or Your Money Back

Alternatively, you can appeal to the human need to avoid pain by showing how readers can reduce or eliminate undesirable things such as discomfort, embarrassment, loss, illness, mistakes, poverty, and boredom, to name a few. Here are a few famous ones that play on that need:

Do You Make These Mistakes in English?

Are You Ever Tongue-Tied at a Party?

You Can Laugh at Money Worries—If You Follow This
Simple Plan

When Doctors Feel "Rotten," This Is What They Do

Do You Have These Symptoms of Nerve Exhaustion?

Do You Do Any of These 10 Embarrassing Things?

All of these successful headlines are compelling. They not only capture the attention of prospective buyers, they also make an immediate connection with them. They give readers a good reason to read on.

The Building Blocks of Winning Web Headlines

Headlines are the starting point of successful web copy. If your headline fails to capture the attention of readers, it doesn't matter how good your body copy is because your readers won't ever get there. According to master direct marketer and author Ted Nicholas, who reportedly has sold $500 million worth of products in 49 industries, a good headline can be as much as 17 times more effective than a so-so headline. Simply changing one word or one figure in a headline can dramatically improve the response.

A successful headline engages or involves the reader by

▶ Offering a strong, compelling promise

How a Simple Formula Has Been Scientifically Proven to Cure Cancer and Virtually All Diseases

▶ Highlighting benefits to the reader

The World's Richest Source of Cash—And How You Can Tap into It to Start or Grow Your Business

▶ Explaining exactly what the offer is

Earn Your Master's Degree Online in 18 Months or Less

▶ Appealing to the emotions

Will These Internet Trends Kill Your Online Business?

▶ Using specifics

Why the Securities Regulators *Forbid* Me to Tell You How to Consistently Earn 151.8% to 301.02% Returns on Your Investments—and how a loophole can enable you to still cash in on these astronomical returns

▶ Arousing curiosity

Words That Command People to Do Your Bidding

▶ Calling out to a specific target audience

The Sales-Closing Techniques of a Self-Made Billionaire

▶ Making an announcement

$2 Million Scientific Project Unlocks the Secret of Aging: How You Can Become Biologically Younger

▶ Asking a question

Does Coral Calcium Really Reverse Aging, Extend Your Life Span, and Cure Degenerative Diseases Like Cancer?

▶ Beginning with the words *how to*

How to Control the Mind of Your Prospects—And Influence Them to Buy What You're Selling

Building Block 1

Web headlines differ from advertising headlines because a web headline doesn't always explain what the offer is. Instead, it wraps the offer in an editorial cushion. Like the body copy, the headline should not read like an ad; rather, it should read like an editorial. Remember that, according to Ted Nicholas, *five times* as many people read editorials than messages that scream out, "I'm an ad!" If an advertorial is prepared in a way that lends credibility, it can pull up to 500 percent more in sales!

Building Block 2

When writing a headline that highlights benefits, remember that there are obvious benefits as well as hidden ones. An obvious benefit is one that is immediately apparent. Even then, the obvious must be articulated in a way that conveys value. For example, say you are trying to convey the money-saving benefit of joining a buyers discount club. Instead of writing a bland headline like "Save 20 Percent on All Your Purchases," I'd write the following:

> Discover How to Give Yourself a 20 Percent Pay Raise—
> Without Having to Squeeze a Single Cent from Your Boss

Do you see the hidden benefit? When you save 20 percent or more on everything you buy as a discount buying club member, it's the equivalent of getting a 20 percent pay raise (and you don't have to pay taxes on that pay raise!). I've stated the obvious in a creative way and added emotion and drama to it by using the action words *discover* and *squeeze*.

A hidden benefit is one that is not immediately apparent and, at first glance, may not seem to be a reason for buying your product or service. "A Tax-Deductible Vacation in Las Vegas" is a hidden benefit of attending a seminar in Las Vegas.

Building Block 3

According to master copywriter and marketer Ted Nicholas, who reportedly spent more than $100,000 testing to find out which copy elements boost response rates, an ad headline draws 28 percent more attention if framed in quotation marks! The ad appears much more important because the impression that someone is being quoted adds credibility, which in turn makes it more riveting and more likely to be read. For example, "You, Too, Can Pick Winning Stocks—with 95 Percent Accuracy."

Building Block 4

Whenever possible, use the imperative in your headline, which is a grammatical mood that (as its name implies) influences the behavior of another or expresses a command.

> Land a Better Job
>
> Create Your Own Channel and Share Video Online [courtesy of MaxCast.com]
>
> Put an End to Migraines
>
> Broadcast Yourself [courtesy of YouTube]
>
> Erase Your Negative Credit Marks
>
> Share Your Photos. Watch the World. [courtesy of Flickr.com]
>
> Cancel Your Debts
>
> Stop the Flu Dead in Its Tracks

An online advertisement for Windows Mobile Phone uses four such imperative statements in succession, as follows:

> *Get more done, stay more connected, explore more places, have more fun.*

The imperative mood commands, leads, or empowers your prospect to do something. It starts with an action verb such as *blast, impress, improve, create*; it assumes the subject is you and ends with the object of the action. If your verb is *blast,* the question is "Blast what?" And the answer is "Your competition." The headline is "Blast

Your Competition." If your action verb is *impress,* the question is "Impress whom?" Answer: "Your friends." The headline is "Impress Your Friends."

CHOOSING YOUR WORDS: TIPS, TERMS, AND CONCEPTS

▼

Once you've written your copy, it is vital that you pay attention to how readable that copy is. Short sentences and simple words make your copy more inviting. They also help to cut up huge blocks of text into bite-size paragraphs that are no more than three or four sentences each.

Microsoft Word has a tool that displays information about the reading level of the document, including readability scores. It rates text on the 100-point Flesch Reading Ease scale; the higher the score, the easier it is for people to understand your writing. Aim for a score of 70 or higher. It also rates your writing on a U.S. grade-school level. For example, a score of 7.0 means that a seventh grader can understand the document. When writing copy, aim for a score of seventh- or eighth-grade-level comprehension.

Words to Avoid in Your Web Copy

You already know that you should avoid using intellectual, rational, or right-brained words, opting instead for emotional words, but there are other categories of words you must avoid using.

Don't use euphemisms in an effort to avoid words that might offend. Doing so insults the intelligence of your audience. While you think you are trying to spare your readers' feelings and sensibilities, using euphemisms may backfire and cause readers to be more offended than if you had just been straightforward. For example, don't call overweight people "metabolically challenged" or people who suffer from hair loss "follicularly challenged" or poor people "economic underachievers." People see through these euphemisms and may think you are actually being condescending.

Don't use buzzwords if the buzzwords don't play an integral part in your selling proposition. In other words, don't use buzzwords just to show people that you're cool, that you're hip to modern lingo, or to impress them with your vocabulary.

Buzzwords sometimes alienate people who don't understand what you are talking about. They may also make you sound pretentious. Even worse, you may be using words that have gone hopelessly out of style (without your knowing it), which makes you appear so outdated.

Don't use corporatespeak. The way you write web copy is distinctly different from the way you would write a corporate communication or even a literary or journalistic work. As I tell my students, "You're not going to win any literary awards for writing excellent web copy, but you are going to win sales." You might pride yourself on writing flowery prose or businesslike correspondence, but those things don't cut it in web copy. For instance, the sentence "We are committed to your success" doesn't mean anything to people anymore. It's tired, it's boring, and it doesn't convey tangible benefits.

Don't use clichés. I believe the avoidance of clichés applies to all genres of writing. They diminish the value of your writing. Clichés make your writing look terribly dated, which in turn may affect how your readers view your offer. If you are behind the times, what does that say about your product or service?

Don't use tentative adjectives. These are words and phrases like *pretty good, very impressive,* or *quite wonderful.* Such words rob your writing of conviction. You must either drop the word or the phrase altogether and simplify your sentence or replace the word with a compelling one that dramatizes the thought you are trying to communicate.

Do communicate. We've all heard the Internet referred to as the information superhighway. In fact, that's practically a cliché. But information is distinctly different from communication. The Internet is filled with people who can inundate you with all kinds of information; the person who has the ability to communicate is the one who will rise above the clutter and the noise—and actually be heard or read.

Author Sidney J. Harris once said, "The two words 'information' and 'communication' are often used interchangeably, but they signify quite different things. Information is giving out; communication is getting through." In marketing, you want to use words that communicate, words that will create interest, trigger enthusiasm, and motivate people to action.

Words to Use in Your Web Copy

Here are some eye-catching words that create positive or engaging images.

Attention-Grabbing Words

Affordable	Challenging
Alert	Competitive edge
Allure	Comprehensive
Applause	Compromise
Avoiding	Concept
	Crucial
Big	
Billboard	Danger
Blockbuster	Daring
Bonanza	Destiny
Boom	Dirty
Bottom line	Distinguished
Brain picking	Dividends
Bravo	Dynamics
Breakthrough	
Buy	Eager
Buyer's guide	Easy

Eat

Economic needs

Effective

Emerging growth

Endurance

Energy

Enterprising

Envision

Epidemic

Excitement

Exercising

Expert

Explain

Exploit

Favorable

Find out

Flex

Flourishes

Focus

Foothold

Forecast

Formula

Fueling

Fundamentals

Funny

Gaining

Gallery

Generic

Get

Giant

Good-looking

Growth

Gut feelings

Happy

Heritage

High-tech

High yield

Hit

Hopeless

Hot property

Hybrid

Huge

Hurry

Idea

Imagination

Inflation-beating

Innovative

Insatiable

Investigative

Just in time

Keep in touch

Kidding

Last-minute

Late-breaking

Launching

Liberated

Lifeblood

Lively

Longevity

Lucky

Luxury

Mainstream

Make

Mania
Marvelous
Masterpiece
Measure up
Medicine
Merit
Monitor
Monumental

Naked
Nest egg
New
Newswire
Next generation
Nostalgic
Novel

Obsession
Opportunities
Overrated

Perspective
Philosophy
Pioneering
Portfolio
Profitable decision
Promising

Recruiting
Remarkable
Reminiscent
Renaissance spirit
Reviewing
Revisited
Revolution

Rewards
Rich
Right now

Sampler
Save
Savvy
School of thought
Scorecard
Security
Show me
Shrewd
Simplistic
Skill
Slash
Smart
Soar
Specialized
Speed up
Spiral
Spotlight
Stardom
Starter kit
Stop
Stubborn
Successful switch
Surefire
Surging
Survival

Tax-resistant
Tech revolution
Technology
Tell
Test-drive

Timely	Upscale
Top dog	Value line
Traces	
	Willpower
Ultimate	Word-of-mouth
Underpriced	
Unlock	Young

DOs AND DON'Ts OF WEB COPYWRITING ▼

Do give a compelling promise early in the body copy that the material viewers are about to read is worth their while. For example:

> Be sure to read every word of this because the secret ingredient for turning your small business enterprise into a mega–success story is hidden in this article.

In the next example, I challenge them to read every word, because if they don't, they'll miss that thing they are dying to know.

> Your first step is to read this article in its entirety. Please don't just skim through it—I don't want you to miss a single word, because when I demystify web copywriting for you, you simply cannot fail to create the sales and profits you want on the web.

Another technique I use is to reveal a little-known fact, anecdote, or case study at the beginning, followed by a statement like this:

> If you think that's interesting, wait 'til you read what I've discovered.

This statement implies that more interesting information is about to be revealed. In the next example, the promise of solid proof is compelling and makes readers continue reading with anticipation.

The career of writing no longer has to be synonymous with starving. An annual income of $100,000 or more—even on a freelance or part-time basis—is now well within your reach. This is absolutely no hype—and I'll give you solid proof in a moment. And if you think that's exciting, wait 'til I show you how you can do it in as little as 6 weeks.

This is how it works when you put it all together: In your introductory paragraphs, tell your readers what you are going to say with a compelling promise. In the body copy, deliver on the promise, and, in a concluding paragraph, remind them of what you just revealed. This boosts your credibility for delivering on a promise and paves the way toward making your reader welcome your offer.

Do establish early in the copy who is writing the piece and why the audience should believe the writer. This is where your (or your client's) credentials, qualifications, or experience become important. They don't necessarily have to be monumental; that is, you don't have to be the leading expert or authority in a particular field, but your credentials must make you (or your client) believable.

One html trick I use to identify the writer (i.e., the person in whose "voice" the web copy is expressed) early in the piece is to make the writer's name a hypertext link. When visitors click on the link, it opens a pop-up window containing the qualifications of the writer.

Do write in the first person. Whenever possible, remove the words *we* or *our* from your web copy and replace them with *I*. By speaking in the first person, it is as though one person is talking to another. *We* and *our* sound more corporate, less intimate and friendly. You can't use this technique all the time, but do use it when it's appropriate.

Do use a drop letter (also called a drop cap) when starting your body copy. A drop letter is an oversized (often bold and ornamental) first letter of the first sentence of your body copy. Generally, it drops down two or more lines into the opening text of your body copy. Tests conducted by Ted Nicholas have proven that starting your body copy with a drop cap increases readership because it draws readers' eyes to it, thereby leading them to start reading the body copy instead of clicking away. In his book *Ogilvy on Advertising,* David Ogilvy writes, "The drop capital increases readership of your body copy by 13%." (See Figure 3.4.)

Do use multiple pricing structures. Always remember that people fall into different price categories. That's why Mercedes-Benz makes cars that cost $30,000, $69,000, $85,000, and more. Most people fail to recognize this when they design their offers. As a result, their offers are static. They usually have just one price and one offer.

Different pricing programs are structured to catch as many people as possible at the level at which they are willing to buy. Remem-

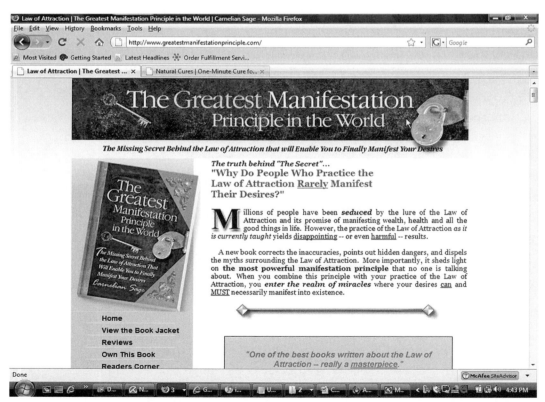

Figure 3.4 Drop capital increases readership.

ber: The value of any merchandise is what someone is willing to pay for it.

People also gravitate to different income promises: If you run a headline that reads "How to Use Website Metrics to Boost Your Conversion Rates to 10%, 20%—Even 30%" you're likely to get more responses than if your headline reads "How to Use Website Metrics to Boost Your Conversion Rate to 30%." Why? Because a broader spectrum of the audience can relate to—and believe—the three levels of improvement (10, 20, and 30 percent). Some people would have trouble believing anyone could get a 30 percent conversion rate, but they might readily believe that 10 or 20 percent is possible.

Remember that when you write web copy. Say I write the following headline to promote a web copywriting course: "Earn $300 Per Hour as a Web Copywriter." Very few people would read any further. The claim sounds unbelievable, even though it's true. Some people think it's not possible for them to earn that much. If, on the other hand, I write "Can You Really Earn $85, $125—even $235 an Hour as a Web Copywriter?" and a subheadline that reads "The Web Price Index Says You Can," that would make more people read on, wouldn't it?

Do call attention to the flaws or shortcomings of your product or service, but only if you can turn those flaws and shortcomings into benefits. When you admit the drawbacks of your product or service, you immediately increase your credibility. People think you are really up front and honest about the not-so-great aspects of your product, not just touting the good things about it. The key here is that you should not call attention to flaws or drawbacks unless you can turn that "confession" into a benefit. Avis said it this way: "We're Number 2. We try harder" and turned a drawback into a unique selling proposition. I'm sure you've often heard this said: "We're not cheap, but we're the best."

Do ask an opening question. I have already discussed the importance of incorporating compelling questions into your web copy to grab the attention of your readers and to force their brains to answer the questions more imaginatively than you can articulate them.

When you open the first paragraph of your web copy with a question, it increases your chances of getting your readers to read on.

A well-designed question causes the prospect's thoughts to focus on what you have to say. Your opening question must, of course, be relevant and important and must speak to the needs of your audience. When crafted skillfully, questions point to the result or benefit of your product or service.

Do craft text links that are engaging and highly clickable. We already know that web visitors often scan the page instead of reading it word for word. When they do, their eyes gravitate to formatting devices such as words in bold print or italics, underlined words, and bullets. Hyperlinks to related websites are also formatting devices. These are even more eye-catching than bold, underlined, or italicized words because they're in another color.

It takes more than a vague "click here" to compel readers to click through to the target destination. In order for the text link to be highly clickable, it must either convey a benefit or employ an embedded command.

Click here to *discover the one-minute cure for virtually all diseases.*

Notice that this example contains an embedded command (more on that in Chapter 7), conveys a benefit, and is written in the imperative mood. These kinds of text links are significantly more clickable. "Give it a try, risk-free" as a clickable link is more effective than "Click here to order."

Do use phrases that take the edge off the act of purchasing, that make it look easy, and that, ideally, convey a benefit:

Submit Your Online Reservation

Unlock the Cash Vault Now

Click Here to Get Your Name in the News

Become an Associate

Get [*product*] Now

Attend the Boot Camp

This enhances the editorial approach to writing web copy. If you can avoid using words like *buy now* or *order* inside your editorial web copy, do it.

THE LONG AND SHORT OF IT: HOW LONG SHOULD WEB COPY BE? ▼

I'm often asked if web copy has to consist of multiple pages in order to sell—especially since most people don't read on the web. While there will always be companies, products, and services for which abbreviated web copy is both suitable and adequate, I believe that when you're trying to convince people to invest any amount of money or time (or both), you need to assure them that they are making the right purchase decision.

Most often, you simply can't do that in a single page or less of copy. That would be like expecting a customer to walk into Circuit City and walk out five minutes later with a brand-new computer after spending 60 seconds with a salesperson pitching that particular brand. That's just not how buying decisions are made, and that's just not the anatomy of the sales process.

How long should web copy be? My answer used to be this: "Web copy should be like the length of a woman's skirt—long enough to cover the subject, but short enough to be interesting." Although that answer may sound clever and does hold seeds of truth, a more accurate reply is "Web copy should be as long as it takes to make the sale. Period."

This policy holds true in offline copywriting as well. In his book *Ogilvy on Advertising*, David Ogilvy wrote: "All my experience says that for a great many products, long copy sells more than short. . . .

Direct response advertisers know that short copy doesn't sell. In split run tests, long copy invariably outsells short copy."

In his first Rolls-Royce advertisement, Ogilvy used 719 words, and he found that the advertisement was thoroughly read. Spurred on by the success of long copy in garnering attention, he used 1,400 words in his second Rolls-Royce advertisement, also with excellent results.

Another well-known example demonstrating the effectiveness of long copy is the Schlitz beer advertisement written by legendary copywriter Claude Hopkins. Hopkins wrote five pages of text, and as a result of that campaign Schlitz moved up from fifth place to first in beer sales.

Seldom have I seen a high-ticket item sold in less than several pages of copy—either online or offline. As a rule, the higher the price of what you are selling, the longer the web copy should be. For example, the web copy I wrote for Jay Conrad Levinson's Guerrilla Marketing Boot Camp took 13 pages to make a $2,500 sale. But when you consider that those hardworking 13 pages sold more than half a million dollars' worth of seminar seats, you begin to under-stand the value of long copy.

When you learn the principles of writing long direct-response web copy, you will be able to write short web copy easily. It's similar to going to medical school and specializing in surgery. If you were a brain surgeon who later decided to become a general practitioner, you could do that.

However, the length is not always dependent on the price of the product or service you are selling. For example, the web copy I wrote to sell an e-class with a ticket price of $1,500 was only six pages long, while the web copy I wrote for a $27 book took all of eight pages. Both sold very well. It all points back to writing web copy that's as long or as short as it takes to make the sale.

The more practice you have writing web copy, the better feel you will have for the rhythm of the sale and the sentiments of your audi-ence, and you'll know instinctively how long or short your web copy needs to be. The warp-speed copywriting exercise in Chapter 1 will fine-tune your instincts.

Of course, there is also such a thing as web copy that is too long. I've seen a 75-page sales letter used on a website to promote an Internet marketing seminar. There may be people who will read something that long, but generally speaking, that length overwhelms most people. Above all, don't use long copy as an excuse to babble on and on. Your web copy needs to be a lean, mean selling machine, even if it is disguised as editorial content. It pays to remember what advertising master John Caples once said about the length of copy: "It can't be too long, only too boring."

The Trifecta Neuro-Affective Principle, which is presented in Chapter 6, provides the option of streamlining your copy to just the essential elements that make the most impact. Since the trend on the Internet is leaning more and more toward shorter forms of copy, it is advisable to master the principle so that you, too, can sell any product or service without having to use long-scrolling webpages' worth of copy.

HOW WELL DOES YOUR WEBSITE SELL?   ▼

In the years I've spent specializing in web copywriting, I've developed a comprehensive formula for mathematically measuring the selling quotient of web copy. I coined the term *selling quotient* (SQ), which is the predictor of a website's sales performance based on its web copy.

You can plug this formula into your existing web copy and determine exactly what kind of a selling job your website is doing. You can also use it as a tool for evaluating web copy that you have written following the guidelines in the first four chapters of this book.

This formula allows you to grade your web copy on a scale of 1 to 100. The real beauty in the formula, though, is that even if your website scores low, you will know exactly how to fix it.

Formula for Mathematically Measuring the Selling Quotient of Web Copy

Rate the following components of your website, giving yourself a possible score of 100 points.

First Screen

Does the first screen give the web visitor a compelling reason—in 5 seconds or less—why he or she should stay and read on? (0–7)

_____

Note: Did you make sure that the logo, company name, header, graphics, and other nonselling features did not take up a sizable chunk of the first screen?

Headline

Does the headline stop readers dead in their tracks? (0–7)

_____

Does the headline read like an interesting editorial—instead of an ad? (0–7)

_____

Does the headline incorporate a compelling promise or point to a benefit that's important to the target audience? (0–2)

_____

Does the headline call out to the target audience? (0–1)

_____

Does the headline cause the reader to read the subheadline and/or the first paragraph of the web copy? (0–3)

_____

Is this the best possible headline for the objective? (0–2)

_____

Is this the best possible headline for the target audience? (0–2)

_____

Is this the best possible headline for the product or service? (0–2)

_____

Does the headline do one or more of the following: (0–1)   _____

- ▶ Appeal to the emotions?
- ▶ Use specifics?
- ▶ Arouse curiosity?
- ▶ Make an announcement?
- ▶ Ask a question?
- ▶ Begin with the words *how to*?

First Paragraph or Opening Statement

Does the first paragraph cause the reader to read the
second paragraph? (0–3)   _____

Does the opening paragraph ask a compelling question
that breaks preoccupation, or grab attention, or point
to the result or benefit of the product or service? (0–2)   _____

Style and Formatting

Is the web copy written in a conversational style? Does
it use contractions, colloquialisms, and easy-to-read
language instead of corporatespeak? (0–1)   _____

Is it scannable? Does it do the following? (0–5)   _____

- ▶ Use bulleted lists to summarize content?
- ▶ Highlight (i.e., bold, italicize, underline) selected
  keywords to help scanners move through the
  web copy?
- ▶ Have meaningful subheads (versus amusing or
  clever ones)?
- ▶ Present one idea per paragraph?
- ▶ Use the inverted-pyramid style of writing (i.e., key
  points and conclusions presented first, followed
  by less important matters and background
  material)?

> ▶ Break paragraphs into two to four sentences?
>
> ▶ Incorporate interesting stories or case studies, significant facts, quotes, or statistics set off in boxes?

Body Copy

Is the body copy written in editorial (versus advertising) style? (0–3) _____

Does the body copy lead readers down the intended sales path? (0–3) _____

Was emotion injected into the body copy? Is the body copy built on proven emotional drivers such as anger, exclusivity, fear, greed, guilt, and curiosity? (0–3) _____

Do all the parts of the body copy compel the reader to read from start to finish? Did you employ the questions "What's in it for me?" and "Who cares?" and "So what?" after writing each sentence—and remove all sentences or phrases that don't satisfy those questions? (0–2) _____

Does the body copy employ the linear path—with minimal distractions and minimal clickable links that don't support the sales process? (0–5) _____

Does it use psychological devices that motivate prospects to buy? Have rational words been replaced with emotional words wherever possible? (0–3) _____

Does the body copy answer the question "Will this product really work for me if I use it?" with an unequivocal "Yes!" Were all possible sales objections addressed? (0–2) _____

Is the writer of the website's information identified early in the body copy? Are reasons given for why the readers should believe the writer? (0–2) _____

Does the web copy convince readers that no other
product or service can compare to the one that's being
sold on the website? (0–2)   _____

**Offer, Testimonials, Bullets, Price, Guarantee,
Bonuses, and Close**

Is the offer crafted in an irresistible manner? Does it
establish a unique selling proposition—and is that USP
featured prominently on the web page?
(0–3)   _____

Does the web copy employ the use of testimonials? Are
the testimonials strategically placed in areas where they
reinforce the selling arguments? (0–3)   _____

Does the web copy employ mouthwatering bullets? Do
the bullets first state the benefit that readers will receive,
followed up with either (1) a brief scenario of how their
life will change when they get that benefit or (2) an
injection of emotion, drama, or intrigue that elevates the
desirability of that benefit? (0–3)   _____

Are free bonuses or gifts offered as an incentive to buy?
(0–2)   _____

Does the close summarize the offer, employ a persuasive
call to action, and inject a sense of urgency by giving
compelling reasons to act now? Is the close written in a
style that assumes the sale? (0–3)   _____

Does the web copy convince the reader that the product
or service is worth the price? (0–2)   _____

Does the product or service being offered have a
guarantee that removes the risk from the purchase?
(0–3)   _____

Other Elements

Is there a mechanism to capture the web visitors' contact information? Does the opt-in offer feature an irresistible and easy way to compel the target audience to give up their contact information? (0–7)   _____

Do the web design layout and graphics support the web copy? (0–1)   _____

Does the order form include the following essential components? (0–3)   _____

- ▶ Check box
- ▶ Summary of offer, bonuses, and guarantee
- ▶ Price
- ▶ Assurance of secure ordering
- ▶ How the product or service will be delivered—and when
- ▶ Testimonial as reinforcement of purchase

TOTAL SCORE   _____

Note: To avoid having to manually add up your worksheet score, you can go to www.WebCopywritingUniversity.com/formula.htm. That webpage enables you to simply plug in your scores, and the CGI script automatically calculates the total for you. (The CGI script is courtesy of Paul Galloway, www.PaulGalloway.com.)

Thomas Carruthers once said, "A teacher is one who makes himself progressively unnecessary." This formula is one of the devices I've used to make myself progressively unnecessary to my web copywriting students and clients. It allows you to dissect your own web copy (or your prospective clients' web copy), evaluate its selling ability, and make the necessary improvements—all in one fell swoop.

E-Mail Marketing
The Internet's Killer Application

It is not your customers' job to remember you. It is your
obligation and responsibility to make sure they don't have the
chance to forget you.
—Patricia Fripp

Whenever I refer to *web copy*, I am using an umbrella term that
includes not only website copy, but also e-mails that sell, opt-in
offers, newsletters, e-zines, online ads (including pop-ups), autoresponder messages, free reports or promotional articles, online video
or audio, search engine listings, signature files, and other online
marketing communications. These can represent as much as 90 percent of the sales you can make online.

Of all the components that make up the web copy mix, e-mail
marketing is one of the most important. For that reason, I believe

writing e-mail copy is crucial to your online success, whether you are a web copywriter or an Internet marketer.

TRAFFIC CONVERSION: TURNING VISITORS INTO CUSTOMERS

▼

On the Internet, there are two fundamental ways of acquiring website sales: The first is to generate traffic to your website (*traffic generation*), and the second is to convert your website visitors into customers (*traffic conversion*).

Web copywriting is the primary element of traffic conversion. Make no mistake about it, as a web copywriter, your primary function is as a traffic converter. After all, what good is all the traffic in the world if you can't get visitors to your site to do what you want them to do when they get there?

Traffic generators are those things that drive traffic to a website. Traffic generators include high search engine rankings, investing in pay-per-click advertising campaigns, affiliate marketing, online video marketing, blogging, e-zine advertising, joint-venture endorsements, and similar devices. There are thousands of ways to generate traffic. When you write marketing communications such as free reports, promotional articles, online ads, newsletters or e-zines, SIG files, and search engine listings, you assume the secondary role of traffic generator.

Wagging the Website

Whenever I discuss e-mail marketing, I always mention *Wag the Dog*, a movie starring Robert De Niro as a political operative and Dustin Hoffman as a movie producer, whose characters come together to promote the sagging candidacy of the president. De Niro's character hatches a scheme that, with the help of Hoffman's character and the magic of Hollywood smoke and mirrors, fools the American public and the highest branches of the U.S. government into believing there is a war going on, setting in motion a huge chain of events. Thus, the tail (De Niro's character) is wagging the dog (the United States). The metaphor of the tail (a small, relatively insignificant appendage) wagging the dog finds parallels in web commerce, particularly in the dynamic between e-mail and a website.

On the Internet, what do online businesses pay the most attention to and spend the most money on? The website, of course, because that's the highly visible component of the marketing mix. The website is where a business displays its products and services; it's where you close the sale and take the orders. E-mail, on the other hand, is not glamorous and is therefore viewed as merely a supporting component of the marketing process, which is a big mistake.

Most online entrepreneurs and writers overlook the significance of e-mail, and as a result, they write e-mails haphazardly, almost as an afterthought. They regard e-mail as something that supports the objectives of the website, or as a vehicle for customer service, or as a way to send out special announcements. In other words, they regard e-mail as a low-cost, inconsequential accessory to their web presence, like the tail of a dog.

While e-mail can and does make a fine supporting actor, used properly it can assume a starring role as the primary sales tool. E-mail can be used to direct what happens on your site, not vice versa. In essence, you can use e-mail to "wag the website."

Why Your E-Mail May Be More Important Than Your Website

I'm not suggesting by any means that a website is *not* important or that you should forget about putting one up. I am saying that if you rely exclusively on a website for your sales without using the power of e-mail to fuel those sales, your Internet business is not going to get very far.

E-mail marketing is a hot item in e-commerce. A layperson may think of commercial e-mail as spam, but to the marketing industry, e-mail is a gold mine that allows companies to speak personally and directly to prospects and customers and to carry on a relationship that contributes significantly to sales.

As you know, chances are that less than 1 percent of visitors to your site will ever buy your product or service. Even the best marketers with the most successful websites seldom convert more than 5 percent of their web visitors into customers when their website is their only marketing vehicle. That's why an opt-in mechanism is vital for capturing your visitors' contact information, developing a relationship with them, and, as a result, dramatically increasing the chance of ultimately making the sale.

In view of this, writing powerful e-mail copy is one of the most important skills required for doing business on the web. You should never write e-mail haphazardly. If you do, you'll be leaving a lot of money on the table. Here's why:

▶ Virtually every person who is online sends and receives e-mail. E-mail provides greater visibility for any Internet marketer. E-mail is also a far better vehicle than a website for distributing and collecting information, as well as for developing a dedicated following.

▶ Relationship marketing is at the very heart of all e-commerce. You simply can't build a relationship solely through your website, no matter how many interactive bells and whistles it has. E-mail, on the other hand, builds relationships. To produce an income, a website relies on people visiting and revisiting the site. You may have heard the saying "The money is in the list." What it means is that when you leverage your relationship with the prospects in your database (your list), you are more likely to close a sale. That's because you give people a chance to know you and trust you. Even if your website gets only modest traffic, you can convert that traffic into more money than you can imagine through e-mail.

► While it's true that a website makes the front-end sale, you'll be missing out on 90 percent or more of the potential profits if you don't use e-mail to fan the flames. The real selling starts after the first sale is made, by multiplying that one sale into many, many more sales through follow-up e-mails. This is why the lifetime value of the customer—not the first sale—is paramount.

Lifetime Value of a Customer

How do you calculate the lifetime value (LTV) of a customer? First, you figure out how many years your average customer does business with you (customer lifetime). Next, you estimate how much business you'll get from the average customer over that period of time (sales per customer). Then you factor in the number of referrals the average customer gives your company and multiply that by the percentage of those referrals who become customers. The formula will look like this:

$$\text{Customer lifetime} \times \text{sales per customer} \times$$
$$\text{number of referrals} \times \text{percentage of referrals who}$$
$$\text{become customers} = \text{LTV}$$

Let's plug in some hypothetical figures for an online bookstore:

Customer lifetime = 10 years

Sales per customer (per year) = $50

Number of referrals made by average customer = 4

Percentage of referrals that become customers = 26%

$$10 \times \$50 \times 4 \times 0.26 \times \$520$$

Next, subtract the cost of books sold—say, $403—and that gives the bookstore a gross margin (gross profit) of $117 per customer. That's the LTV of one customer to that bookstore.

If each customer has an LTV of $117, then the bookstore can easily determine how much it can reasonably spend to acquire each new customer and still make a profit over the lifetime of that customer. The profits probably won't come with the first sale. They may not even come in the first year, since the cost of acquiring a customer can be high, but if you build strong relationships and offer quality products and services, over the life of the customer, you should reap handsome rewards.

Note: If the bookstore sells other things—CDs, DVDs, stationery, greeting cards, and so on—each new category introduces new revenue streams and significantly increases the potential lifetime revenue from a customer.

1. E-mail helps you keep the customers you have. It costs much less to keep an existing customer than to acquire a new one. According to *eMarketer,* it costs five to ten times as much to find a new customer as it does to retain an existing one. Additionally, loyal customers are more profitable to your business because they usually buy more of your company's products, are less sensitive to price, and often refer other customers. They usually take less of your customer service time because they're already familiar with your company.

2. An increasing number of traditional brick-and-mortar companies are discovering that a website is simply not sufficient for success in e-commerce. The Internet's killer application— e-mail—is the primary vehicle for interactive marketing. Why? E-mail is a high-response-rate vehicle because it's in-your-face, immediate, and inexpensive. It sells, promotes, informs, creates buzz, acquires and retains customers, reinforces branding, and provides customer service all in one fell swoop.

   With an estimated 39 trillion pieces of e-mail being sent out each year at the time of this writing, 80 percent of

which are spam mails, it makes sense now, even more than
ever before, to maximize the impact of your e-mail messages, or you'll be buried alive in the mountains of e-mail
that people get.

Having a mailing list of prospects does not mean you will automatically make money. That's *not* what "The money is in the list"
means. The money is indeed in the list, but only if you know how to
leverage that list through e-mail copy that deepens your relationship
with the members of your list. You do this first and foremost by getting them to like you and gaining their trust.

In your e-mail, you can also use psychological devices (as will be
mentioned in Chapters 5, 6, and 7) when writing web copy, but if
you fail to get your e-mail audience to like and trust you, you won't
make sales. It's as simple as that.

How many times have you bought products that you didn't particularly like, want, or need just because you liked and trusted the
people who were selling them to you? Dr. Ralph F. Wilson, who,
according to the *New York Times,* is "among the best-known publishers and consultants who preach the responsible use of e-mail
for marketing," exemplifies this premise. Among the practices he
advocates are (1) using a confirmed or double opt-in mechanism to
keep from getting bad e-mail addresses or getting unwilling recipients on your list, (2) providing quality content in every e-mail
communication, (3) avoiding overpromotion and modulating
e-mail frequency, (4) providing e-mail recipients with an easy way
to unsubscribe in the event they no longer wish to receive e-mail
from you, and (5) safeguarding your reputation in the context of
e-mail. That's why, in addition to Dr. Wilson's practice of providing
outstanding marketing content on his website, Wilsonweb.com, he
is also well liked, trusted, and respected by more than 100,000 subscribers to his popular e-mail newsletter *Web Marketing Today,*
something that undoubtedly contributes to the success of his
online enterprises.

THE FRAME-OF-MIND MARKETING METHOD FOR WRITING E-MAILS ▼

Empathy is defined as the capacity to understand, be aware of, be sensitive to, and vicariously experience the feelings, thoughts, and experiences of another person. Frame-of-mind marketing grows directly out of that feeling of empathy. While many seem to be born with that ability, the good news is that empathy is not a genetic trait but, rather, a skill that you can easily develop.

The ability to view things from the perspective of your audience is valuable not only in copywriting and marketing, but for all social interactions. The more sensitive you are to people's frame of mind, the more persuasive you can be, the more rapport you can have with them, and, consequently, the more they will trust you and agree with you.

Let's examine the frame of mind of people who are in the process of opening their e-mail. The easiest way to do this is to put yourself in the shoes of your average e-mail recipient. Write down the thoughts that normally run through people's heads as they open their e-mail in-boxes. Here are some examples of typical thought processes:

Okay, who sent me e-mail today? They are curious and eager to receive e-mail. According to AOL's fourth annual Email Addiction Survey, 51 percent check their e-mail four or more times a day (up from 45 percent in 2007) and 20 percent check it more than ten times a day.

I'm busy and I just have enough time to read the good stuff. They scan their in-box for (1) important business e-mail, (2) personal e-mail, and (3) other things that they have time to read, usually in that order.

Let me delete all the junk mail so that it doesn't clutter up my in-box. People are inundated with commercial e-mail, free newsletters,

and e-zines—and their forefinger is positioned over their
mouse, ready to click on the delete button.

*My in-box is my private, personal space, and I don't want strangers
and salespeople invading my privacy.* Their in-box is a sacred place,
and they are protective of it, inviting only friends, relatives,
colleagues, and selected business acquaintances to enter.
Some people may have additional reasons, but these are
nearly universal. Most of us probably feel the same way.

For this reason, the cardinal rule for writing successful e-mail copy
is to review the frame of mind of your audience *before* writing a single word. Clearly, when we want to sell our ideas or products to
others, we need to create rapport, and one good way to do this is by
aligning ourselves with them, which simply means being like them.
People develop a bond with you because they see a reflection of
themselves in you. An effective way to do this is by mirroring the
language in which your target audience communicates, which allows
you to gain instant rapport with them. The result is that they
instantly like and trust you, although they may not know why. Can
you see how useful this can be in the selling process—online as well
as offline?

People online are used to the up-close-and-personal language
that is prevalent in e-mail, instant messaging, and text messaging.
There is a one-on-one, in-your-face kind of intimacy in e-mail, and
you have to work with it and not against it. You must understand
who your audience is and speak their language. At the same time,
you should make it personal and conversational. Even if you are
speaking to CEOs, you don't have to use the language of the board-
room. Speak to your reader's level of intelligence and comprehension, but keep it friendly.

Just as in writing copy for your website, don't begin your e-mail
messages with formal corporatespeak: "We at Widgets.com have
been in business for 15 years, and we are the industry's premier
source of widgets." Not only does that kind of language sound
pompous, but it deliberately keeps your audience at arm's length. It's

also boring, so your readers are likely to tune out. Furthermore, how does the fact that your company has existed for 15 years fill the needs of your audience? What's in it for them?

Breaking the Sales Barrier

There's another part of the equation that is rarely mentioned: Getting your prospects to like you is important, but what's even more important is letting your clients see that you like them. When that occurs, sales barriers really come down. When we know someone likes us, we believe that they won't cheat, lie to, or take advantage of us, but instead will give us the best possible arrangement or the best possible deal.

For this reason, it's crucial to write your e-mail as though you are writing to just one person that you're fond of, not 1,000, 10,000, or 100,000 at once. Don't speak at or to your reader, but *with* him or her.

Since your audience's e-mail in-box is a sacred place where only trusted people are welcome and invited, it is also the place where you can create the closest, strongest bond that can be forged between marketer and audience. You must never damage that bond by abusing your readers' trust in you. If they opted in to receive marketing tips from you, and if you don't deliver on that promise but instead give them sales pitches for various products, you blow it. If you treat their e-mail in-box as a dumping place for junk mail, you will also blow it.

People form opinions about you based on the e-mails you send them. Often, you don't know what those opinions are unless people happen to be vocal about them. Sometimes people brag about the size of their mailing list, but as the saying goes, "It's not the number of eyeballs that matter, it's the frame of mind behind those eyeballs that really matters." Just because you have a list of 50,000 or 100,000 e-mail addresses doesn't mean that those people care a whit about you. I'd rather have a list of 1,000 devoted subscribers with whom I have a first-name relationship than 100,000 who couldn't care less about me. That's because I'd be more likely to make a significant number of sales from 1,000 loyal readers than from 100,000 strangers.

THE FUTURE OF E-MAIL MARKETING ▼

Anyone who has been online for any length of time is aware of the alarming proliferation of spam e-mail. The trend is expected to continue, as an increasing number of marketers, eager to cash in on the free marketing medium, exploit the situation without giving any thought to the bandwidth they are wasting and the people they are annoying. Add to that the growing fear of computer viruses, worms, scams, and pornography, and you begin to understand the vigilance that organizations and the government are exercising to put a stop to spam.

The CAN-SPAM Act (Controlling the Assault of Non-Solicited Pornography and Marketing Act), which was signed into law back in 2003 (and revisions to which went into effect on July 7, 2008), sets forth a framework of administrative tools and civil and criminal penalties to help America's consumers, businesses, and families fight spam. In addition, spam and virus filters have become standard on e-mail servers, permanently blocking suspicious and obviously unsolicited e-mail.

Some people are predicting that, with the rise of flooded e-mail in-boxes and spam filters that can block even legitimate opt-in messages, the demise of e-mail as a marketing and publishing channel is not far behind.

Is e-mail marketing on its way out? Not by a long shot. There's still a lot of marketing juice left in e-mail.

However, gone are the days when marketers could compose an e-mail message, push the Send button, and expect everyone on their mailing list to receive it. Marketers need to become more sophisticated about the medium in order to make their e-mail marketing as effective as it was prior to spam phobia. The rest of this chapter reveals some of the cybersmarts that you need to navigate the changing e-mail landscape.

HOW TO MAKE SURE YOUR E-MAIL IS DELIVERED

▼

Do you know the most important objective when it comes to sending e-mail? Many experienced marketers say, "Getting your e-mail opened." Actually getting your e-mail opened is the second-most-important thing. The most important is getting your e-mail delivered.

As a service to their users, more and more e-mail providers offer filters intended to radically reduce the amount of spam their users receive. What is a legitimate e-mailer to do? Let's say you send a mailing to your opt-in list, some of whom have e-mail services that block bulk mail and redirect it to the recipient's bulk mail box, the equivalent of sending it to Siberia. This happens frequently, especially if you have a huge mailing list. If your list is large, you may avoid such filters by breaking up your mailings into smaller chunks.

In addition to blocking bulk mail, a majority of e-mail programs allow their e-mail users to filter out spam and other junk mail. People can, for instance, ask to have e-mail that contains certain words such as *sex* or *girls* or *one-time mailing* in the subject or even in the body of the e-mail filtered from your in-box or sent to the trash bin. More and more people are availing themselves of such filtering capabilities, which is why popular e-mail services such as Gmail and Yahoo! Mail, and e-mail applications like Eudora and Outlook come with built-in filtering capabilities. People can also filter out specific mailers, that is, create a blacklist of unwanted e-mail senders. This is good and bad news, since they can also opt to let certain e-mailers in (i.e., create a whitelist of e-mail addresses or domain names from which an e-mail blocking program will allow messages to be received), but this often takes a specific action, and not all recipients are aware of this feature.

Some e-mail programs, like Outlook, automatically filter out e-mail that has the word *free* in all-capital letters in any part of the e-mail. If they find sales@anydomainname.com in the From field, they filter that out, too. Ditto for *extra income* or *for free* with a question mark or an exclamation point.

How to Avoid Spam Blockers

Spam blockers and filters used by the majority of e-mail providers have become increasingly restrictive, and this often causes even legitimate e-mail to be relegated to recipients' bulk e-mail boxes or prevented from being delivered altogether. Therefore, before you press the Send button on your promotional e-mail, newsletter, or e-zine—stop. Give it a once-over and see if it contains any of the following offending words and phrases:

Amazing

Amazing stuff

Buy now

Cable converter

Cash bonus

Collect child
support

Compare rates

Compete for your
business

Congratulations

Credit bureaus

Dear friend

Dig up dirt on
friends

Free

Free grant money

Free installation

Free investment

Free leads

Free preview

Great offer

Guarantee

"Hidden" assets

Investment

Maximize

Money

Multilevel
marketing

New

No investment

Opportunity

Order now

Powerful

Profit

Promise you . . . !

Removes wrinkles

Reverses aging

Sale

Search engine
listings

Serious cash

Special Promotion

Stock disclaimer
statement

Stop snoring

Tells you it's an ad

Winner

In addition, customary phrases like *Click here, Click below, Unsubscribe,* and *To be removed* are also blocked, because these phrases are frequently used by spammers and other purveyors of spam. Following is a list of other words and phrases that also resemble spam. They may not necessarily be flagged as spam by spam filters when used only once in the body of an e-mail, but it would be advisable to use them in moderation or avoid using them altogether, if possible.

Accept credit cards
Act now! Don't
   hesitate!
Additional income
All natural
Apply online
As seen on
Avoid bankruptcy

Be amazed
Be your own boss
Being a member
Big bucks
Billing address
Billion dollars
Buy direct

Call free
Call now
Calling creditors
Cancel at any time
Can't live without
Cash bonus
Casino
Cents on the
   dollar
Check or money
   order

Consolidate debt
   and credit
Credit card offers
Cures baldness

Direct e-mail
Direct marketing
Do it today
Don't delete
Drastically
   reduced

Earn per week
Easy terms
Eliminate bad
   credit
E-mail marketing
Expect to earn

Fantastic deal
Fast Viagra delivery
Financial freedom
For instant access
For just $ (some
   amount)
Free sample (or free
   anything)
Full refund

Get it now
Get paid
Get started now
Gift certificate

Have you been turned
   down?
Home employment
Human growth
   hormone

If only it were that easy
Increase sales
Increase traffic
It's effective

Join millions of
   Americans

Limited time only
Long-distance phone
   offer
Lose weight
Lower interest rates
Lower monthly
   payment
Lowest price
Luxury car

Mail-in order form	No inventory	Order status
Marketing solutions	No medical exams	Orders shipped by
Mass e-mail	No obligation	priority mail
Meet singles	No purchase	
Member stuff	necessary	Pennies a day
MLM	No questions asked	Please read
Money back	No selling	Potential earnings
Moneymaking	No strings attached	Pure profit
Month trial offer		
More Internet	Offshore	Real thing
traffic	Offer expires	Refinance home
Mortgage rates	Offers coupon	Requires initial
	Offers extra cash	investment
Name brand	Once in lifetime	Risk free
Nigerian	100 percent	Round the world
No age restrictions	guaranteed	
No claim forms	One-time mailing	Satisfaction
No cost	Online biz	guaranteed
No credit check	opportunity	Save $
No experience	Online pharmacy	Save big money
No fees	Only $	
No gimmick	Opt in	

If you've included any of these words—or any dollar signs, exclamation points, or anything in all-capital letters, for that matter—in your outgoing e-mail, you may want to rethink what you have written.

That's because SpamAssassin (and other, similar programs, like SpamGuard, which come integrated in e-mail providers like Yahoo! Mail) may inadvertently identify your e-mail as spam and block it from being delivered. SpamAssassin, one of the most popular open-source antispam applications, has several hundred spam filters and allows mail administrators to customize which e-mails get through and which ones are automatically blocked and sent to spam limbo, meaning they are redirected to the recipient's bulk mail bin or purged altogether.

Even if the e-mail you are sending is legitimate opt-in e-mail that the recipient has requested and wants to receive, it can be hijacked by e-mail providers or Internet service providers (ISPs), who are becoming increasingly vigilant about protecting their clients from junk e-mail.

You can see how easy it is to get caught in the crossfire and end up in the same dump as spammers. The sad fact is that some legitimate e-mail marketers and newsletter and e-zine publishers don't even realize that their e-mail is being rerouted to spam limbo, and they wonder why their click-through and conversion rates are dismal.

How do you get around this? You can either play by the rules and not use the offending words and phrases altogether or you can devise creative ways to conceal the words and phrases from the spam radar. You can insert symbols within the words; for example, use "fr^ee" or "fr*ee" instead of "free." Don't get too creative; your sentence or thought must still be understandable to your readers.

Another matter worth noting is that the deliverability of e-mail is often dependent on the spam-blocking strength of e-mail services or ISPs. Yahoo! Mail, for instance, uses aggressive server-level spam filters that do a great job at reducing the amount of unsolicited e-mail messages, but they also erroneously flag legitimate e-mails as spam and send them to the recipients' bulk mail folder. Other ISPs like MSN Hotmail and Juno, on the other hand, have less vigorous spam filters that allow all but the most blatant spam to reach recipients' in-boxes. It's worthwhile to keep abreast of the major ISPs' server-side filtering so that you can send out e-mails accordingly. For example, if you're planning to send out a promotional e-mail to your mailing list, it might be wise to segment that list by ISP (sort according to their domains, for example, those addresses ending in "@yahoo.com" or "@msn.com" or "@aol.com") and tailor each e-mail for each segment of your mailing list so that each e-mail works within the parameters of each ISP's spam-filtering rules. Although this might seem like tedious work to you, consider the alternative. If you send one universal e-mail to all recipients in a single bulk mailing—

without segmenting your list and without taking the spam rules of the receiving ISPs into consideration—the majority of your e-mail could land in your recipients' bulk mail files.

If you want your e-mail to be read and not filtered out as spam or junk mail, you must pay attention to these guidelines and keep up with the constant changes ISPs make.

Does Your E-Mail Test Positive as Spam?

My favorite strategy for sanitizing my e-mail of items that might trigger a false positive is by running it through Lyris's ContentChecker before sending it out. This is a free service that uses SpamAssassin's rules to rate your e-mail. You can find it at www.lyris.com/content checker.

When you get there, paste your text into the form provided on the website, and you'll instantly get a score. If your score is greater than five, it's an indication that your e-mail strongly resembles spam and might be blocked or filtered by major e-mail providers or ISPs. If it's less than five, you can be reasonably assured that your e-mail will be delivered without incident. Lyris will also send you a detailed analysis of what led to your score, identify the offending elements, and make recommendations on how to revise your message to conform to industry antispam criteria.

There currently exists no program, application, or utility that can guarantee with 100 percent certainty that your outgoing e-mail is spam-proof. Lyris ContentChecker only checks your e-mail against the spam-filtering rules of SpamAssassin, which, although arguably the most widely used antispam application, does not represent the spam-filtering strength of all e-mail services and ISPs. This is why it is necessary to stay informed about the major ISPs' constantly changing e-mail rules.

HOW TO WRITE E-MAIL THAT'S READ ▼

Let's assume your e-mail gets through those e-mail filters. How do you appeal to the actual e-mail recipients themselves? I've read tens of thousands of e-mails, and I've written thousands more over the past ten years. I've found that the e-mails that do a great job of selling contain seven elements.

Seven Elements of E-Mails That Sell

Element 1: A Compelling Subject Line. The subject line must be irresistible and must beg to be opened, *not* because of hype or overly commercial language, but because it is compelling. What's more, your subject line *must not* appear to be an advertisement, which, even if it somehow got through the filters, would have the same effect as asking readers to watch a commercial.

Remember that each of us is bombarded with an average of 3,500 commercial messages per day—from TV, billboards, radio, the Internet, and practically everywhere we turn. The last thing we want to see when we open our e-mail (or visit a website) is yet another ad. Yes, that applies even when we gave a company permission to send us e-mail.

Here's a simple exercise that will give you the best education you can get when it comes to writing subject lines that are impossible to ignore. This exercise puts you smack-dab in your prospects' shoes or, more precisely, in their frame of mind. Go to your e-mail in-box and check your incoming e-mail. You need to actually do this; don't be tempted to just do it mentally or you'll defeat the purpose of the exercise. This is positively eye-opening.

Once you have your e-mail in-box in front of you, what do you see? You see the sender, subject, date, and size columns. Where do your eyes go first? Some people glance at the sender column, but if you're like most people, you'll tend to scan the subject column to see which e-mail you want to open first, right? Which subject lines are you most likely to open first, and why? All the tests I've been involved in show that e-mail recipients from a confirmed opt-in list are at least five times more likely to open those that have the appearance of personal e-mail versus commercial e-mail and those that have a friendly tone rather than a corporate, businesslike tone. Which of the following e-mails would you open first?

Subject: Online Marketing Gazette

Subject: Avon Spring Specials

Subject: Are the rumors about you true?

Subject: 30% Discount on Eyewear!

Subject: Holiday Bonanza

Subject: You got me worried

Subject: Save up to 70% off at Overstock, 40% at Amazon, and more!

I'm betting you'll open the e-mail with the subject line "Are the rumors about you true?" or "You got me worried" first.

It's obvious which e-mails are personal and which are commercial, and it's easy to see that if the subject line of your e-mail looks like it's coming from a friend, it's more likely to be opened first.

Here are a few more examples of subject lines that give the appearance of personal e-mail:

Subject: This got my attention . . .

Subject: Did you get my message?

Subject: This finally came . . .

Subject: Not sure if you got this?

Subject: I'm not quite sure about you . . .

Subject: About your website, [*FirstName*] . . .

Subject: Here's what I promised . . .

Subject: Here's the formula . . .

Subject: I almost forgot . . .

Subject: Sorry, I goofed . . .

When your eyes zero in on the subject line, they also dart quickly (if not peripherally) to the sender field of the in-box. Therefore, the subject and the sender *must* agree with each other. Suppose you craft a subject line like the following in an attempt to trick the recipient into thinking it is a personal e-mail:

Subject: Hey, was that you I saw?

If the name in the sender field is "Internet Profits Weekly," your otherwise friendly and curiosity-provoking subject line is negated when your recipient realizes it's a ploy. Above all, be real.

Some say that this technique is deceptive because the recipient is not really your friend but, rather, a prospect, a customer, a subscriber, or just someone who has opted into your list. The fact is, your e-mail recipient *should* perceive you as a friend. That's the heart of relationship marketing. That's the reason you ask viewers for their e-mail addresses in the first place—to start a relationship with them so they can get to know you, trust you, and eventually buy from you.

There's a very thin line between creating a riveting subject line and one that is deceptive. The new rules of the CAN-SPAM Act require that the subject line of any commercial e-mail not be deceptive. Therefore, do not use the bait-and-switch ploy of using a subject line that is designed for shock value or for the sole purpose of getting recipients to tear open your e-mail if the content of the e-mail bears no relevance to the subject line. Furthermore, if you use trickery to get recipients to open your enticing message, they may bite once or twice, but when they recognize the pattern, the game's over. They're likely to ignore all future e-mails from you, they may ask to be removed from your list, they could report your e-mail as spam, or they might blacklist your e-mail address via their spam filter, preventing your message from getting through to them. There are no hard-and-fast rules in e-mail. When you do your own intelligence work, the frame of mind of your audience will become apparent to you, and writing subject lines that are noticed will be a snap.

When you get a feel for the language used in e-mails that get maximum readership (personal e-mails), you've won half the battle. Reading this, you might think that creating a personal-sounding e-mail does not seem difficult. After all, you e-mail your friends all the time. Shouldn't it be a simple task to write marketing e-mails the same way? One would think so, but it's not. Somehow, when we sit down to write marketing e-mail, many of us try to be clever and creative or we inject a big dose of marketese and, as a result, lose our friendly, personal tone, as we subconsciously switch to writing in a commercial or corporate style. That puts us way off the mark when it comes to e-mail communications.

To make matters interesting, I'm going to throw you a curveball. I recently wrote a successful subject line that read "Why the FDA Is Suppressing the One-Minute Cure for All Diseases." That doesn't sound friendly or conversational at all. It's a straightforward "what's contained within," editorial-style subject line.

When sent to the appropriate target audience, it works because it suggests a benefit to the reader and arouses curiosity (what is the one-minute cure and why is the FDA suppressing it?). Furthermore, it reads like an editorial, not an ad (even though the body of the e-mail promotes a book titled *The One-Minute Cure*). This subject line appeals to the audience's information-seeking mind-set. Again, there are no hard-and-fast rules—only guidelines. What is true is that it's essential to pay attention to the frame of mind of your audience and the medium in which they will be viewing your message, and to assess the impact you're making. Here are a couple of examples of editorial-style subject lines designed for specific target audiences:

Subject: Venture Capitalists Explain How to Get Funded

Subject: Warren Buffett's Favorite Foreign Stock Picks

Subject: This Company May Be the Biggest Threat to Your Family's Health

Subject: Vitamin E Linked to Cancer

Personalizing E-Mails—Not All It's Cracked Up to Be. We've established that, above all, e-mail subject lines need to be as friendly, human, and personable as possible, but do they need to be personalized? I have long advocated personalizing subject lines, but I was in for a shock when I opened my e-mail in-box and found five e-mails from five different senders with the following subject lines:

Subject: Maria, this Friday

Subject: Maria, will you be part of this test?

Subject: Will you be near a phone tomorrow, Maria?

Subject: Maria, your account

Subject: Maria, last chance!

The e-mails came from five different senders. That was a real eye-opener. I realized that the tactic of using the recipient's first name as a way of personalizing the subject line had become so widespread that instead of making me want to open the e-mails, it made them candidates for deletion! Any one of these subject lines on its own might have been an effective device for getting people to open your e-mail, but when viewed in the context of the recipient's in-box, it lost its punch.

This may seem minor, but it has major repercussions for your marketing, not only in terms of this particular device, but as it applies to other techniques that might, over time, become overused.

What would happen if you weren't constantly in tune with your audience's frame of mind or weren't paying attention to the trends as they emerge? If you rely on what others are doing and continue to blindly use the same tactic, your e-mails will fail miserably and you might never know why your response rates dropped.

About two years ago, I received an e-mail from a well-known Internet marketer whose subject line was as follows:

Subject: It's not _____ that made Bill H. an online millionaire, it's _____ . . .

At first, I thought the subject line was brilliant because it made me tear open the e-mail to satisfy my curiosity. It's interesting to note that the Internet marketer who sent out the e-mail is also a professional teleseminar host who always makes it a habit to distribute advance teleseminar handouts filled with intriguing, fill-in-the-blank statements—statements to be completed with information presented at the teleseminar. That seemed to me a terrific strategy for getting people curious enough to attend the teleseminar (see "Incomplete thoughts" under "Crafting the All-Important Subject Line" later in this chapter)—and the fill-in-the-blanks subject line he employed was equally effective in getting the reader to open his e-mail. Just as I predicted, the e-mail did, indeed, get a high readership and a high click-through rate. But after the fill-in-the-blank tactic was repeated a few times (and copied by dozens of other Internet marketers to boot), the e-mails that employed the tactic were no longer being opened and, instead, were largely ignored. There was nothing intrinsically wrong with the psychological device used, mind you, but its execution (fill in the blanks) became overused, and that rendered it ineffective.

Part of deciphering the frame of mind of your prospects is observing what they're wising up to, what they're becoming immune to, and which tactics are no longer working. You will be well served if you also observe what e-mail spammers are doing. Spammers often resort to devices that attempt to disguise the fact that their e-mails are unsolicited (such as using phrases like "at your request"). Those devices start becoming recognizable to your target readers, who then begin ignoring or deleting the messages. If those devices start to resemble yours, you need to adjust lest your e-mails be mistaken for spam.

Crafting the All-Important Subject Line.   Recall that I mentioned the most important element of a website: the *first screen*. In an e-mail, the subject line is the most important element.

Direct magazine reported that an American leatherware firm sent out a marketing e-mail to their mailing list and accidentally omitted the body copy. Their e-mail was sent to their entire list with nothing but the subject line. Much to their surprise, that mailing generated the largest response rate they had ever had! When writing subject lines, keep these things in mind:

▶ *This.* The word *this* in the subject line of an e-mail is proven to get e-mail recipients to open their e-mail.

Subject: This is what I was talking about . . .

This is so powerful because it arouses the recipients' curiosity, and they must open the e-mail to find out what *this* is. Of course, not all subject lines containing the word *this* will be opened. For example, "This is the best moneymaker in the world . . ." would most likely be recognized as spam and immediately deleted. Other powerful e-mail openers are *here* and *about your . . .*

▶ *Ellipsis points.* Whenever possible, I use ellipsis points at the end of my subject lines. This creates a sense of incompleteness, which makes readers want to rush to open your e-mail.

▶ *Incomplete thoughts.* Presenting an incomplete thought in the subject line, especially about a topic of particular interest to your target audience, causes what I call a "brain itch." Scientifically, it arouses the *reticular activating system* (RAS) in the brain, which is the part of the brain that dislikes incomplete information and does not rest until it finds the information it needs to close a topic. This "brain itch" can be relieved only when the reader opens the e-mail to complete the thought. The thought, of course, must relate to the topic of your e-mail. Otherwise, recipients will click open your e-mail just to satisfy their curiosity, then click away when they realize it was simply a ploy to get their attention.

Words to Avoid Putting in the Subject Line. Strangely enough, some of the attention-grabbing words that you would use on a website are some of the very words you must avoid in an e-mail subject line:

Buy	Power
Discount	Powerful investment
Free, Maximize	Profit
Money opportunity	Sale
New	Special

Words like these reek of advertising or commerce, when your goal is to appear friendly and personal. While these are the magic words advertisers and direct marketers swear by and use liberally in their copy, they are not effective when used in e-mail. This is an area in which what works well in offline marketing (direct mail, radio and TV, print ads, or infomercials) does not work well on the web. Chances are, these words will fail miserably on the web, not to mention that they might be censored by spam filters.

Permission-Based E-Mail: Not a License to Be Bland. I'm often asked whether it is advisable to put the name of the company or newsletter in the subject line of an e-mail. My answer is that permission-based e-mail doesn't give you the liberty to be bland.

Much has been said about the recipient's permission being the foundation of e-mail marketing. Back in 2001, Brann Worldwide, a marketing agency, conducted a national survey and found that 92 percent of U.S. consumers feel positively toward companies that ask their permission before sending them information. But that was in 2001, and the online population's attitudes have changed since then. Most people dislike e-mails they once gave permission to but now no longer wish to receive. Q Interactive, an online marketing services provider, and Marketing Sherpa, a marketing research firm, conducted a joint e-mail survey, published in March 2008, about how people's definition of spam has changed from *unsolicited* e-mail to *unwanted* e-mail. One of the most striking findings is that 56 percent of the survey participants no longer regard spam as simply e-mail that violates permission-based regulations, but now includes any e-mail that causes consumer dissatisfaction. Therefore, most people now consider the following types of e-mail to be spam: (1) marketing messages from known senders if the message is just not interesting to them, (2) too frequent marketing messages from companies they know, and (3) e-mails that were once useful but aren't relevant anymore.

The majority of marketers are as yet unaware of this change in people's attitudes toward e-mail; therefore, they continue to operate on the premise that their e-mails are welcome as long as their recipients have given their permission. Proceeding on this inaccurate premise, some marketers believe that the subject lines of their e-mails must identify who they are in order to remind the recipients that the e-mails contain requested information.

In an environment where most e-mail recipients can't remember whether or not they asked for this or that information, you don't have the luxury of playing it safe by using a bland subject line that consists of nothing but the name of your company or newsletter. The objective of the subject line is to give the recipient a compelling reason to open your e-mail *now*. Instead of using the all-important subject line to state *who* you are, it's far better to use the sender field or the first sentence to identify yourself.

Element 2: The First Sentence. The next thing you need is an opening line that identifies who you are and establishes rapport. Your e-mail must have a real person behind it; it can't be a faceless piece of communication. You can start by saying something that you would say to a friend. I've seen an Australian newsletter publisher, for example, start an e-mail by describing the wonderful weather they were having in Australia and briefly describing the idyllic setting where he lives and works. A famous Internet marketer started an e-mail by saying that he just got back from a successful trip, followed by a short description of that trip. Brevity is the key; just a couple of ice-breaking sentences should suffice.

Some copywriters and marketers skip this seemingly insignificant gesture because they want to get to the point and not waste their audience's time. As a result, they miss the opportunity to bond with their readers and gain rapport with them. Some of the most success-ful e-mails are the ones that elicit the reaction from people that makes them say, "I feel like I know you!" This is your opportunity to get your audience to like you, and if they like you they're more inclined to buy from you.

Element 3: Stay on Point.   This is the gist of your marketing message or the promise of a benefit to come. A good way to do this is by using a journalists' device called the *inverted pyramid* (an upside-down tri-angle, with the narrow tip pointing down and the broad base at the top). The broad base represents the most significant, newsworthy information, and the narrow tip the least important information. Following this method, you put the most important information at the beginning and the least important information at the end of your e-mail. As with most journalism, brevity and clarity get high marks, so get right to the point. Your readers are busy, and they don't want you wasting their time.

Whatever you do, don't make the mistake many Internet entre-preneurs make and start your e-mail with a lengthy reminder that the e-mail is not unsolicited, that the recipient has agreed to receive your mailing or newsletter, and then offer instructions on how to opt out. While this statement acknowledges the permission-based aspect of your relationship, it wastes the first screen of your e-mail, which is the prime area for starting your sales process. Put instructions for opting out at the end of your message.

Element 4: Just One Message.   Don't litter your e-mail with a slew of subjects and topics. Stick to a single message so that you can lead your reader down your intended sales path.

When average recipients receive an e-mail, particularly a lengthy one, they don't read it sequentially. They scan it looking for things that may interest them. If three or four topics grab their attention, they make a mental note of them and start reading the one that interests them most. As they read that part of your e-mail, their brains are unable to pay full attention to what they're reading. Various other ideas start competing for attention. This can easily work against you, especially if you are trying to sell something. Not only will you *not* have your readers' full attention, but also they are not likely to go down your intended sales path or take action of any kind, because the brain is compelling them to read the other things that attracted them.

Multiple messages in a single e-mail, combined with the fact that readers have short attention spans, make for an unholy alliance when it comes to e-mail marketing.

Element 5: Provide Value.   Give your e-mail recipients something of value in return for their undivided attention. This could be something free or at a discount, or some useful information or a special offer.

Element 6: The Benefit.   It's not enough just to tell your readers what your offer is; you must demonstrate how it will benefit them. An easy way to do this is to state the offer and follow it up with " . . . so that you can [*fill in the blank*]." A travel website, for instance, can say, "Try our complimentary fare-tracking service so that you can be informed weekly of all the unpublished, hard-to-find bargain fares to Boston—without having to scour the web."

Element 7: A Call to Action.   Many e-mail marketers go to great lengths to create well-crafted e-mails that make a compelling selling argument about their product or service, but at the last moment, when the prospect is just about ready to take the next step, they drop the ball by failing to ask the prospect to take action. The action can be a request to click, sign up, register, or buy, but whatever it is, you must make sure you tell the reader what to do next. This is true not only for your e-mails but for your website and *all* marketing communications.

PUT THE COMPETITIVE EDGE INTO
YOUR E-MAIL MARKETING

▼

Forrester Research analyst Jim Nail underscored how important it is for e-commerce players to use e-mail to create a dialogue and deepen intimacy with customers in order to maintain the response rates that e-mail marketing often enjoys. He emphasized the importance of starting slowly and gradually building rapport, which allows you to gain additional personal information that in turn helps you fine-tune your marketing and sales message.

Creating a dialogue, deepening intimacy, and building rapport take us back to frame-of-mind marketing and the importance of knowing your prospects' and customers' frame of mind. Once you've identified and written down all the aspects of your own list members' frame of mind, you are ready to write an effective e-mail.

The following technique takes the struggle out of writing e-mail.

Step 1: Write down the three words that best describe the message you're trying to convey. Not a three-word sentence, mind you, but three individual words or phrases that summarize the thought you are trying to communicate—for example, a smell, a benefit, an emotion, a color, a mood, a texture, a sound, a flavor, or an adjective that describes your message. If I were writing an e-mail about a hair restoration product, I might choose *patent, scientific,* and *side effects.* Or I might choose *clinical, success rate,* and *track record.* (See Chapter 6 for a more detailed explanation of the magic of three.)

Your three words help narrow your focus and keep you grounded. After you select your words, start writing your e-mail, paying attention to these simple rules:

- ► Focus on the frame of mind of your audience, and write in a way that appeals to that frame of mind.
- ► Write the way you speak.

> ▶ Don't try to be creative or formal.
>
> ▶ Write the letter as though you're writing it to one person only—and that person is your friend.

Step 2: Give yourself five minutes to write the letter, making sure you use your three keywords in the letter. *Don't* edit the e-mail as you write. Here's a trick that makes editing your e-mail painless: When you are finished writing, e-mail it to yourself. The perspective you'll gain from this experience is priceless. You'll see firsthand how you'd perceive your subject line relative to other subject lines in your in-box. Would *you* pick it out among the rest of your incoming e-mail? Would you open it and read it? You'll read it in a whole new light: from the point of view of your recipient. With every sentence, ask yourself, "Is this something that I would say to a friend?" If the answer is no, revise what you've written.

Similarly, you will discover the nuances of language and whether you've succeeded in gaining rapport and persuading your prospects to take the action you want them to take. All the rough areas that need work will become apparent, and you will see exactly what needs to be fixed.

Adapt as Your Audience's Frame of Mind Changes

When you send a series of e-mails to your list, the recipients' frame of mind is slightly altered with each mailing, as your previous communications influence their expectations and predispositions. They may have warmed up to you and begun to trust you more, or, if you have misread their frame of mind, maybe just the opposite.

All too often, marketers assume that each e-mail gets the same kind of attention as those that went before. This is a mistake. You must never write in a vacuum or regard each e-mail as an isolated piece. You must think of each e-mail as part of a conversation in an ongoing relationship.

When you have a good grasp of your prospects' frame of mind at every stage, you are in a better position to monopolize their attention. Since you know what your prospects' predispositions and expectations are, you have the opportunity to find ways to engage them. For instance, you can use the element of surprise to delight or intrigue them, or you can find ways to arouse their curiosity in order to make them look forward to future e-mails.

The variations are practically infinite. Just consider the unique frame of mind of your own list members and you can come up with ideas that may have never occurred to you before and that are custom-made for your list.

Using E-Mail to Get Attention

Earlier we discussed the reticular activating system (RAS) in relation to subject lines of e-mails and the brain's need for closure, its need to complete incomplete thoughts. The RAS, in essence, is the attention center in the brain. It is the key to turning on the brain and is considered the center of motivation. It determines what we pay attention to.

Here's an example of how the RAS works: Do you remember the last time you decided to buy a new car? Let's say you decided that you wanted to buy a Ford Explorer. All of a sudden you started seeing more Ford Explorers than you'd ever seen before. That's not because people are buying Explorers in record numbers; it's because the RAS of your brain made you aware of them, whereas previously you ignored them.

The RAS receives thousands of stimuli and messages every second, and since it is not possible for the brain to pay attention to everything, it filters or blocks out most of the messages, allowing only certain ones to come to our attention. You can immediately see how valuable it would be if you could get your e-mail messages to rise above the avalanche of messages that your recipients receive. Here are some of the ways you can stimulate your prospects' RAS in order to transition them to a receptive frame of mind:

1. *Ask your reader to write something down.* The act of writing something down helps trigger the RAS. In her book *Write It*

Down, Make It Happen (Fireside, 2000), Henriette Anne Klauser writes, "Writing triggers the RAS, which in turn sends a signal to the cerebral cortex: 'Wake up! Pay attention! Don't miss this detail!' " What you ask readers to write down depends on the nature of the product or service that you sell. I have a client who is a director of a discount buying club that offers up to 18 percent in rebates whenever members purchase from among 200-plus online stores with more than 250,000 products. An e-mail I wrote to encourage members to shop in these stores included the words "I'm sure you're eager to get started, so make a list of all the things you need to buy in the next three months, such as [I listed a dozen items]," and concluded with the words "Go ahead and write them all down."

The simple act of writing down the items puts them at the forefront of your readers' minds and makes them receptive to going the next step and doing what you ask them to do. Think back on your own experience. Isn't it true that whenever you had a written list of things you needed to buy (whether you carried that list with you or not), your mind subconsciously zeroed in on those items when they came into your field of vision? Your mind may have tuned out those things had you not written them down.

2. *Create a small, but entertaining or interesting, activity.* This provides a refreshing diversion from the usual barrage of commercial e-mail. Make sure the activity leads up to a well-crafted marketing message that invites readers to click through to your website or otherwise carries them along your intended sales path. When you lead off with a noncommercial activity, you get recipients to agree to something. When you subsequently get them to click through to your website, that's another *yes*. In effect, you are breaking a large buying decision into several manageable steps to which the reader can say "Yes!" Professional salespeople use this technique all the time.

One marketer who sells software for installing website audio sends out an e-mail inviting recipients to send a free personalized audio postcard to three friends. It is an ingenious (and fun) activity that also demonstrates the ease of producing an audio recording, displays its excellent sound quality, and thereby paves the way to the sale of the software.

Another marketer, who sells a book for dog lovers and owners entitled *Your Dog's Love Letter,* sent out an e-mail inviting the members of her list to view a heartwarming video on YouTube.com about a dog trainer who sings five puppies to sleep in less than a minute.

Subject: This dog video is priceless—a must-see . . .

Hi [*FirstName*],

I hope this letter finds you well and enjoying the summer. ☺

I just thought because you're a dog lover, that you'd enjoy this 1½-minute video. You won't believe it 'til you see it. This is a must-see for dog owners.
http://www.youtube.com/watch?v=G4KWZJ4tOsA

Let me know what you think of it.

All good wishes,
Coy Meadows

As a result of sending this e-mail to the 145 people on her mailing list, the video she uploaded to YouTube.com was viewed by over 8,571 people in just 14 days. Apparently, her e-mail recipients had forwarded the video link to other dog lovers and owners. The interesting thing is that she didn't even own the video. It belonged to someone else who already had the video on YouTube and had received over 4 million views. All she did was ask permission to use the video and repurpose it for her marketing campaign by embedding her website address in it. Viewers of the video caused her website traffic to spike and sales of her book to increase significantly—even though there was no call to action in the e-mail whatsoever.

3. *Invite your recipient to participate in a quick poll or a one-question survey.* This is an involvement device that gets your readers to pay attention to a subject on which you want them to focus. The subject of the poll or survey should be one that is of particular interest to your list members, one that gives them a chance to interact with you and express an opinion about something that is important to them, as well as one that gives you the opportunity to segue into your marketing message. As an incentive, you might offer to give participants access to the poll or survey results. (Create e-mail surveys for free at www.freeonlinesurveys.com—see Chapter 12 for details.)

4. *"Please forward."* The Association for Interactive Marketing (AIM) discovered a technique for encouraging pass-along readership of its newsletter. AIM simply added "Pls. Forward" to the end of its newsletter subject lines. The association reports that this little device has more than doubled its circulation numbers.

What *Really* Works on the Internet Sometimes Doesn't

There are rarely absolute truths when it comes to Internet marketing. There are only conditional truths, based on the frame of mind of the marketplace or your audience. What was true yesterday, last week, or last year may not be true today. This is especially true in the changing online climate of Web 2.0.

With direct mail, when you track and test your mail pieces and identify your control piece, you can roll out the control piece and virtually predict how much money you will make with mathematical certainty. On the Internet, results are not as predictable, because things change rapidly. While I'm an advocate of tracking and testing online, my test results may or may not apply to you, and you should be wary of those who offer sweeping generalizations.

No one website strategy, e-mail tactic, or marketing message works all the time. Ultimately, you alone can determine what will and will not work, depending on the frame of mind of your own audience and the results of your own tracking and testing. There are e-mail marketing services that have the ability to evaluate the effectiveness of your e-mail campaigns by tracking how many of your e-mails were opened, replies, length of time opened, specific links clicked on, bounces, unsubscribes, and even orders completed. In my opinion, these services are invaluable not only because they show unequivocally what's working and what's not working, but because they also enrich your knowledge of your audience's frame of mind in real time.

SIG File: Your Online Business Card

A signature file, also known as a SIG file, is, quite simply, your digital signature. It's the part of your e-mail message that appears at the very bottom and tells your story—who you are and what you do—or features whatever product or service you are promoting. A SIG file can be delivered in html or plaintext.

Think of it as your online business card, which you can use as a marketing tool because it gives you the opportunity to advertise your website, your product, or your services with every e-mail you send, at no cost to you. Most free e-mail service providers such as Gmail, Yahoo! Mail, and MSN Hotmail enable users to load their SIG files onto the e-mail account settings so that the digital signature is automatically appended at the end of all outgoing messages. Likewise, most e-mail applications like Eudora and Outlook enable users to create a SIG file that is appended to each outgoing e-mail, and they also give options such as graphics, stylized text, and even a virtual business card.

Example
> Bob Grant, L.P.C.
> "The Relationship Doctor"
> http://www.RelationshipHeadquarters.com
> E-mail: bob@RelationshipHeadquarters.com
> = = = = = = = = = = =
> Get your F.R.E.E. Report: "The Mistakes Women Make That Cause Men to Leave Them." How many mistakes are you making? Send a blank e-mail to mistakes@domain.com and the report will be sent to your e-mail box instantly.

How Your E-Mail Reputation Affects E-Mail Deliverability

Clearly, e-mail marketing still offers one of the best dollar-for-dollar returns on investment (ROIs) in the entire field of marketing, although ROIs are diminishing rapidly. According to a 2007 report of the Direct Marketing Association (DMA), ROI on e-mail marketing has dropped 20.2 percent since 2005.

	SALES GENERATED FROM EACH $1 SPENT ON E-MAIL MARKETING	PERCENTAGE DROP SINCE 2005
2005	$57.25	N/A
2006	$51.58	Down 9.9%
2007	$45.65	Down 20.2%

While the sales generated from each dollar spent on e-mail marketing still compares favorably to those resulting from offline marketing media (including direct mail), open rates have dipped to all-time lows, and e-mail recipients have become all too eager to click the Report As Spam button on commercial e-mails.

The main reason for this growing animosity and lack of responsiveness, of course, is that the number of commercial e-mails being sent out every day (including those that are unsolicited and unwanted) has reached record highs. Internet users are tired of being inundated and have begun tuning out instead of being responsive the way they used to be. Moreover, people are tired of being sold to, talked at, or pitched practically every minute of the day by marketers. Today's consumer is not only a victim of information overwhelm but is also becoming increasingly guarded when it comes to marketing. For your e-mails to impact this audience, it's imperative that they be engaging, informative, and beneficial, as suggested by the guidelines contained in this chapter.

There is a practice prevalent among ISPs to block not only incoming e-mails that resemble spam but also e-mails coming from specific e-mail senders whom they identify as spammers. According to the ClickZ Network, AOL routinely blocks and deletes around 75 percent of incoming e-mail it identifies as spam. This points to yet another issue that e-mail marketers need to pay special attention to when it comes to ensuring e-mail deliverability—and that is one's *e-mail reputation*.

E-mail reputation is similar to the conventional concept of reputation except that it has to do with your e-mail-sending practices and behavior. ISPs use your online reputation *score* to decide whether or not to deliver the e-mails sent by you. Online reputation has two fundamental aspects:

1. *Recipient reputation.* This represents your track record with your e-mail recipients and incorporates such factors as including a readily identifiable sender in the From field, ensuring the appropriate frequency of e-mails, providing relevant content, sending only to people who opted in or subscribed, providing an easy way to unsubscribe, and honoring unsubscribe requests on a timely basis.

2. *ISP reputation.* This is your track record with ISPs that monitor whether the e-mails you're sending are addressed to accurate,

live e-mail addresses, that there is a consistency in the From addresses and IP address(es), and that your e-mails are opened by and clicked on by recipients.

Companies like IronPort, Habeas, and Return Path regularly monitor hundreds of millions of e-mail senders daily—their infrastructure, e-mail-sending behaviors and practices, whether or not they're blacklisted by the major ISPs, and a multitude of other e-mail-related factors. You could be blacklisted by the major ISPs due to some e-mail behavior you exhibited in the past and not even know it. If you're blacklisted by an ISP—Yahoo!, for instance—all e-mail you send to recipients that use Yahoo! Mail will be blocked. Unsuspecting marketers often have low open rates and click-throughs on their e-mail campaigns because they have poor e-mail reputation scores.

How sure are you that your e-mail is making it to your recipients' in-boxes? How do you find out what your e-mail reputation score is? There are a variety of ways. Habeas.com offers a free e-mail reputation check at https://secure.habeas.com/rar/reg.php?s=repcheck_blacklist. Among the things they check for are real-time feedback from the ISPs (including user complaints about you) and whether you are on 50 of the top blacklists of domains or addresses from which the industry filters and blocks e-mails.

Another way to check your e-mail reputation score is by sending an e-mail to reputation@IronPort.com. IronPort, a SenderBase e-mail reputation service, will provide you with your reputation score between −10 and +10. The lowest (most negative) scores are almost certainly flagged as spammers, and the highest (most positive) scores represent sources of legitimate e-mail.

Just as your credit score determines whether or not creditors will extend credit to you and what interest rate you'll get on your loans, your e-mail reputation score determines whether ISPs will allow your outgoing e-mails to be delivered to your recipients. Sometimes ISPs like AOL even go to the extent of restricting member access to sites run by spammers and locking down accounts that generate spam.

So how do you prevent yourself from getting a low e-mail reputation score—and what should you do if you discover that you already have a low reputation score? Following are a few tips for improving your e-mail reputation and, consequently, your e-mail deliverability:

1. Use confirmed opt-in lists (or double opt-in, whenever possible) to ensure that only willing recipients subscribe to your list and to prevent the accumulation of inaccurate, inactive, or fake e-mail addresses.

2. Make sure your e-mail content is relevant to the interests of your list members and that it coincides with the topic that they gave you permission to send them. Irrelevant e-mail content may cause your recipients dissatisfaction and deem your e-mail spam, thereby degrading your e-mail reputation.

3. Limit the frequency of your e-mails. When subscribers receive an excessive number of e-mails from you, they might not unsubscribe, but they will begin to ignore most of them. ISPs such as AOL, MSN Hotmail, Yahoo!, Gmail, and AOL are able to track both open rates and click-through rates—and fewer opened e-mails and click-throughs will hurt your e-mail reputation.

4. Send e-mail in smaller chunks to keep excessive volume from being blocked by ISPs. ISPs do not like large numbers of e-mails to be sent simultaneously because not only do excessive e-mails take a heavy toll on bandwidth but large mailings are usually characteristic of spam. You are likely to be suspected of being a spammer if you don't get into the practice of sending your e-mail in smaller segments.

5. Instruct your subscribers to whitelist the e-mail address from which you routinely send your e-mails. A *whitelist* is a list of

e-mail addresses or domain names from which an e-mail blocking program allows messages to be received. Important: Because most people do not know how to whitelist an e-mail address and the instructions are not always easy to find within the e-mail account, you must provide specific instructions.

6. Consider paying for e-mail reputation management services such as Habeas and Return Path, or send out mail via a third-party agency such as Goodmail. E-mail reputation management services like Habeas help ensure that your e-mails adhere to industry best practices, and as a result your e-mail reputation improves and your in-box deliverability is maximized. Goodmail sends your e-mail on your behalf via CertifiedEmail™, which is marked in the in-box with a unique blue-ribbon envelope icon, enabling your recipients to distinguish your message as coming from someone with whom they have a preexisting relationship. It is the only class of e-mail available that ensures delivery of all opt-in e-mail messages to your recipients' in-boxes, with links and images intact.

7. Refrain from sending commercial e-mail to mailing lists other than your own. Most marketers are unable to resist the temptation of buying third-party opt-in lists, especially when they don't have sizable lists of their own. Third-party opt-in lists are big business these days. Those who build and sell these lists usually entice people to join their list by offering them a reward such as a travel certificate, a chance to win a grand prize, a gift card that can be used at a store or restaurant, or one of many other freebies. When people opt into these lists, they usually fail to read a notice in fine print that says the company has the right to sell or trade their e-mail addresses with others, or they just blindly agree to continue receiving e-mails from the company and other third parties in exchange for the freebies. Therefore, when you buy such third-party opt-in lists and send commercial e-mail to them—even includ-

ing a reminder that they've agreed to receive information from third parties—you have unwilling e-mail recipients who have usually been bombarded by all the other commercial enterprises who also bought those lists. There was a time when third-party opt-in lists might have worked to legitimize your unsolicited e-mails, but these days, as ISPs become overzealous about open rates, click-through rates, and spam complaints from e-mail recipients—even though the list you bought is a confirmed opt-in list—you could land on the blacklist of the major ISPs with a single mailing. If that happens, your e-mail reputation score will plunge, which will render most, if not all, of your subsequent e-mails undeliverable.

8. Make it easy for your list members to unsubscribe from your list. Although including an opt-out notice is now a requirement under the new rules of the CAN-SPAM Act, it is even more important for you to ensure that the mechanism for unsubscribing is easy. It should be no more difficult than sending a reply e-mail or visiting a single webpage. Although every e-mail marketer dreads having list members opt out of their list, if you don't make it easy for them to unsubscribe, the Report Spam button is infinitely easier for your e-mail recipients to click. Always remember that a list member's request to unsubscribe from your list does not affect your e-mail reputation, but a spam complaint will. In the final analysis, you won't want to keep unwilling recipients subscribed to your list anyway because they're not likely to respond to your offers.

9. Include your postal address with all your commercial e-mails. The rules of the CAN-SPAM Act require senders of commercial e-mail to include the sender's current physical address. This need not be the actual physical address of your business, but according to the new rules under this act, a post office box or private mailbox is acceptable. This requirement is intended to ensure that both e-mail recipients and law

enforcement authorities are able to contact senders. If you don't comply with this requirement and an ISP decides to take issue with it, or a recipient complains about your non-compliance, you risk not only getting a poor e-mail reputation but also incurring federal penalties.

Now that you've learned the key strategies for writing web copy and online marketing communications, it's time to learn how to make your web copy even more compelling through the use of psychological devices that can turn skeptical prospects into willing buyers.

5

Using Psychology to Motivate Prospects to Become Purchasers

What power there is in a drop of ink, which falling like dew
upon a thought produces that which makes thousands,
perhaps millions think.
—Lord Byron

Step 4 of our web copy blueprint called for adding the psychological devices that transform readers into buyers. These are tactics that fly beneath the radar of your readers' perception, producing an almost hypnotic effect that actually makes them want to buy what you are selling—often without knowing why. These devices are extremely powerful and, if used inappropriately, can be dangerous. I urge you to use them judiciously, responsibly, and ethically.

Using psychology to sell is not about conning people into giving you their hard-earned money. It's not about manipulating people to do something against their will. It is about using your understanding of human nature to make your readers voluntarily and willingly become happily involved in a buying decision that you have made painless, even enjoyable. The fact is that all the psychological devices and triggers in the world won't amount to anything if you fail to speak to the needs of your target audience—and your target audience's frame of mind.

THE "REASON WHY" ▼

In his book *Influence: The Psychology of Persuasion* (rev. ed., Collins Business, 1998), Robert Cialdini, Ph.D., discusses an experiment conducted by Harvard social psychologist Ellen Langer in which she demonstrated that people like to have a reason for doing something. Her experiment was simple. People were waiting in line to use a copy machine at a library. Langer's colleague asked those waiting if she could go ahead of them, saying, "Excuse me, I have five pages. May I use the Xerox machine because I'm in a rush?" Interestingly, 94 percent of those asked complied. Note the word *because,* which introduced a reason for the request.

The experiment was repeated with a new group. This time Langer's colleague said, "Excuse me, I have five pages. May I use the Xerox machine?" Only 60 percent agreed, a significant decrease. When the requester did not offer a reason, significantly fewer people complied.

They repeated the experiment a third time, saying, "Excuse me, I have five pages. May I use the Xerox machine, because I have to make some copies?" Although the reason was not a convincing one (everyone in line had to make copies), 93 percent of those asked said yes. Just the semblance of a reason introduced by the word *because* was enough to persuade people to comply.

In selling a product or service, always tell your readers why they need to do what you're asking them to do. Something as simple as "You must act now because this offer expires on December 31, after which we can no longer accept orders" is sufficient.

THE ZEIGARNIK EFFECT

The Russian psychologist and theorist Bluma Zeigarnik (November 9, 1900–February 24, 1988) is best known for having discovered a phenomenon called the Zeigarnik effect. She first took an interest in the phenomenon when her professor, Gestalt psychologist Kurt Lewin, observed that waiters at a local eatery had better recollections of orders that had yet to be served than of those that had already been served. From that observation, she theorized that people have a tendency to remember things that are unfinished or incomplete. The Zeigarnik effect refers to the state of mental tension and unbalance caused by uncompleted tasks.

When website visitors arrive at a website and are met with many options and links leading to various items of interest, mental tension and unbalance occur for as long as they aren't able to complete the task of clicking on those items of interest. When applied to writing web copy, this means that you shouldn't litter your website with a slew of subjects and topics that will distract your reader. You must stick to a single message so that you can lead readers down your intended sales path. This is the *linear path* method of writing web copy.

To understand this better, let's examine the thought processes of website visitors: When web visitors arrive at your site, they scan through the entire site looking for things that interest them. If several buttons and links grab their attention, they make a mental note of them and start reading the one that interests them most. Now, here's the interesting thing: While they are reading that page, the Zeigarnik effect takes over, creating the mental tension and confusion that come from uncompleted tasks, which, in the case of your visitor, is the urge to click on those other buttons or links.

Since the brain is unable to pay full attention to the topic at hand until those other tasks are completed, this can create a problem, especially if you happen to be in the middle of making a selling proposition when the effect takes over. Not only will you lose your readers' attention, it is unlikely they will go down your intended sales path or take action of any kind, because their brains are compelling them to do the other tasks. That's why it's advisable to minimize the number of unnecessary links and buttons on your website—to keep your reader on the linear path.

Likewise, mental tension may appear when, in the course of reading your copy, your readers come across unfamiliar concepts or terms. To combat this, I employ small pop-up windows to explain concepts that might create mental tension. That way, readers can click on the link, quickly relieve the tension by reading the brief explanation in the pop-up window, and continue reading what I want them to read. The other way, they might be tempted to click away, never to return.

Both the linear path concept and the Zeigarnik effect are very powerful concepts that many web copywriters and website owners fail to understand. If you're ever tempted to include advertising banners on your website, or Google AdSense ads, or reciprocal links with other websites, or links to other unrelated pages in your website that don't contribute to the sales process, remember that you are violating the linear path concept and allowing the Zeigarnik effect to kick in.

THE CLIFFHANGER
▼

The cliffhanger is one of my favorite devices. If you've ever watched the season finale of a TV series, or heard teasers for TV news or news-magazines that say things like "Is green tea the new miracle cure for cancer? Film at eleven," you already understand the concept.

This is a variation of the Zeigarnik effect. The uncompleted thought demands our attention. As a result, we eagerly sit in front of our TV sets to see the season premieres of our favorite shows just to find out what happens next or listen to an entire news broadcast just to hear that 30-second snippet that answers the question that's been bugging our brains.

You can imagine the impact this principle has on web copy. Whenever I break my copy into multiple webpages and it's essential that readers click through to the next page, I use a cliffhanger to get them to click. For example, "The secret ingredient of branding that can single-handedly turn a small business enterprise into a mega-success is hidden in Tommy Hilfiger's story. Did you catch it? Here it is . . ." (followed by a button designated Next Page).

HYPNOTICALLY PERSUASIVE LANGUAGE
▼

Neurolinguistic programming (NLP) is the science of how the brain codes learning and experience. This coding affects all communication and behavior. NLP involves the use of proper syntax (or language). Using it properly can make all your written communications more persuasive. There are several NLP devices that I often use in writing web copy. Among them are embedded commands, presuppositions, linguistic binds, and reframing.

Embedded Commands

The objective of web copywriting is to generate a response of some kind, such as getting your readers to pick up the phone and call your business, subscribe to your newsletter, sign up for your mailing list, or buy your product or service. Using embedded commands entails crafting the action you want your reader to take and wrapping it in the cushion of a casual, innocent-looking sentence.

Consider the following sentence:

I wonder how quickly you are going to buy this product.

It seems harmless enough. Your reader might consciously take it as a hypothetical comment. But notice the embedded command, which is quite hypnotic in effect: *you are going to buy this product.*

Using embedded commands in speaking calls for altering your tone of voice. You would lower your voice and speak the command part of the sentence more slowly for emphasis and to produce a hypnotic effect.

In writing, however, you can use boldface, quotation marks, italics, or even a different color to set off or delineate your command. When you write "I wonder how quickly **you are going to buy this product**," use boldface type for the command, "you are going to buy this product." The bold type plays a role in how effectively the command is communicated. A person will respond to that part of the sentence as a command and will follow the command without consciously realizing it.

In this way, you gain compliance effortlessly. Your readers don't even perceive that they've been given a command. Typically, they will obey your command as though they had received it directly, without any resistance whatsoever. Clearly, this is a very powerful tool. Because embedded commands evade the scrutiny of the left brain (the critical, logical side of the brain), readers are not aware of what is causing their desire.

Embedded commands motivate people to take action and compel readers to come to a quick decision. Advertisers have known this for years, and that is why they write slogans like "Aren't you glad you use Dial? Don't you wish everybody did?" The embedded command, of course, is "use Dial." The same is true of "Wouldn't you really rather have a Buick?" Of course, the embedded command used in the sentence is "have a Buick."

Writing Embedded Commands

Start by constructing your command. This is usually three to seven words articulated in the imperative mood; that is, you begin with an action verb that presupposes the subject "you."

Some examples of commands are

Get your hands on this [*name product*].

Act on my advice.

Say yes to this offer.

Learn this secret.

Pick up the phone.

Next, simply embed the command in a sentence and set it off in bold type. For example, if the action you want your readers to take is to "read every word of this article," your sentence could go like this: "As you **read every word of this article**, you will discover advanced psychological tactics that will boggle your mind."

Presuppositions

Powerful as the brain is, it usually can focus on only one major thing at a time. Therefore, when bombarded by multiple thoughts, it is forced to presuppose (assume) and accept suggestions as facts. This is why using presuppositions in your web copy is such a powerful technique.

The question "What will you do with the extra $2,500 you'll earn next month?" is an example of a presupposition. Your brain is asked the question "What will you do . . . ?" By its very nature, the human brain is compelled to answer it. It's an involuntary, spontaneous reaction. When your brain is asked a question, it instantly goes to work in search of an answer. If you've ever had the experience of waking up in the middle of the night with the answer to a question you were thinking about earlier in the day, then you've experienced the profound effect questions have on the brain. The brain keeps working on the question subconsciously until it comes up with an answer (if not verbally, then mentally). The answer may not always be correct, but the brain is satisfied only when it has produced an answer that it considers valid.

The question, "What will you do with the extra $2,500 you'll earn next month?" assumes that you will earn $2,500 next month simply by asking what you're going to do with it. This is called an *adjacency pair,* and the reader's/listener's brain pays attention only to the first part ("What will you do . . .") of the pair. A significant percentage of language processing takes place subconsciously. To understand a question or sentence, we must subconsciously make assumptions in order to make sense of what is being asked or said. Therefore, in order to answer the question, your brain has to assume that the second part of the question, "the extra $2,500 you'll earn next month," is an established fact. Do you see how smoothly that just slides into your consciousness?

Presuppositions are often seen in the leading questions prevalent in courtroom dramas, as well as police interrogations. These leading questions imply the existence of something when, in fact, its existence has not been established. Consider the following question:

Why did you steal the money?

The question assumes the existence of a sum of money. It further assumes that the money has been stolen, that you have stolen it, and that you have a reason for having stolen it. When questions such as these are delivered by a lawyer or law enforcement officer skilled in the syntax of presuppositions—especially when fired in rapid succession (stacked presuppositions), the listener is often forced to tacitly accept the implied meaning of the questions, even when the adversarial questioning was designed to introduce damaging arguments.

Here's another example of a presupposition: What will you do when the government imposes a five-cent surcharge on every e-mail that you send out? The brain focuses on the first part of the adjacency pair ("What will you do . . ."), which means it has to presuppose that the latter part of the sentence (about the government imposing a five-cent surcharge on every e-mail that you send out) is an established fact, when it actually is nothing but a rumor.

Here's another example: "Are you one of the 325 million people in America who's tired of the nine-to-five corporate grind, who wants to start her own business?" The question presupposes that there are 325 million people who want to start their own business in America, when that fact hasn't been established. Heck, that figure even exceeds the total population of the United States!

Not all presuppositions come in the form of questions. You can use presuppositional phrases like "As you know," "I'm sure you know," "Everybody knows . . ." and presuppositional words like *clearly, obviously, evidently, undoubtedly, easily, readily, automatically,* and *naturally.* Any statement you put after any of these words is more likely to be received or accepted by your reader without resistance. For example, "Obviously, these triggers usher in a revolutionary—and immensely more effective—era of selling that you simply can't miss out on," or "Clearly, investing in ViralVideoWizard.com's services is the fastest way to get Page 1 Google rankings and send massive traffic to your website in as little as 24 hours."

Clearly and all the other presuppositional words and phrases impart a halo of credibility around what you are saying and lead the reader to assume that the ensuing statement is true. It makes the statement take on the appearance of fact and therefore makes your sales argument go down smoothly.

I am not suggesting that you use this device to tell lies, use weasel words, or slip your readers a Mickey. I believe in telling the truth in advertising and abide by the adage "Advertising is truth well told." As with any powerful psychological device, you have to use presuppositions ethically and judiciously.

Linguistic Binds

A linguistic bind is a form of syntax that makes your reader say, "Why, of course, what you're saying is true!" and is another powerful tool in the art of persuasion. Let's analyze this linguistic bind: "While you're sitting there reading this letter, you begin to understand why you can't afford to waste any more time getting less than everything that life has to offer."

It consists of two parts. Part 1 states something obvious ("you're sitting there reading this letter"), and part 2 states what you want your reader to think, say, or do. It is the command. Curiously, this pattern makes your reader believe that what you are saying is logical when, in fact, parts 1 and 2 of your sentence are not linked by logic at all. Nevertheless, this device can make people agree with practically anything you say.

Here are some more examples of linguistic binds:

> "Now that you've read this special report, I'm sure you realize that you must get a copy of *The One-Minute Cure: The Secret to Healing Virtually All Diseases* now so you can find out how to heal yourself and your loved ones."

> "As you sit there reading this, I know that you're thinking about all the ways you can turn your book into a bestseller as a result of attending Mark Victor Hansen's Book Marketing University."

> "As you think about what you really need in your business, you begin to realize that you have only one choice to make, and that is to invest in this [*product or service*]."

There are other variations of linguistic binds. One is "The more you A, the more you B" syntax. For example:

> "The more you understand the power of this one psychological trigger, the more you'll realize that you need to get all 30 of Joe Sugarman's *Psychological Triggers.*"

> "The more you read, the more you won't want to be without this incredible product."

Another is the cause-and-effect syntax: "Taking advantage of this free trial of our water purifier in the comfort of your own home will cause you to fully understand why buying bottled water is simply not the way to go."

Reframing

Reframing is the process of altering one's perception of a person, place, or thing by changing the context in which it is viewed. Consider reframing in its literal sense. Imagine an ordinary photograph in a plain metal frame hanging on a wall. You would probably not regard it with any more importance than, say, a typical poster. Now imagine that same photograph reframed in an ornate museum-quality, solid-hardwood frame with custom moldings. Suddenly, you perceive it as a photograph of distinction, significance, and importance.

Our perception of a person, place, or thing is altered simply by changing the context—the frame—in which it is viewed. In verbal or written communication, perception can be altered by using the technique known as *reframing*.

Reframing in the context of copywriting is a technique for communicating a flaw, a shortcoming, an imperfection, or a disadvantage in a way that transforms its meaning to one that is pleasant, desirable, or advantageous. Advertisers often abuse this concept by saying misleading things like "When you purchase this camera, you will also get as a free gift this genuine, handsome, imitation-leather carrying case." There is nothing genuine about imitation leather. Don't reframe in this way because it will insult the intelligence of your audience.

The key to successful reframing is to shift the reader's focus to a desirable, sometimes hidden, aspect of a disadvantage and turn it into a plus. You may be surprised to discover how just about anything can be reframed into something desirable when you look at it in a different light or, more accurately, with a fresh set of eyes.

Reframing is an excellent tool to use to justify the price of what you're selling. In the following example, reframing was used to justify the $1,595 price tag for a one-day speakers' workshop:

> What price can you put on learning how to get as many speaking engagements as you can handle? $25,000? $15,000?

$10,000? (Believe it or not, that's how much other speaker trainers charge!)

If you paid me my standard consulting fee of $625/hour for the 7½ hours I'm giving you at the Speakers' Workshop on October 18, it would cost you $4,687.50.

Would you believe it if I told you the workshop won't even cost you $4,000? No, not even $3,000. Your investment in your speaking career—*and* your life—is only . . .

$1,595.

You'll most likely earn at least **twice** that much on **your very first speaking engagement.**

Here, the price of the workshop ($1,595) is compared to: (1) how much other speaker trainers charge ($25,000, $15,000, or $10,000), (2) the cost in consulting fees to receive an equivalent 7½ hours of training ($4,687.50), and (3) how much the buyer would earn on his or her first speaking engagement (twice as much as the price of tuition to attend the speakers' workshop). When reframed in this context, what could appear to be a prohibitive amount of money to spend on a one-day workshop suddenly seems reasonable—even inexpensive.

The preceding example also illuminates an interesting aspect of consumer psychology. When a prospect is presented with a high-priced product or service, followed by the presentation of a second, lower-priced product or service, the latter will be deemed *considerably less expensive* than if it were presented all by itself without a basis of reference. For example, if you're selling a software program that is available in a Standard Version (priced at $49) and a Professional Version (priced at $79), and you present the higher-priced Professional Version first, followed by the lower-priced Standard Version, prospects are likely to think the Standard Version is a bargain because they're comparing it to the price of the Pro Version. Had you presented the Standard Version all by itself, it wouldn't have seemed like a bargain at all because they would have no basis for comparison.

Applying this to web copywriting, in order to appeal to this aspect of consumer psychology, you should simply mention the higher-priced option first, if one exists, before you present the price of the actual product you really want the prospect to consider buying. In the minds of your prospects, the higher-priced option would be the expensive version and the lower-priced model the low-cost or cheaper version. Now, just when you think you've got your prospects all figured out, and you predict they'll choose the lower-priced product, they may choose the more expensive model instead. This actually happens a significant percentage of the time, and it's because prospects are often propelled by an inexplicable psychological compulsion to buy the deluxe version instead of settling for the cheaper one. Either way, you win because prospects are more likely to buy one version or the other.

Another way to apply this concept in copywriting is by elevating the *value* of your offer in your prospects' eyes before mentioning the price. That way, they will expect it to be priced at a premium and will be pleasantly surprised to know it's much less, that is, a bargain. For example:

> What would you expect to pay for a software program that combines the functionality of the best html editors plus 12 of the most popular Internet marketing applications? You would have to buy 15 products to match the power of WebGenius—and they would cost you more than $850. But WebGenius doesn't even cost half of the combined cost of all those products. Your investment, including lifetime upgrades, is only $99. That's only a small fraction of the cost of all those other programs that don't do half as much as WebGenius does.

THE APPEARANCE OF CONSISTENCY ▼

Humans have a nearly obsessive desire to be—or to appear—consistent to others and to ourselves. Once we've subscribed to something, voted for something, bought something, or taken a stand on something, we are under tremendous pressure to behave consistently with that commitment in order to justify our earlier decision.

I use this technique in writing web copy by first helping my readers express a firm stand or opinion about something, then presenting my product in a way that it plays to the stand my readers have taken. I first construct a question to which readers could not possibly answer no, such as "If I could show you a way to double or triple your sales closing rate—and teach you how to sell 50 to 100 percent of all prospects you come in contact with—are you willing to spend an entertaining 63 minutes to learn it?"

By asking this question I have, in effect, extracted an unspoken commitment from the readers, even if I receive no audible reply. Next, I tell them to read the rest of the article, where I give the details of my offer. After I've given the sales pitch, I say something like:

> Earlier on, I asked you the question: "If I could show you a way to double or triple your sales closing rate—and teach you how to sell 50 to 100 percent of all prospects you come in contact with—are you prepared to spend 63 minutes to learn it?"
>
> Since you're still reading this, I'm going to assume you answered, "Yes." Well, now that I've shown you unequivocally how Brian Tracy's 24 Techniques for Closing the Sale can deliver on that promise—and have also shown you Brian's first-rate credentials and the rave reviews he's received—it's time for you to act on this.

As you can see, I remind readers that they need to behave consistently with the commitment they've made. This is one of the most powerful weapons of influence.

CONTRADICTORY THINKING

▼

The best way to explain this concept is to tell you a story—actually, a fable. You probably remember this Aesop's fable. There once was a fox who tried in vain to reach a cluster of grapes dangling from a vine above his head. Although the fox leaped high to grasp the grapes, the delicious-looking fruit remained just beyond his reach. After several attempts, the fox gave up and said to himself, "These grapes are sour, and if I had some, I would not eat them."

This fable illustrates what former Stanford University social psychologist Leon Festinger called *cognitive dissonance*. Cognitive dissonance (or contradictory thinking) is the distressing mental state in which people "find themselves doing things that don't fit with what they know, or having opinions that conflict with other opinions they hold."

The fox's withdrawal from the pursuit of the grapes clashed with his thinking that the grapes were tasty. By changing his attitude toward the grapes, however, he was able to maintain an acceptable explanation for his behavior.

You can put this to effective use in your web copy by giving your readers a compelling reason to buy early in the sales process. This, in turn, makes them more likely to buy when confronted with the actual buying decision. Your readers have to be able to take ownership of that promise and cling to it so tenaciously that no other thought can pry it away from them. Any doubts or obstacles that may occur to them during the sales process are overcome by the original belief, paving the way to a home-run sale.

Robert Cialdini once wrote about a presentation he attended where two presenters tried to recruit new members into a Transcendental Meditation (TM) program. The presentation began with a compelling selling argument. However, when it came to the question-and-answer portion, an attendee demolished the presenters' arguments, and the presentation collapsed. The rest of the audience, however, instead of being turned off, rushed in record numbers to plunk down their $75 deposit to attend the TM program.

Cialdini thought that the other attendees hadn't quite understood the arguments or the logic of the dissenting attendee, but after interviewing those who signed up, he learned that they had had good reasons for considering signing up for the TM program before attending the presentation. Apparently, the dissenter's remarks, instead of dissuading them, compelled them to sign up; otherwise, they might go home, think about the dissenter's arguments, and never sign up, which would have contradicted their original commitment to TM.

Driven by their needs, they were desperately searching for a way to solve their problems, and they very much wanted to believe that TM was their answer. Rather than face the tedious task of finding another solution to their problems, they opted for the comfort of staying with their original belief, despite evidence to the contrary.

How can you use cognitive dissonance in your web copy? In the beginning of your web copy, you have to get your readers to say, "Yes, that's exactly what I need!" You can do this by crafting a well-articulated promise and inserting it very early in the body copy. Next, get readers to take ownership of that promise and cling to it so tenaciously that no one can pry it away from them. That way, any doubts or obstacles that might arise during the sales process will be squashed by the original belief, thus paving the way to clinching the sale. Here are examples of well-articulated promises:

> By the time you finish reading this article, you will know how to consistently pick the hottest stocks that are on the upswing right now—so you can make a killing on the stock market every time.

> What if I told you I could show you how to increase your ability to ethically influence others, naturally, without sounding like you're making a sales pitch? How much more money and success could you create with that skill?

THE CYRANO EFFECT

▼

The value of emotion in web copy cannot be overemphasized. I've repeated the principle "People buy on emotion and justify with logic" often—for good reason. Emotion is such a powerful element of the online sales process, one that is intricately connected with the psychology of the Internet buyer, that it would require an entire book to devote to its intricacies. I've encapsulated those intricacies into one psychological device that I call the Cyrano effect.

If you were to ask a sports car owner why he bought his car, he might tell you something along the lines that the car is a technological marvel, that it goes from 0 to 60 in five seconds, that the engine represents a breakthrough in German engineering, that the car has won many awards—or that he got a good deal for it. What he probably won't tell you is that the real reason he bought it is because of how he *feels* when he steps behind the wheel of the car—that it makes him feel powerful, virile, young again, and maybe even superior to others. Neither will he tell you that he bought it because it would make him feel good to be the envy of his neighbors, to impress women, or to get the respect of his associates. Then there are other subconscious emotional reasons that he may not even realize, much less verbalize—some of which have roots that go back to his childhood.

The preceding example indicates that to a great extent, a sale is made based on the salesperson's ability to stir as many emotions in the prospective buyer as possible. This is true in auto sales as well as in virtually all selling situations, and even more so in selling online, where attention is difficult to capture. Inasmuch as emotion is the single most important reason why people buy, the most important objective of a salesperson, marketer, or copywriter is to deliver an *emotional experience* during the sales presentation—or the test drive (in the case of auto buying). When people visit your website, for instance, they buy the vivid emotions you give them with your web copy. People have the need to be stimulated, not just intellectually but emotionally. In an increasingly technological world, they want to be taken out of their ordinary, day-to-day existence and temporarily transported to a place where they can feel alive, victorious, proud, accomplished, gratified, noble, responsible, or just plain happy.

This certainly goes hand in hand with what John Naisbitt, author of runaway bestseller *Megatrends* (Warner Books, 1982) wrote in his book *High Tech High Touch* (Broadway Books, 1999): "Focusing on the effects of technology in reshaping society, the book brings together a mountain of evidence implicating technology in relentlessly accelerating our lives and stirring profound yearnings for a more emotionally satisfying existence."

Now, here's the important lesson that you must learn from this glimpse into human nature: Although buyers want physical satisfaction, which they hope to obtain from the benefits of your product or service, what they *really* desire is emotional satisfaction. When you're able to satisfy them emotionally during the sales process, the virtues of your product or service become secondary.

When you engage your prospect's imagination successfully, it often eclipses the gratification they get from actually having your product or service. It is to the illumination of this concept that I've coined the term the *Cyrano effect*. This is derived from the title character of a French play written by Edmond Rostand, *Cyrano de Bergerac.* Cyrano was an ordinary-looking man with an overly large nose, who wooed the beautiful Roxanne on the behalf of his handsome but less articulate friend Christian de Neuvillette by writing beautiful letters that made Roxanne swoon. The story of Cyrano de Bergerac actually shines the light on this truth about advertising: An extraordinary product without emotionally engaging copy may only have a slim chance of selling well, while an ordinary product with emotionally engaging copy can sell incredibly well.

When marketers and advertisers speak of adding value to their offers to make them irresistible (as I've suggested in earlier chapters), one might think they're appealing to their prospect's logical mind, which knows a good deal when it sees one. Actually, when you dissect the matter further, the desirability of anything you offer for sale still boils down to how well you make your prospect's heart beat a little faster. Again, it's the emotional experience that you're really selling, and a value-added offer that your prospect "simply can't resist" is only an offshoot of the emotion you've successfully stimulated.

I've seen the Cyrano effect in action on countless occasions, both in my personal experience as well as in the experiences of many online marketers that I know. On one occasion, I wrote the copy for a company that sells a turnkey business-in-a-box that is licensed to market a variety of downloadable audiobooks on the Web. I didn't find the product particularly exciting at first, but as I began to develop the copy, I renamed the product a *franchise* to replace the bland business-in-a-box concept. Almost as soon as I called it a franchise, my imagination took flight. I found a sudden spark of inspiration that enabled me to write an emotionally driven copy piece. The peculiar thing about it was that I myself became excited about it and even planned to buy one of the franchises for my stepdaughter, but decided to wait until later. The product was launched at noon on November 16, 2006, a buying frenzy ensued, and 2½ days later the franchises were all sold out and my client had made $1 million! In fact, there was not a single franchise left for me to buy for my stepdaughter, and I regretted having waited too long. Looking back, it dawned on me that the excitement generated by the prospect of owning a franchise captured people's imaginations (including my own!), and what people actually bought was that emotional buzz, that temporary high that made them feel how they wanted to feel. For a considerable percentage of the buying population, that buzz is worth any amount of money you could ask for. This is reminiscent of the old sales aphorism "Sell the sizzle, not the steak."

Is this deceptive advertising then? Of course not. It's simply marketing that takes the psychology of online buyers into consideration. As I've mentioned earlier, I prescribe to the maxim "Advertising is truth well told." Advertising is not about telling lies, misrepresenting the virtues of one's product or service, or dispensing hype or exaggerated claims—although many unscrupulous advertisers have given advertising that reputation. It is actually contingent upon advertisers and copywriters to position their product or service in the best possible light so that it becomes desirable to their target audience. There's no deception in that. In truth, you're actually giving your customers what they *really* want—an emotional experience.

Now, here's an interesting phenomenon that happens as a result of providing an emotional experience in your web copy or sales process: Once you've successfully engaged your prospects' emotions, and your prospects consequently buy your product or service, more often than not the satisfaction they experience after the purchase has very little to do with the product or service they bought. The satisfaction persists even if buyers never use the product or service! Mind you, this phenomenon does not happen in most buying situations. We all know countless people who have bought products from emotion-driven infomercials and end up being remorseful and unhappy about their purchases. The satisfaction phenomenon happens only when you skillfully provide your buyers with an indelible emotional experience and, more important, you've succeeded in getting customers to *like* you. This goes hand in hand with the principle discussed in Chapter 4 (in the subsection entitled "Traffic Conversion: Turning Visitors into Customers") about how people often buy products that they don't particularly like, want, or need just because they like and trust the person who is selling the product to them.

Joe Girard, who was named the World's Greatest Salesman by *Guinness World Records,* operated on the tandem concepts of this satisfaction phenomenon. He sold an average of 6 cars a day, sold a total of 13,001 cars at a Chevrolet dealership in Detroit between 1963 and 1978, and was inducted into the Automotive Hall of Fame. Joe accomplished this not because he sold the most desirable cars in the world, not because he worked in the only car dealership in town, and not because he was the stereotypical fast-talking salesman. He did it by giving his prospects an emotional experience and getting them to like him. He made it his policy to tell every prospective customer who came into the dealership that he liked them, sometimes by admiring something about them, something they were wearing, their attitude, their smile, and so on. People like people who like them. Joe's prospects felt flattered (emotion!); they instantly liked Joe and wanted to do business with him because he liked them. He also made it a point to tell them, "I'm not excited about selling you this car today. You know what will excite me is if you come back and buy from me a second time." This made people feel that Joe cared more about making them happy (more emotion!) than merely selling a car. Joe was also famous for sending out greeting cards *every single month* to every person who ever bought a car from him (more emotion!), and he constantly assured them that he would take care of any auto service needs they might have. With the twin practices of providing an emotional experience and getting people to like him, Joe became the only car salesman in history who sold cars by appointment only. Customers had to wait between seven and ten days to book an appointment with him just for the privilege of buying a car from him. That's because they had heard about how he treats his customers and they, too, wanted to have that emotional experience.

I've seen this satisfaction phenomenon firsthand countless times, but the instance that I will never forget is the case of an Internet entrepreneur, whom I will call Peter, to protect his privacy. Peter offered a career counseling program on his website consisting of 15 audio CDs that he sold for $900. Since I was hired to write his website copy, I set about creating excitement for his prospects, giving them a remarkable emotional experience just from reading the copy. (Stimulating emotions is even more indispensable when it comes to selling high-ticket items.) As a result, Peter sold over 500 copies of the program in less than three months. It wasn't until after they started shipping out the audio sets to his customers that Peter learned of the serious error made by the company that produced the audio CDs for him. Apparently, CD #5 was completely blank! Instead of sending out an apology to all the people who bought the program, he waited for customers to complain about the blank disk and planned to send a replacement CD only to those who asked for it. Out of over 500 customers, only 8 notified Peter that CD #5 was blank and asked for a replacement! And not a single customer returned the program for a refund.

This case study illustrates that when web copy successfully delivers emotional satisfaction *before* the purchase is made, this often translates to satisfaction *after* the sale—even in cases where there may not be sufficient reason to be satisfied. Emotionally satisfied customers are also likely to ignore or underestimate the faults of a product or service. Naturally, there also exists the possibility of buyer's remorse once the customer climbs down from the emotional high, but by and large, buyers remember the emotional experience that caused them to buy in the first place, and that effect stays in place once they own or use the product or service.

Those who are experts in branding know this effect all too well. The De Beers diamond cartel launched a branding campaign over 70 years ago with the slogan "A diamond is forever" and supported it with the emotion-stimulating theme that diamonds are the symbol of enduring love, which is how they justified the high cost. Who could put a price on eternal love after all? Then came the brilliant slogan "She already knows you love her. Now everyone else will, too." As a result of manufacturing a relationship between emotion (love) and diamonds, 80 percent of American grooms give their brides diamond engagement rings, which average $3,000 in price. Women who receive a diamond engagement ring, or any gift consisting of diamonds, often float on a cloud of emotional satisfaction—and they feel "like a million bucks" long after they receive the expensive gift that proved to them how much they were loved. And the men who gave them the diamonds derived their emotional satisfaction from the feeling of proving their love through the gift of diamonds, not to mention the happy reaction they received from the ladies. In reality, the emotional satisfaction that both the men and the women experience has little to do with the intrinsic value of the diamond. The desirability of natural diamonds is emotional, not rational. A large part of diamonds' allure is their high cost and supposed rarity. In actuality, diamonds are plentiful and would probably cost no more than semiprecious stones were it not for De Beers's stockpiling them, rather than selling all of them, in order to prevent prices from falling. So in the final analysis, the only thing De Beers is really selling is not rare, expensive gems; they're selling emotional satisfaction, which endures long after the purchase is made.

When you consider how De Beers built a trillion-dollar business by simply fabricating preciousness out of people's emotions, you begin to realize how powerful emotional satisfaction is in driving sales. This is worth paraphrasing Ralph Waldo Emerson's famous saying "Build a better mousetrap and the world will beat a path to your door" as "Stimulate people's emotions and the world will beat a path to your website." If you fail to provide emotional satisfaction, you fail to make the sale.

So how do you create an emotional experience and provide emotional satisfaction in web copy?

You can do it by articulating your target audience's 3 Ps—their problem, pain, or predicament—as accurately as possible, or you paint a picture of what their lives could be when their problem, pain, or predicament is eliminated. Consider the following headline:

What Will You Do When Your Family's Assets Are Wiped Out to Pay for Nursing Home Expenses?

Another thing you can do is install involvement devices in your copy that engage your website visitors emotionally. Here's an example of an emotional involvement device employed by a client of mine who sells a Career Success Manual: (The following screen capture is courtesy of UltimateCareerGuide.com.)

Which of the following statements describe you?
(Check all that apply.)

❏   Your career is **unfulfilling** or you're stuck in a **dead-end job** where you're not growing professionally or personally.
❏   You **don't know exactly what you want** in a career, but the work you're doing now certainly isn't it!

- ❐ You're eager to get promoted or advance within your industry, but you're **having trouble "breaking through."**
- ❐ You're **dissatisfied with your job,** and you want a way out—but you don't know how to go about it.
- ❐ You're **unemployed** or afraid you might be **laid off** soon, and you want to find a new—and better—job as soon as possible.
- ❐ You feel **burned out, overworked, or underpaid,** and you want to find an enjoyable job that pays what you deserve.
- ❐ Your **career is not a good fit**—and you yearn for work that would more closely match your interests, personality, and skills.

In the preceding example, the emotions you're trying to stimulate are frustration, dissatisfaction, defeat, and even despair. You not only effectively get your website visitors involved with your website, causing them to stay there longer, but also get them to identify themselves as your prospects when they check the items that apply to them. Most important, you stir up emotions in them that will go a long way toward keeping them glued to your web copy.

A client of mine who has the reputation of being a stock-trading whiz kid offers a service called First Hour Trading, which is a type of day trading wherein he pinpoints "Bull Trap" stocks that have the highest probability of experiencing price movements during the first hour of the trading day. He and the subscribers of his service who follow his trades average at least 1 percent returns on their investments every day. However, because he's prohibited by the Securities and Exchange Commission (SEC) from making income promises to prospects, I installed the following Earnings Calculator in his web copy.

⬇⬇⬇

NOTE: Type $25,000 in the Initial Investment section (this is the minimum investment amount for day trading). To calculate how much you'll earn in a month, *type 22* in "Number of Trading Days" (since there are *22 trading days a month*).

Your Earnings Calculator

(*no commas*) Initial Investment $ [   ]

(Daily) Rate of Return % [1]

Number of Trading Days [   ]

Your Initial Investment Would

Grow to This Amount → $ [   ]

Your Net Earnings (Compounded) $ [   ]

[Clear]

When website visitors type in the amount of their initial investment and the number of trading days, they're effectively involved in
the sales process already. When the form automatically calculates
their potential earnings for the month, it comes to $4,894 per month
even on the minimum investment amount—and yearly earnings of
$256,612! If that doesn't get their hearts pounding faster and make
them emotionally involved, I don't know what will. The best part is
that we didn't have to make any income promises. We simply gave
the website visitors a tool with which to do their own math.

Another method you can use to create an emotional experience
is to get your website visitors to imagine for themselves how it would
feel to own or use your product or service. Here are a few examples:

Service: Weight Loss Clinic
How *proud* will you feel when you attend your high school reunion being in the best shape of your life? Imagine the look on your former classmates' faces.

Service: Interior Design
Imagine having an interior designer who can create your living environment in a way that transforms . . .

> . . . the way you view the world when you wake up in the morning
>
> . . . the mood you have throughout the day, and
>
> . . . even what you dream of at night.

Product: Day Trading Workshop
How will your life change when you begin getting a 10%, 12%—even 15% return on your investments every month? What kind of car will you be driving? In what part of town will you live?

Product: Time Management Seminar
How much more quality time will you have with your family and the people you care about when you discover how to get your job done in half the time?

Product: Language Learning Program
How *confident* will you feel when you arrive in Rome able to speak Italian fluently?

Product: Business Opportunity
How *satisfying* would it feel to be able to do the things you never had time to do before—the things that are truly important to you—and still be making the kind of income you want?

In my experience, I've seen website sales double or even triple with the judicious use of any one of the devices I've described in this chapter. This is why psychological and linguistic devices are an integral part of your web copy. Strategically employing these devices wherever possible in your copy is essential if you want to maximize the sales generated.

6

The Art of Changing Your Prospects' Minds

At any given point in your online sales process, your prospect has a level of interest that ranges from apathy through mild interest, medium interest, strong interest to sold. (See Figure 6.1.)

Your prospects also have various levels of skepticism ranging from extremely skeptical to distrustful, reserved, accepting, believing, and, again, sold. (See Figure 6.2.)

The Trifecta Neuro-Affective Principle that I present in this chapter is designed to take your prospects from wherever their present interest or skepticism levels may lie and transform them into not only enthusiastic believers but willing buyers. When used on your target audience in tandem with the five-step blueprint in Chapter 2, this principle can accelerate your prospects' decision-making process, thereby dramatically minimizing the time it takes for them to buy what you're selling.

Levels of Interest

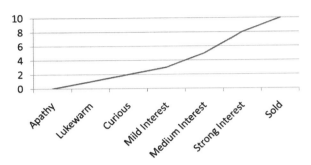

Figure 6.1 Levels of interest.

What exactly does it take for your prospect to change his or her mind about your product or service—and act on the basis of that mind shift?

I wish to emphasize that it is not my intention to teach you how to cause your online prospect to think favorably of your product or service—and consequently want to buy what you're selling—through compulsion, nor through deceptive or manipulative approaches.

Having stated that, the secret to changing your prospect's mind—or any other person's mind, for that matter—is to produce a shift in his or her mental representations. A mental representation in the context of this discussion is defined as a presentation to the mind

Levels of Skepticism

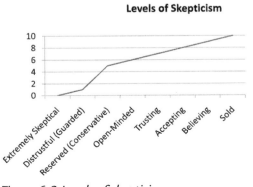

Figure 6.2 Levels of skepticism.

The Trifecta Neuro-Affective Principle

The term *trifecta* is derived from a type of horse-racing bet, in which the bettor must select the *first three finishers in exact order*. In like manner, it is contingent upon web copywriters and online marketers to select which three representations of their sales proposition they should use—and in which sequence—in order to make the sale.

The word *affective* means "arousing feelings or emotions," and *neuro* refers to the billions of nerve cells in the brain (called *neurons*). The term *neuro-affective*, therefore, denotes the *connection between the mental and emotional states*.

To the extent that you arouse emotions in human beings, you also alter their mental representations of reality, effectively changing their minds. I owe this insight to philosopher and scientist Alfred Korzybski (July 3, 1879–March 1, 1950) and his work on general semantics, which states that a person's experience is not reality but a representation of it, based on the structure of the human nervous system and the structure of language.

---

in the form of an idea or image. It's the specific way in which an individual perceives, codes, retains, and accesses information in the brain.

One extremely powerful method of changing someone's mind is by presenting multiple versions of the same concept. In my experience, as well as in most cases that I've observed, the optimum number of versions that has the highest likelihood of making an impact is three. When three forms of representation are offered, especially when each of the three conveys a well-rounded spectrum, a change erupts dramatically in the consciousness of your prospect as a result of the subtle mental-emotional processes that crystallize.

Consider the following: Ken Kragen, who successfully managed the careers of some of the world's most important entertainers, including Kenny Rogers, Lionel Richie, Trisha Yearwood, Olivia Newton-John, the Bee Gees, and the Smothers Brothers, uses the *magic of three* to catapult his clients to stardom. He determined that it takes three highly visible media events occurring within a short period of time to take a person from obscurity to fame. It's clear to see why this is so. Imagine hearing about an up-and-coming actress three times this week. The first time you hear about her is in a feature article written about her in *People* magazine, the second time as a guest on *The View,* and the third time on *Entertainment Tonight,* where she's shown walking down the red carpet at a movie premiere accompanied by a famous actor. When these three things happen in the span of one week, you don't just sit up and take notice—you're likely to think she's someone who matters in Hollywood, and you might be led to believe she's an A-list actress, even if you've never heard of her before this week. The buzz around the water fountain at work may now even include her: "That actress whom Dylan Maynard is dating now" or "I heard she led a rally against the resumption of commercial whaling" or just casual banter like "Did you see the Armani dress she wore at the premiere?" If the actress happens to have a movie coming out in theaters this weekend, you might go see it, even if you would never have considered seeing it had it not been for the three-event strategy engineered by her brilliant manager!

The magic of three has captivated our imagination not only in Hollywood but also in the stories we've read or been told since childhood, as well as in titles of bestselling books, idiomatic expressions, and advertising slogans.

"Goldilocks and the Three Bears"

The Three Musketeers

A Christmas Carol (and its three spirits of Christmas)

The Chronicles of Narnia: The Lion, the Witch and the Wardrobe

"The Three Little Pigs"

"Hear no evil, see no evil, speak no evil"

"Three Blind Mice"

Eat, Pray, Love (bestselling book by Elizabeth Gilbert)

"I came, I saw, I conquered" (*"Veni, vidi, vici"*—Julius Caesar)

Be, do, and have

Healthy, wealthy, and wise

Snap, Crackle, and Pop

"Spray, brush, and go"

"Hire specialists. Work together. Pay for results." (tagline of Elance.com)

Play. Love. Grow.

Why is a series of three so powerfully persuasive?

One reason might be because three is the most abbreviated way to convey a spectrum—such as in the threesomes of good, better, best; morning, noon, night; thoughts, words, actions; minimum, maximum, optimum; birth, life, death. The spectrum, which also delineates a continuum, then affords us a sense of completion, and anything more would be superfluous. We get the whole picture already, albeit in shorthand.

Another reason might be because three is the minimum number that human perception considers a pattern. If something happens once, it's merely a fluke. If it happens twice, it's a coincidence. But if it happens three times, people begin to draw conclusions. Are you beginning to perceive the unlimited usefulness of threes in web copywriting—and even sales and marketing in general? The principle I'm about to teach, however, goes way beyond just the power of threes.

Our brains are wired to respond to threes because three represents a digestible bite. It's also easy to remember a sequence of three. This may be due to the oral tradition by which information was handed down long before the age of the written word. We can remember the joke about the rabbi, the priest, and the minister walking into a bar, but if we add a fourth guy, he may fall just outside the parameters of our memory and tends to weaken the impact of the triad altogether.

In the realm of online selling, when you present three irrefutable sales arguments to your prospect, it causes subtle processes in the brain to coalesce into an emotional experience, and that emotional experience in turn goes a long way toward advancing the sale. (See Chapter 5 for an in-depth discussion of emotional experience and the Cyrano effect.) Since people buy on emotion and justify their purchases with logic, when your buyers are prompted to give a reason why they bought your product or service, it would be easy for them to declare, "I had three good reasons," and then recite them quite effortlessly. This memory goes a long way toward cementing customer satisfaction. A surprising side effect of this exchange is that when your customer recites the three reasons to other people, those reasons may resonate with the other people because they, too, will feel a sense of completion. It might convince those other people to buy your product or service because further considerations would seem superfluous. And it may even cause them to recite the three reasons to other people as well, thereby creating a snowball effect. Following is an example of three sales arguments presented in one digestible bite:

> *The One-Minute Cure: The Secret to Healing Virtually All Diseases* will show you . . .
>
> → a remarkable, *scientifically proven natural therapy* that creates an environment within the body where disease cannot thrive—and enables the body to cure itself of disease.
>
> → why over *6,100 articles in European scientific literature* have attested to the effectiveness of this simple therapy in not only killing diseased cells but also simultaneously revitalizing and rejuvenating healthy cells, thereby creating vibrant energy and well-being.
>
> → how this *safe, inexpensive* and *powerful* healing modality has been administered by an estimated *15,000 European doctors, naturopaths, and homeopaths* to more than 10 million patients in the past 70 years to successfully treat practically every known disease.

WHAT ROLE DOES EMOTION PLAY IN MIND CHANGING?

▼

Emotion plays a reciprocal role in both the installation of beliefs and the replacement of old beliefs with new ones. The more emotional your prospect's commitment is to an existing belief, the more difficult it is to change his or her mind. Conversely, the more emotionally engaging your web copy is, the easier it is to install a belief that endears your product or service to your prospect.

Some of the most influential people in the world, including political leaders, evangelists, public speakers, authors, and sales professionals, instinctively employ the Trifecta Neuro-Affective Principle—often without even knowing that their use of the principle is the reason they're successful at changing the minds of large numbers of readers, voters, educational institutions, and even nations.

How can you employ the Trifecta Neuro-Affective Principle in your web copy and online marketing communications? The formula that is most effective for changing prospects' minds on the Web is the use of multiple entry points—ideally, three. You need to streamline your concept, topic, or sales proposition to the essential triad. When you distill it in this manner, you'll find an extraordinary concentration of power that can produce extraordinary results. Your concept will shine like a raw diamond stripped of all its debris, and it will have optimum impact.

The key to harnessing the power of the Trifecta Neuro-Affective Principle is to determine which three of the many possible presentations you should employ. This may take some deliberation because you face the challenge of becoming ensnared in your own personal preferences instead of those of your target audience (which was the primary shortcoming of using the five-step blueprint). The mind-changing encounter can be successful only when you set aside your own point of view and, instead, engage the psyche of your prospect. The more you know about the mental representations and resistances of your target audience, the more you can engage them fully, and the more likely you will be successful in changing your prospects' minds in your favor.

THE THREE PRINCIPAL TRIGGERS OF MIND CHANGE
▼

Different people have different ways of processing information that is presented to them—and different people may find one representation easier to decode and embrace than others. It would be a futile endeavor to tailor one's web copy to cater to all the diverse triggers of mind change. However, a shift of mind is likely to coalesce when you employ three principal triggers. Precisely calibrating the delivery of your concepts with the use of these triggers literally alters your prospects' behavior and increases the likelihood that they will act in favor of your product or service.

The three principal triggers of mind change are resonance, redefinition, and resistance.

Emotional Resonance

Whereas logic and rational thought stroke the cognitive side of the human brain, resonance arouses the emotional side. Therefore, when an emotional trigger is employed, that's when your prospects feel they *resonate* with you or your message. That also means your concept, topic, or sales proposition feels right or is a good fit for their particular situation, and it convinces your prospects that they need look no further than your product or service to fulfill their needs. That feeling often happens at an unconscious level.

Another aspect of the resonance trigger is the phenomenon that psychologists call *identification*. When your prospects perceive similarities between themselves and you (or your spokesperson or representative), they identify with you, tend to resonate with your ideas, and sometimes even model their behavior around yours. Therefore, to the extent that you're able to have your prospects believe that you're just like them or that you understand their problems, pain, and predicaments, you have the power to influence what they will believe and how they will act. Skilled copywriters and marketers are able to exploit the phenomenon of identification in order to bring about the mind shift and action they want from their prospects.

Redefinition

Your sales proposition becomes convincing to the extent that you can redefine the prospects' understanding of a concept in a way that causes them to see things in a brand-new way—that is, *your* way. It becomes even more convincing when it lends itself to representation in a variety of forms, with each form reinforcing and rounding out the others. Since every human being has multiple intelligences, entry to the belief system via a number of different routes corresponding to our different human intelligences is essential. For example:

> ► *Narrative:* consists of telling a story or case study related to the sales proposition or the people and circumstances surrounding it
>
> ► *Quantitative:* consists of using finite, measurable examples that support the sales proposition
>
> ► *Logic:* consists of identifying the key elements or factors that come into play and exploring logical outcomes that support the sales proposition

Other possible forms of representation include graphic, linguistic, humorous, aesthetic, numerical, experiential, and even existential. If you can present a concept in three ways, each one appealing to a different sensibility or intelligence, you make your concept accessible to more people. After all, some of your prospects are more likely to embrace concepts explained to them in a narrative fashion, for instance. Others may be moved primarily by argument, with its logically ordered propositions, while still others might relate to quantitative entries.

Resistance

While the triggers of resonance and redefinition represent factors that facilitate mind change, there also exists one important factor that hinders the progress of mind change. The major paradox in getting a prospect to change his or her mind in favor of your product or service lies in the strong beliefs, views, and perspectives that are resistant to unfamiliar, contrasting, or opposing propositions. Therefore, identifying objections or resistances and overcoming them is essential in enabling the facilitating factors of resonance and redefinition to create the mind-changing effect you want.

When the triggers of resonance, redefinition, and resistance are engaged, and they are represented in three forms that reinforce and round out each other, that combination creates the perfect storm of mind-changing conditions. The "perfect storm" refers to the simultaneous occurrence of events that, taken individually, would be far less powerful than the result of their deliberate combination. Likewise, the triggers constituting the Trifecta Neuro-Affective Principle, taken individually, do not yield the effect of changing people's minds that their combined power produces.

Sales professionals who possess the uncanny ability of turning even the coldest prospects into enthusiastic buyers usually hit upon this perfect storm by chance and without realizing they're employing any principle at all. Knowing the elements of the Trifecta Neuro-Affective Principle enables you to utilize it with conscious deliberation, thereby making the sale a probable occurrence and not a stroke of chance.

I've examined many successful sales processes of companies, professional salespeople, and marketers, both online and offline, and analyzed what made them successful. Invariably, I'd find a *trifecta* that cause people to buy from them, usually without any hesitation or second thoughts. Every one of them had employed a variation of the Trifecta Neuro-Affective Principle.

Here's a real-life case study that shows the precise and successful use of the Trifecta Neuro-Affective Principle. The actual name of the entrepreneur in the following case study has been changed to protect his privacy.

Product: The product was a one-day seminar in Chicago introducing a breakthrough weight loss program. (No physical product was actually being sold—just information regarding the revolutionary weight loss methodology presented by one person.)

Particulars: Erik Morgan, a famous and highly respected best-selling author of seven books and a well-known consumerist known for exposing the unethical practices of the FDA as well as pharmaceutical companies and the food industry, sent out a one-page e-mail on April 17. In the e-mail, he told the personal story of how, after struggling with excess weight all his life and trying diet after diet that didn't work, he suddenly lost 25 pounds in less than two weeks and has kept the pounds off for almost a year without dieting, exercising, or taking drugs or fat-burning pills. He said that he did it through a revolutionary breakthrough that many people are calling the greatest nutritional discovery of the century. It makes people lose up to 10 pounds in 48 hours and at least 30 pounds in 30 days without dieting, exercising, or taking weight loss drugs or fat-burning pills. He further claimed, "This discovery is the best, fastest, easiest, and most powerful way to get you to lose unwanted pounds and keep them off forever. This is the miracle I have been looking for my whole life." He went on to say that the drug companies are scrambling to hide this unbelievable way of losing unwanted pounds from the public because they are trying to turn this discovery into a drug that they can patent and sell for billions of dollars. He also stated that the government won't allow him to sell this nutrient, but that the discovery is so powerful, safe, and effective that it makes people lose the unwanted pounds so fast that they end up needing a completely new wardrobe just a few weeks after starting on the program. Erik said the only way he could provide the information about the discovery was through a one-day (12-hour) seminar to be held in Chicago on May 27. The seminar tuition fee was $1,000, and for those who couldn't attend the live seminar, reservations could be made to buy the audio CDs of the seminar recording at a price of $250.

Results: On the basis of that e-mail alone, which consisted of only six paragraphs (473 words), hundreds of people gladly forked over $1,000 to attend the seminar, sight unseen. The one-day seminar was scheduled to be held 40 days into the future at an undisclosed venue in Chicago. No one except those who paid the $1,000 were given the location of the venue. There wasn't even a webpage giving additional details about the seminar—just the one-page e-mail with a link to the online order form. From what I could ascertain, that e-mail campaign generated over $320,000 in seminar tuition fees, not including another $65,000 in revenues from the advance orders of the $250 CD set.

Analysis: It's not my objective to make a judgment call about the quality of the underlying products (seminar and audio CDs) that were sold by Erik Morgan in this example. My only goal is to illustrate the anatomy of a successful mind change, and identify the factors present in Erik's e-mail campaign that squashed people's skepticism and dramatically increased their interest to the point that they were willing to make a $1,000 buying decision (or $250, in the case of the audio CD set) in the time it took them to read the e-mail. Those kinds of results, of course, are the stuff that marketers' dreams are made of—that is, to be able to convey just three things in the right sequence and consequently cause people to fall all over themselves to buy whatever you're selling. I'm not at all surprised by the phenomenal response Erik got, because the Trifecta Neuro-Affective Principle was firmly in place. Here's how the three principal triggers were engaged.

Resonance: The recipients of Erik's e-mail were able to identify with Erik's lifelong struggle with being overweight because they themselves battled excess weight. They got excited hearing about Erik's weight loss—especially the part about maintaining the weight loss without having to diet, exercise, or take diet drugs or pills. Furthermore, they regarded Erik as a respected authority figure, one whom they could look up to and emulate. Since Erik had the reputation of being a consumerist, he was credible to them. They couldn't imagine him fabricating his story about permanent weight loss. Any skepticism that they might have entertained upon hearing this too-good-to-be-true news dissipated. First base.

Redefinition: Erik redefined the accomplishment of weight loss and positioned it as the greatest nutritional discovery of the century. He also mentioned that the drug companies are scrambling to hide from the public this unbelievable way of losing unwanted pounds because they are trying to turn this discovery into a drug that they can patent and sell for billions of dollars. This logically ordered proposition talleyed with what they already knew about Erik as someone who exposes the hidden tricks that drug companies employ to fool the public. Therefore, it passed through to their belief system with no resistance. Second base.

Resistance: Erik stated in his e-mail that the government won't allow him to sell the weight loss nutrient, but that the discovery is powerful, safe, and effective. This addresses the objections prospects might have had about the danger of ingesting this new nutrient. Since Erik also said the *only* way he could provide the information about the discovery was through a one-day seminar in Chicago, they were able to justify the high price tag in their minds because the information wasn't available anywhere else. And if they couldn't afford the $1,000, Erik had given a less costly option: the $250 audio CDs. Third base.

With all the triggers engaged, the only question left for the prospects to answer was which one they should opt for—the seminar or the audio CDs? Whether they chose one or the other, the e-mail campaign was a home run for Erik.

Here's something interesting that happens when you employ the Trifecta Neuro-Affective Principle. More often than not, you simultaneously satisfy the five-question blueprint for writing killer web copy (see Chapter 2). The answer to Question No. 1 (What's the problem?) is stubborn excess weight that won't go away. The answer to Question No. 2 (Why hasn't the problem been solved?) is that diets don't work. The answer to Question No. 3 (What is possible?) is that permanent weight loss is now possible without the need for diet, exercise, weight loss drugs, or fat-burning pills. The answer to Question No. 4 (What's different now?) is that now there's a revolutionary breakthrough that many people are calling the greatest nutritional discovery of the century, which makes people lose up to 10 pounds in 48 hours and at least 30 pounds in 30 days without dieting, exercising, or taking weight loss drugs or fat-burning pills. Finally, the answer to Question No. 5 (What should you do now?) is this: Sign up for the $1,000 seminar in Chicago or reserve your copy of the seminar recordings for $250.

To illustrate how easily anyone can apply the Trifecta Neuro-Affective Principle to just about any product or service, I've randomly selected a website that sells a healing program based on the principles of energy psychology. The target audience consists of adults who are battling an illness or disease or have people they care about who are suffering from an illness or disease. The product consists of a set of DVDs, audio CDs, and manuals that teach people how to administer a simple healing mechanism to themselves or others to cure diseases and illnesses ranging from the flu to cancer. It's priced at $800. As you read the following copy (see Figure 6.3), notice how the three triggers (resonance, redefinition, and resistance) are engaged and why the copy is rendered irresistible by them. Again, the names of the individuals and the company have been changed for privacy reasons.

Analysis: The web copy in Figure 6.3 not only succeeds in employing the three emotional triggers of resonance, redefinition, and resistance but also presents the sales proposition in three formats that appeal to various human intelligences: narrative, quantitative, and logic.

The entire web copy is presented as the first-person narrative of a doctor who holds three credentials—M.D., Ph.D., and D.O. *Resonance* is achieved because the target audience is likely to deem the

"I Should Already Be Dead."

These are the words of Dr. Lone Thomas, a triple-certified doctor (M.D., PhD and D.O.) who was diagnosed with Lou Gehrig's Disease in February 2003. "It was a diagnosis worse than even cancer or AIDS," he continued, "because Lou Gehrig's disease is an incurable motor neuron disease that attacks the nerves and muscles, and is fatal. I considered the diagnosis a *death sentence* since 80% of people who suffer from it die within 5 years, and no one has ever survived for 10 years.

"I had been suffering from the disease for three years when I heard about a doctor of Psychology, Dr. Aaron Mercer, who had discovered a healing modality that he called the **THC method**, which brings the body to a state wherein it *heals itself*. My symptoms had become *almost unbearable* by that time—I had severe fatigue, constant fasciculation, or twitching of the muscles, and my voice was so weak I could barely speak. Being a doctor, I knew I only had a few months to live.

"But Dr. Mercer's words gave me *hope*. He described the simple healing protocol used in the THC method, which consisted of pointing the fingertips of both hands on four different healing centers in the body in a specific sequence. It didn't require any equipment or supplies whatsoever. The whole process he described only took a few minutes, and it was to be done a few times a day depending on one's particular disease or illness, and its severity.

"I had nothing to lose so I signed up for Dr. Mercer's THC training program in Dallas, which back then cost thousands of dollars. But to me, no amount of money was too much to spend to save my life. Thereafter, I began practicing the THC healing method on myself, **and within 6 weeks, I was healed of Lou Gehrig's Disease!** The speed in which I became symptom-free was *incredible* compared to the amount of time it usually takes for medical treatments to work on serious diseases of utmost severity. I've remained symptom-free for almost 3 years, and if I were examined today, it would seem that I never had the disease.

"The most startling thing about the THC method of healing is that no one—neither Dr. Mercer nor I, nor anyone else for that matter—could explain *why* it heals practically any illness or disease, whether it be physical, mental or emotional. We just knew that its effectiveness had its roots in energy psychology—and that it *works!*

"Being a doctor, as well as the head of my own medical center that specialized in alternative treatments for cancer, I did a lot of research to figure out why the THC method works. Dr. Mercer allowed me access to his files, and there I found hundreds of cases that, from a medical standpoint, seemed like miraculous healings. The files were overflowing with letters from people who were healed of **Parkinson's Disease**, terminal **leukemia**, lymphoma, and other kinds of **cancers**, fibroids, dementia, and a wide variety of mental conditions like **clinical depression**. Just about every disease known to man had been healed by the THC method—and it even works on pets.

"After much research, Dr. Mercer and I uncovered the medical explanation for the efficacy of the THC healing modality. Our research revealed that the reason why the THC method works consistently and predictably is because it activates a physical function in the body that removes what the Stanford University Medical School calls the **#1 cause of 99% of all illness and disease** in the body. When you eliminate its cause, you eliminate the disease.

"Many other respected health experts whom we interviewed concurred with this finding. But the most convincing discovery we made was that the Heart Rate Monitor, which is a widely used medical apparatus, actually proves that the THC method removes the #1 cause of 99% of all illness and disease in the body. We conducted dozens of experiments wherein we took measurements with the Heart Rate Monitor before a subject did the THC method, and then again after the THC method is administered. And there it was—solid proof that the THC method did indeed dramatically reduce—or eliminate altogether—the primary cause of what makes people sick. Even more stunning is the fact that the Heart Rate Monitor is immune to the placebo effect, which means that the results we obtained were not tainted by a psychological effect.

"At first, I was concerned that people who really needed to be healed wouldn't be able to afford the $5,000 it cost to attend Dr. Mercer's live training. But Dr. Mercer decided to distill all the information he taught in the training workshop into a set of DVDs, audio CDs and manuals that are priced quite affordably.

"Learning the THC method itself is *easy*. In fact, in as little as a few minutes after you view the first DVD, you can turn to the index of the manual, look up the condition you want to heal, and find the page number where you can find the specific protocol to treat that disease or illness. Then, it's just a matter of sitting comfortably on a chair or sofa, or lying down on your bed, if you prefer that, doing the prescribed protocol for the number of minutes specified. The method is so simple that *even a seven-year-old child can do it*. The THC method is designed to be either self-administered, or administered on others who can't do the protocol for themselves, such as extremely ill or immobilized people, young children or pets.

"No family should be without the THC method of healing. It's like the cheapest form of health insurance you can buy, but one with the best likelihood of keeping you and your family healthy. You see, the THC method is not just for healing you when you suffer from a disease or illness. You can also use it to prevent you and your loved ones from getting sick in the first place.

"So in parting, I want to tell you the first 5 words that I said at the very beginning. I should already be dead. But instead, here I am alive and well—with not a single hint that I ever suffered from a disease that had a death sentence attached to it. I'm absolutely sure that whatever disease or illness you and everyone you know are battling right now could not compare to the seriousness and severity of my previous condition—unless you have Lou Gehrig's Disease yourself, of course. So imagine how much more easily the THC method will work in your particular condition. Remember, the THC method does not heal disease or illness. It simply REMOVES what the Stanford University Medical Hospital and many of the country's top health experts declare as the #1 cause of disease and illness. I'm certain you'll want to do that for yourself and your family—and pass this priceless knowledge on to future generations. Your life and the life of your loved ones might very well depend on this.

"I wish you and yours the best of health!"

Lorne Thomas, M.D., PhD, D.O.
www.StanfordCure.com

Figure 6.3 THC copy.

narrator a reliable source, an authority figure, and someone who's respected and can be trusted. Dr. Lorne Thomas talks about his harrowing health ordeal in a dramatic way, starting with the riveting words "I should be dead by now." (*That really strikes an emotional chord, doesn't it?*) The ensuing description of his suffering further causes the reader to identify with Dr. Thomas, while at the same time making the readers feel subconsciously that whatever disease or illness they or their loved ones are suffering from pales in comparison with Dr. Thomas's suffering. (*"It was a diagnosis worse than even cancer or AIDS."*) When Dr. Thomas tells how he was healed by the THC method in six weeks, beyond his medical comprehension, and explains the mechanics by which healing via the THC method occurs, he redefines the concept of healing for readers. Redefinition is achieved through quantitative representation: ". . . it activates a physical function in the body that removes what the Stanford University Medical School calls the #1 cause of 99% of all illness and disease in the body." It is further achieved by stating that the Heart Rate Monitor has scientifically proven without a doubt, and without the possibility of the placebo effect, that the THC method does eliminate the number one cause of 99 percent of all illness.

The objections that are likely to arise in readers' minds are the following:

"But will it work for me (or my loved one)?"

"Does it take a lot of time to do the THC method? If it does, I know I won't do it because I don't have a lot of extra time in my day as it is."

"Is it hard to do?"

"Does it cost a lot of money?"

"Will I have to buy special equipment or supplies for the rest of my life if I were to decide to use this healing method?"

All the objections have been identified and successfully countered by Dr. Thomas's declarations that: (1) the THC method has been used to heal practically all diseases and illnesses (as evidenced by the flood of letters); (2) the THC method takes only a few minutes to do; (3) it's so simple to do that even a seven-year-old child can do it; (4) it's affordable, especially compared to the $5,000 one would have had to pay for the live training and considering the fact that it's the "cheapest health insurance" one could ever find; and (5) no special equipment or supplies are needed. By addressing all the possible objections, the resistance trigger was employed.

Finally, not only did the copy present the sales proposition in a narrative and quantitative form of representation, it also appealed to the reader's logic (see Figure 6.4). The logically ordered proposition was accomplished with the sales device most copywriters forget to utilize: the *feel, felt, found* sequence. In essence, Dr. Thomas was saying to readers, "I know how you *feel* because I *felt* the same way. But I *found* a revolutionary healing method that eliminated the cause of my disease and thereby healed me. Now you can do the same."

Since the copy succeeded in employing the three triggers of resonance, redefinition, and resistance *and,* at the same time, reinforced the sales proposition through the three principal forms of representation (narrative, quantitative, and logic), it rendered the product irresistible. I wouldn't doubt that after reading the ten paragraphs of web copy a good percentage of the readers who are suffering from an illness or disease—who also have access to $800—would be ready to buy without reading another word.

Notice that the ten-paragraph sales copy contained virtually no sales pitch. It was just a straightforward narrative telling the story of someone who was healed of a painful and incurable disease. The call

3 Triggers of the Trifecta Neuro-Affective Principle™

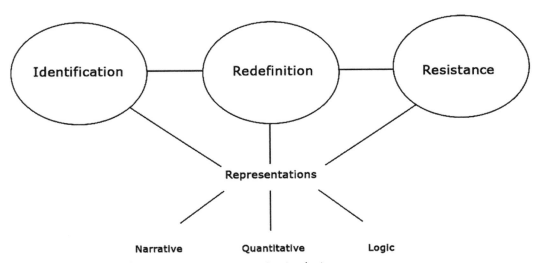

Figure 6.4 Trifecta schematic: narrative-quantitative-logic.

to action comes across more as advice to the reader than as an invitation to order. And yet it dealt a powerful selling punch!

One important thing to remember is that putting the Trifecta Neuro-Affective Principle in place is not necessarily equivalent to writing web copy in its entirety. Rather, it is a shortcut strategy for presenting the most salient points of your sales proposition in the most compelling manner in the least amount of time. There may be times that fleshing out your copy further, presenting other benefits and testimonials, or including other copy elements is called for (see Chapter 3 for a discussion of the other essential components of winning web copy). What the application of the Trifecta Neuro-Affective Principle does is successfully grab the attention, maximize interest, create desire for your product or service, and, oftentimes, cause your prospect to act (i.e., buy, order, or purchase), thus completing the AIDA cycle in a single pass. At other times, the Trifecta Neuro-Affective Principle may capture attention, interest, and desire, but your prospects might still need to acquaint themselves with all the details of your offer before they actually buy. At the very least, when they do click through to your order page (or a page that gives the details of your offer), they arrive in a presold frame of mind and with a willingness to buy your product or service if the price is commensurate to the perceived value of your offer and is affordable to them.

Following is another example of how the Trifecta Neuro-Affective Principle can be applied to yet another product by engaging not only the three triggers but also three forms of representation:

Product: A book that teaches companies how to use the 80/20 principle to maximize the return on their advertising dollar.

Target audience: Companies that have an advertising budget of $50,000 a year or more.

Analysis: The copy starts off with a quote that expresses the "secret sorrow" of practically every advertiser—that of wasting advertising dollars and not knowing what to do about it. More

emotions are aroused later in the copy when it is
established that there is nothing safe about casting a wide
net when it comes to advertising. This employs the
resonance trigger, because the readers know that problem
only too well—and identify with it.

To convince readers of the applicability of the 80/20 principle when it comes to advertising expenditures, an ordered list of ten advertising media employed by Silhouette Cosmetic Surgery Centers is presented in Figure 6.5, followed by a description of the principle in words, and, finally, a bar graph. Presenting multiple versions of the same concept is an extremely powerful way of turning something abstract and elusive (such as the 80/20 principle) into something familiar and accepted. That's because it's expressed in various depictions (numerical, linguistic, and graphic)—and it is likely that one, two, or all three of them will resonate with readers (see Figure 6.6). Additionally, the simple act of repeating a concept three times in different contexts is often sufficient in installing and ingraining a concept into someone's belief system. This then employs the redefinition trigger because it paints a picture of the principle in a compelling way that the reader hasn't encountered before.

Finally, the objections that the reader probably has would run along the lines of "I've seldom been able to pinpoint exactly which of my advertising works, and which doesn't. What would I learn from the book that I don't already know?" That unspoken objection is countered by the statements that convey that there is now "a wide array of mechanisms at our disposal" and that the book reveals "little-known tools and resources" that enable one to identify advertising that makes the company money or causes it to lose money. This then employs the resistance trigger.

As was shown in the previous example, the copy in Figure 6.5 doesn't contain much of a sales pitch. There are no psychological

"I know that half of the money I spend on advertising is wasted, but I can never find out which half."
-- John Wanamaker, the *Father of Modern Advertising*

Most advertisers operate under the unconscious "50/50 principle" of spreading advertising dollars equally across various media. In 1897, Italian economist and sociologist Vilifredo Pareto discovered what has since been called the "80/20 principle," which states that in most situations, 80% of the output will be generated by 20% of the input. Translated in advertising terms, **80% of the desired revenues an advertiser earns as a result of advertising will be generated by 20% of the advertising budget**.

That means John Wanamaker's assertion that half of the money spent on advertising is wasted is actually conservative. It's actually <u>more than half</u>.

Consider the case of the Silhouette Cosmetic Surgery Centers in the following illustration:

The 80/20 Principle - Revenues Generated by Advertising
Silhouette Cosmetic Surgery Centers

Type of Advertising	Percentage of Total Revenues Generated	Percentage of Advertising Dollars Spent
Direct mail – Postcards	31%	6%
Co-op Advertising - Val-Pak Coupons	27%	6%
Direct mail – Salesletters	23%	7%
TV – Cable Stations	5%	16%
Radio	3%	9%
Internet Advertising	3%	10%
Outdoor Advertising - Billboards	3%	8%
Outdoor Advertising - Bus Stop Benches	2%	9%
Print Ads - Magazines	2%	11%
Print Ads - Newspapers	1%	18%
TOTAL	100%	100%

It's apparent from the above list that **81% of the company's revenues** were generated by only the 3 of the advertising media (postcards, co-op advertising and salesletters) which only comprised **19% of the advertising spending**. It's also interesting to see that newspaper advertising, which represents 18% of all advertising spending contributes the least (1%) to the company's revenues. The company is therefore losing a significant amount of money in not just one, but <u>two</u> ways: 81% of their spending is wasted on ads that don't yield maximum revenues, and **they're also losing 400% additional revenues they could be generating** if they allocated all their advertising budget on direct mail and co-op advertising!

The sobering truth is that most advertisers don't have a clue as to whether their advertising is cost-effective or not. They often *play it safe* by "casting a wide net" hoping they'll have a big catch. What they don't realize is that there is nothing safe about casting a big net!

As illustrated above, chances are, only 20% of your advertising buys are adding significantly to your bottom line – and the rest are <u>not only</u> a poor investment of money, but they also prevent you from re-allocating those precious advertising dollars towards the revenue-generating 20% of your advertising campaigns.

Thankfully, in this age of technology, we're no longer as helpless as John Wanamaker was a century ago. Today, we have a wide array of mechanisms at our disposal that allow us to **measure people's responsiveness to our advertising messages** – both on and off the Web -- and enable us to track and test the effectiveness of our advertising.

Wouldn't you want to find out which 20% of <u>your</u> advertising buys are working, and the 80% which aren't? How would your company's profitability change when you do more of what's working and eliminate all the wasted advertising – and consequently get a substantially greater return on your advertising dollar?

The Pareto Advertising Model is the only book that shows you how to use the 80/20 Principle to maximize the return on your advertising dollar -- whether you want to **spend less** on your advertising while **earning more revenues** for your business – OR spending the same amount on your advertising and **generating up to 400% more revenues**. No matter how you look at it, it's a *win-win situation*. *The Pareto Advertising Model* reveals little-known tools and resources that enable you to identify your company's advertising campaigns that make you money and cause you to lose money, so that you can **spend less and earn more**. Any one of the tools or resources you learn from this book could pay for its price thousands of times over. When would you like to maximize the sales results you get from your advertising dollars?

Figure 6.5 80/20 copy.

3 Triggers of the Trifecta Neuro-Affective Principle™

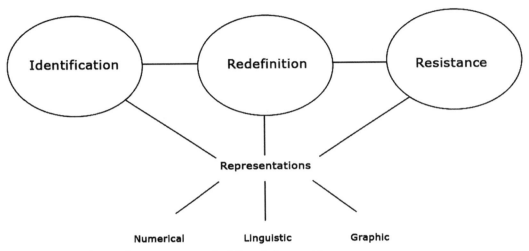

Figure 6.6 Trifecta schematic: numerical-linguistic-graphic.

devices, involvement devices, or other essential copywriting elements employed. That's because when you complete the trifecta, prospects arrive at a point where they realize that further explorations are not necessary—you've told them enough. Then a peculiar thing happens: Prospects actually sell themselves on your product or service. That's the power of the Trifecta Neuro-Affective Principle in action.

I was recently interviewed by a top public relations professional, whose company is the leading provider of experts and authors to the media. During the interview, she voiced her dislike for overly long sales letter types of copy that she considers overkill. "I don't need to read multiple pages of web copy for me to make a buying decision," she said. "I want to be given just the facts, then I'll decide whether I'll buy or not. Some marketers just write pages and pages of words when they already had me at hello."

There are many reasons why a copywriter would find it necessary to write long copy as opposed to short copy (see Chapter 3). It usually has less to do with the copywriter's preference and more to do with the nature of the product or service, the target audience, the price point, the competition, and many other considerations. However, when short copy is identified as the best route to take, the Trifecta Neuro-Affective Principle can be used to deliver just the facts to your prospects in the most compelling method and sequence. Yes, you can have them at hello. Everything else after that is just details.

THE TRIFECTA NEURO-AFFECTIVE PRINCIPLE IN SHORT COPY

Blaise Pascal, the seventeenth-century French mathematician, physicist, and religious philosopher, once wrote: "I have written you a long letter because I did not have time to write a short one." This goes along the same lines as something Mark Twain once said: "It usually takes me more than three weeks to prepare a good impromptu speech." Most outstanding and impactful presentations—especially sales presentations—require much time and preparation, no matter how easy or spontaneous they might look. Anyone with the gift of gab can fill an hour's worth of speaking time at a moment's notice, but only someone who's well prepared and who knows the key principles of communicating succinctly, clearly, and memorably can give a three-minute presentation that has maximum impact. That's why when individuals are about to be interviewed on a national TV program they often need a media trainer to teach them how to speak in sound bites.

On the Internet, there is also a need for this kind of brevity in a number of copywriting applications, such as product descriptions on catalog-style websites, banner ads, pay-per-click ads, blog posts, and other marketing messages where there are space restrictions and a limited amount of text allowed. How can you make an impact with words in such marketing environments? By presenting information in *cyber bites*. I've coined this term to mean web copy in bite-size pieces that pack a powerful selling punch.

Just like sound bites, cyber bites must make the maximum impact in the minimum number of words or characters—but they also need to accomplish one more thing that sound bites are not necessarily required to do. They have to *sell*.

So how do you go about writing cyber bites that sell? If you were put to the task of writing product descriptions for a catalog-style website, for instance, how would you choose, from a long list of specifications and benefits, which highlights to include in the catalog entry? If you were asked to write an advertisement of 50 words or less, how would you whittle a voluminous amount of information down to the essential information that would cause your prospect to want to buy your product or service, or at least take a closer look for the purpose of making a buying decision? If you were allowed to include only three benefit bullets among the dozens that your product or service offers, which three would you choose?

The answer most copywriters would give is invariably one that involves your personal judgment or opinion. No matter how experienced you are in marketing or copywriting, or how well you know your product or service, using your own judgment seldom hits the mark. The way to increase the likelihood of hitting the bull's-eye is by applying the Trifecta Neuro-Affective Principle.

Before you attempt to apply the Trifecta Neuro-Affective Principle in writing a cyber bite, however, you must first put on your customers' hat so that you can gain consumer insight—what your target consumers are saying and thinking and what truly matters to them. As Robert Collier once wrote, "You must *enter* the *conversation* that's *already* happening in your *prospect's mind*." Only when you have this consumer insight can you develop a unique selling proposition (USP) that highlights the benefit sought by your target customers, and one that speaks to their needs. (See Chapter 3 for a complete discussion on USPs.) This USP then becomes the central concept that you need to present compellingly via the three principal triggers of the Trifecta Neuro-Affective Principle.

Following is an example of an effective cyber bite:

Permanent Hair Removal <u>Without</u> the Pain of Electrolysis
—and at a Fraction of the Cost of Laser Hair Removal

▶ Patented handheld hair removal appliance sends a painless radio frequency to the hair shaft, deadening the hair at the root—unwanted hair is gone forever and won't grow back!

▶ Approved by the FDA as Medically Safe Technology

▶ 5,000 of these appliances sold out on QVC in less than 5 minutes!

It's easy to see why this advertisement is irresistible. It not only articulates its unique selling proposition in the headline but also employs the resonance, redefinition, and resistance triggers in its three benefit bullets.

The ad redefines the technology of permanent hair removal (a radiofrequency that deadens the root), causes readers to identify with the 5,000 people who bought the appliance on QVC, creates excitement and a sense of urgency through the mention of how fast the appliance sold, and addresses the common objections to permanent hair removal, that is, pain, cost, and safety.

Following is another example of a cyber bite for a software program presented in two lengths: a bulleted product description and a 50-word advertisement.

Here's how a cyber bite would look in a bulleted product description:

WebGenius is the only website development software that lets you build a high-performing website that is equipped with powerful Internet marketing functionality—in as little as 15 minutes. Your website will practically market itself!

▶ Users call this "the most intelligent website creation software ever designed for Internet marketers."

▶ 83% of users switched from using Dreamweaver or
FrontPage because of WebGenius's powerful and easy-
to-use suite of applications no online entrepreneur can
do business without.

▶ Combines the functionality of the best html editors on
the market and 12 Internet marketing programs and
applications—you'll never need to hire costly
programmers or web designers again!

This copy presents its unique selling proposition in the first two sentences and then employs the three triggers in the benefit bullets. The
reader identifies with the users who called WebGenius "the most
intelligent website creation software ever designed for Internet marketers" because the prospect is an Internet marketer himself. Further
resonance is established with the mention of the 83 percent of users
who switched from using Dreamweaver or FrontPage, since there's a
very high likelihood that the target audience is using one of those
programs and is wondering why someone would want to switch to
another website creation software program. The ad redefines website
creation by mentioning that the software combines the functionality
of the best html editors on the market and 12 Internet marketing programs and applications. The prospect's resistance is countered by the
presentation of the "easy-to-use" technology and the possibility of
creating a high-performing website "in as little as 15 minutes." The
final bullet addresses another unspoken concern of the Internet marketer: the cost and hassle of hiring a website designer and programmer to get his website to look and function the way he wants it to.

Here's how this cyber bite can be abbreviated into a 50-word
advertisement that still employs the three triggers:

"The most intelligent website creation software ever designed
for Internet marketers." 83% of users switched from using
Dreamweaver or FrontPage. WebGenius combines the function-

ality of the best html editors and 12 Internet marketing applications. Easy-to-use, intuitive—lets you create a website in 15 minutes. You'll never hire web designers/programmers again.

It bears repeating that whenever possible, you must present a concept in three ways—not just *any* three ways but *the* three ways in the right sequence that give people a sense of completion. Together, they must hit the main cornerstones that constitute a satisfying purchase decision. And those cornerstones are the three principal triggers of the Trifecta Neuro-Affective Principle.

Take a look at the following three bullets that a copywriter might consider using to convey the benefits of owning the WebGenius website creation software:

▶ Create a high-performing website in a small fraction of the time it currently takes you. What would normally take *10 hours* per website in *Dreamweaver, FrontPage,* or another web design package will take 1/10th of the time with *WebGenius.*

▶ Optimize your new websites to rank well with the search engines, increase your websites' "findability" on the Web—and drive a consistent flow of traffic to your website.

▶ Make changes to your website with the greatest of ease. With the Page Layout section of WebGenius, make all the changes you wish to make—and all the changes will be instantly reflected in all your existing pages and any new pages you create.

While these bullet points convey benefits that the prospect might find desirable, they're all leaning toward employing only the redefinition trigger (i.e., they redefine what website creation would be like with the use of WebGenius). Since the bullets don't attempt to cause the prospects to *identify* with the product or its users, nor do they overcome the objections that might be lurking in prospects' minds, they will get a sense that something's missing. They may not be able to put it into words, but it's the vague feeling that you haven't told them enough for them to take the next step toward buying. It is that incompletion that renders your sales arguments powerless. If, on the other hand, you convey your benefits in a way that employs the three triggers (such as in the cyber bite examples given in the previous pages), you cause a subtle but powerful mind shift that prompts your prospects to change their minds in favor of your product or service. And when that happens, they are more likely to act on the basis of that mind change.

In many ways, the Trifecta Neuro-Affective Principle is similar to debate procedure in that it encompasses more than just logical argument and the presentation of research findings; it also includes persuasion that appeals to the emotional responses of the audience. In a debate, the central topic that the opposing sides seek to resolve is called the *proposition* or *resolution*. In selling situations, its counterpart is the unique selling proposition of a product or service. The arguments of those in favor—the affirmative side—in a debate are very much like sales arguments that utilize the Trifecta Neuro-Affective Principle. The principal objectives of both the debater on the affirmative side and the salesperson/marketer/copywriter are

- ▶ To support, prove, and defend their respective propositions through reason buttressed with research (redefinition)
- ▶ To destroy the opponent's arguments (resistance)
- ▶ To appeal to the audience's emotions (resonance)

Successful completion of the three objectives constitutes the critical mass that wins the debate or closes the sale.

7

Increasing Sales Through the Use of Involvement Devices

The real voyage of discovery consists not in seeking new landscapes but in having new eyes.
—Marcel Proust

Involvement devices are devices that get people involved with your copy. They move people to read every word of your copy. Getting your website visitors to read your copy is job number one if your objective is to sell them something. When you use involvement devices, you effectively own your audience; that is, you hold your audience captive.

In the first edition of this book, involvement devices were featured in the same chapter as psychological devices. However, due to the escalating challenge of getting people's attention in the over-crowded streets of cyberspace, involvement devices have become more important than ever before and warrant a chapter all their own.

If the struggle to gain attention on the information superhighway was fierce back in 2004, it has only become even more so now that the number of indexed websites has multiplied five times! You need to know about every involvement device that will cause your website visitors to stay longer than the eight seconds a website is usually accorded. Nowadays, I rarely write copy that doesn't include the use of one or more of the involvement devices discussed in this chapter.

I tested an involvement device on the website of a client who sells affirmation software. This client's web copy had a decent conversion rate, so I rewrote his copy and added the involvement device shown in Figure 7.1. I installed this involvement device in the first screen of my client's website, and his sales tripled the next day. During subsequent weeks, he maintained sales that were 200 to 300 percent more than the previous daily sales—including days when he sold six times as much product as he had previously.

The original headline, "Learn how to be prosperous, successful and happy in just 10 minutes a day," was an attempt to get at what he thought were the hot buttons of his target audience, but,

But first, I want you to name the **top 3 things** you desire to have, or wish to improve, in your life right now -- examples: money (name the *specific* amount you want), a loving relationship, an ideal job, perfect health, your dream house, a brand new car, etc.

(Type the 3 things you desire in the box below.)

Okay, are you done typing the 3 things you want?

What if I told you that there's a way that you can achieve those 3 things -- *and anything else you desire* -- by using the power of your computer for just **10 minutes** a day.

In the next few minutes, I will show you an **advanced technology** that enables you to manifest everything you want through the results-amplifying use of *computerization*. This information is not available anywhere else on the Web -- or the world, for that matter. So I urge you to **read every word** of this article because the secret that can single-handedly turn your desires into reality is **hidden** in this web page -- and I don't want you to miss it.

Figure 7.1 Example of an involvement device.

although reasonably successful, the headline sounded vague, and it definitely was not riveting. It didn't call out to the real desires of his target audience.

The involvement device asked readers to identify their wants, needs, and dreams. What could be more riveting to your target audience than their specific dreams, the dreams they might not dare tell another living soul? The involvement device asked them to name their dreams, and it gave them a safe place to do it because they knew that no one would ever see their responses. Bringing the readers' desires into focus allowed us to present the product (affirmation software) as the means of achieving those desires.

Do you see how powerful that is? Involvement devices break people's preoccupation with other things. At any given moment, a person's attention is occupied with dozens of things—everything from how they're going to pay for their children's college education to what they're going to have for dinner that night. Think of your prospect's mind as an antenna that receives signals from everywhere. Like a radio tuner, an involvement device gets people tuned in to only one signal, one station, or one channel—in this case, your sales message or your web copy. Getting someone's attention on the Internet is probably the biggest challenge you face, because attention is in short supply—with over 175.4 million webpages clamoring for it.

In an effort to capture attention in the overwhelming marketplace of the Internet, an increasing number of websites in various industries have begun to employ involvement devices. For instance, I've seen a retailer of loudspeakers feature a Home Theater Wizard on its website. The Home Theater Wizard asks a few simple questions of the web visitor, about budget, room characteristics, listening preferences, and equipment setup. The web visitor clicks on check boxes to answer the brief questionnaire, thereby becoming effectively involved. Based on the answers given, the Home Theater Wizard recommends one of the company's preconfigured home theater systems customized to the customer's wants and needs. Since there's no way the company could know what web visitors are looking for in a home theater system, and it offers more than 350 different combinations of speakers from which to choose, the involvement device gets visitors to participate in customizing a system for their needs. In the process, the device causes casual web visitors to stay on the website (instead of clicking away) and take a close look at its product offerings.

The Jewelry & Watches division at Amazon.com employs a similar involvement device. Its website uses a wizard that enables visitors to create a diamond ring to their specifications by answering four questions (visitors click on radio buttons to select their preferred shape, number of carats, type of metal for the setting, and the setting style). When a web visitor answers all four questions, he or she can preview the ring, then select the diamond quality and ring size. The wizard recommends a ring from the jewelry inventory and gives the price of the ring and ordering instructions. This is a more effective approach to choosing a diamond ring than viewing hundreds or thousands that are available. Figure 7.2 shows an example of an involvement device used on a website that sells a real estate

What's your Real Estate IQ? Take this **simple eye-opening quiz** -- then learn **specific, cutting-edge** secrets for making **instant cash in real estate**. Answer True or False:

1. In order for you to accumulate a fortune in real estate, you need excellent credit or a lot of money.   TRUE ☐   FALSE ☐

Click here for the correct answer.

2. **Clearly,** real estate investing has created more millionaires than any other industry known to man, but it's a slow process - taking years to acquire massive wealth.   TRUE ☐   FALSE ☐

Click here for the correct answer.

3. 99.32% of today's **elite real estate millionaires** made their fortunes by buying/renting single-family homes.   TRUE ☐   FALSE ☐

Click here for the correct answer.

Figure 7.2 A questionnaire-type involvement device.

investment course. The quiz does two things: It gets prospects involved and makes them curious enough to click on a text link ("Click here for correct answer") to learn something they don't know—something that whets their appetite for the product being sold. When respondents click on the text link, a small pop-up box reveals the answer. They are not taken to another webpage, which potentially could take them away from the intended sales path. This is essential when designing a device like this one. You won't need to know anything about programming in order to create involvement devices. Your web designer can usually help you install simple devices, or you can post the job you want done on freelance websites like Elance.com or Guru.com. In the Project Description, you can specify whatever kind of interactivity you want in plain English, and you will receive bids from programmers all over the world, who'll do the work for you inexpensively and even install the device on your website, if you wish.

The website *www.OneMinuteCureForAllDiseases.com* utilizes an involvement device (Figure 7.3) in which website visitors are asked to check the boxes next to the diseases that they or the people they know are suffering from. This device effectively compels website visitors to raise their hands and identify themselves as being the prospects for the e-book the website is selling. This is a superior way to grab visitors' attention rather than simply making a catch-all claim that the information in the e-book could potentially cure the whole gamut of diseases. When you narrow their focus on their specific problem you make them believe you're speaking to their particular needs, and they're more likely to pay attention to your sales message. This type of involvement device does not entail programming at all, since the check boxes are simply graphical and do not cause anything to happen other than the placement of a checkmark in the check box selected. The only purpose of the check boxes is to involve the website visitors with your copy and compel them to pay attention to your message.

The same website employs a second involvement device in the part of the web copy where an attempt is made to close the sale.

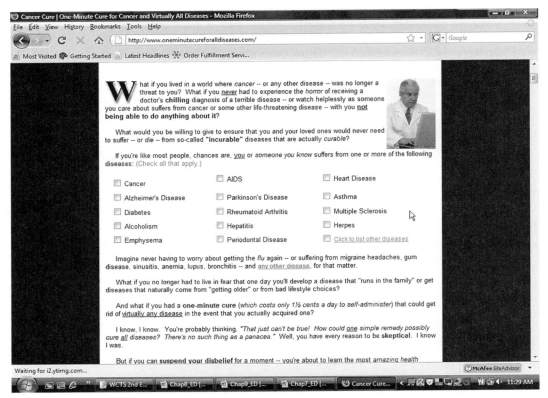

Figure 7.3 An involvement device using check boxes.

Now, the only decision you need to make is *this*: Which of the following would you rather entrust your healing (and the healing of your loved ones) to? Check *one*.

❏ Pharmaceutical drugs that alleviate only the **symptoms** and the **pain** of diseases, but *don't* cure (and often *harm*)

❏ Elaborate, *expensive* and often *invasive* treatments and procedures offered by organized medicine

❏ A simple, **low-cost** therapy based on a *natural* oxygenating substance that is *easy* and **painless** to use at home—and which is **scientifically proven** to prevent and cure virtually all diseases *without* adverse effects

For your sake, I hope you'll make the right decision in partner-ship with your doctor or a qualified health care professional.

In the preceding example, when website visitors click on the third check box signifying that they've made their decision in favor of buying the e-book, they are taken directly to the order page. This type of simple interactivity can be accomplished by installing one line of the html code of your website, which any website designer or anyone with a working knowledge of html can do for you if you're unfamiliar with html.

Interactive software programs are now available through which you can have a multiple-choice involvement device, such as the pre-ceding one, on your website. When your website visitor checks one of the options, the ensuing copy on the webpage *dynamically changes* and is personalized with appropriate benefits and an offer suitable for that specific target audience. One example of such software is called *Interactive Sales Letter,* developed by interactive software developer Scott Stevenson. Using my Web Copywriting Mastery Course as an example, I could conceivably use the following involve-ment device on my website:

Countless people from all walks of life wish to learn the skill of writing killer web copy for a variety of reasons. What is your reason? Select one below . . .

☐ I am an Internet marketer, entrepreneur, or website owner who sells (or plans to sell) a product or service online.

☐ I am a writer (or copywriter) who wants to transition to the lucrative specialty of web copywriting.

☐ I am a marketing professional who's in charge of my company's online sales operations.

Go ahead—click on one of the radio buttons . . .

With the interactive software installed, when a website visitor clicks on one of the radio buttons, the software loads a prewritten copy piece designed to speak to the specific needs of that website visitor, depending on which radio button he or she clicked on. This is far more powerful than trying to create one web copy piece for a diverse array of target audiences.

The sky's the limit when it comes to involvement devices. You're limited only by your own creativity. The Earnings Calculator featured as an emotional mechanism in Chapter 5 (see "The Cyrano Effect" section, page 161) is yet another example of a device that effectively involves people with your copy, giving them another reason to stay at your website and find out what you have to offer.

Figure 7.4 shows an involvement device that uses the power of commitment. Why is this powerful? According to Robert Cialdini, "Writing is believing." When you ask your readers to write down (or, in this case, to type out) the things they desire, they admit the need for your product or service. In addition, a written commitment is more lasting than a mental commitment. When you write out a commitment, you have a greater likelihood of following through than if you don't write it. Notice that I also make readers close the sale themselves by making Megabolic Weight Loss part of their commitment statement.

Now that you know that Megabolic Weight Loss is the surefire way of losing all your unwanted weight, now all that's left is for you to do what it takes to succeed. In order to do that, you need to **get leverage on yourself**.

Quite frankly, *Megabolic Weight Loss* simply cannot fail when it is implemented <u>exactly as prescribed</u>. But no weight loss program, no matter how powerful, will work if there isn't the **power of commitment** behind it.

So **type your name, the number of pounds you want to lose, and the reason/s you want to lose the weight** in the blanks below, and read the completed statement out loud to reinforce the commitment that will lead to your ultimate success:

I, _____ , have decided I want to lose ____ pounds, because _____ " and I'm committed to following the *Megabolic Weight Loss Program* until I reach my desired weight.

Figure 7.4 An involvement device that uses the power of commitment.

INVOLVEMENT DEVICES AND
THE RECOVERY PRINCIPLE
▼

An involvement device I invented several years ago makes use of the recovery principle of marketing. It not only gets people involved in the sales copy and makes them raise their hands and prequalify themselves as your target audience, but also captures their contact information. The recovery principle is not new. It's something used often in direct-response marketing.

Here's how it works: If you fail to sell your web visitors on your primary product at the full price but succeed in selling them the same product (or perhaps a different product) at a lower unit of sale, you recover the effort and cost of getting viewers to your website and plug them into your income stream. Even if you don't make as much profit on each of these sales, you recover costs, which adds to your overall profitability. More important, you turn someone who might otherwise never have done business with you into a customer, and, of course, those customers have a lifetime value since they will be buying future products from you. (See Figure 7.5.)

The recovery involvement device that I used on a website that sells a $2,650 water ionizer accounted for over 115 additional sales to customers who were given a 25 percent discount. That amounted to $228,562 in sales they would never have made if the recovery involvement device had not been installed. Once you understand that you don't have to offer your product at only one price but you can adjust your offer on the fly, you can make far greater profits than if you had not employed a recovery device, which can dramatically improve your website's profitability.

Another example of a recovery involvement device is one that I saw on a website that was selling an online video submission service package for $97 a month. If the visitor attempts to leave the website without signing up for the service, the window shown in Figure 7.6 pops up.

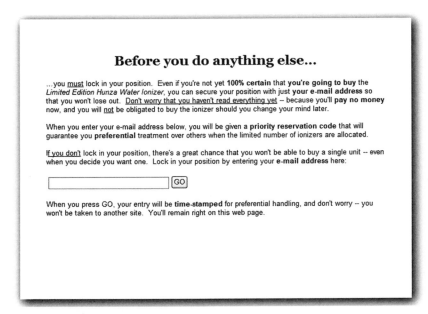

Figure 7.5 A recovery involvement device.

A prospect who clicks on the OK button is given a 14-day trial of the $97-per-month service for just $1. The company is willing to forgo half a month's revenues (approximately $48.50) in the hope that once prospects try their video submission service, they will become subscribers paying $97 per month.

A software developer named Dave Guindon took the recovery involvement device to a whole new level by creating an automated chat solution called Virtual Smart Agent. Once you have the software installed, a virtual agent appears whenever a website visitor attempts

Figure 7.6 Recovery Pop-up.

Figure 7.7 Virtual Smart Agent.

to leave your website without having bought your product or service. The virtual agent offers your departing visitor any discount that you want to extend. (See Figure 7.7.) When this happens, up to 40 percent of your prospects are saved and converted to happy customers. Even if you don't make as much profit on each of those discounted sales as you'd like, you still recover costs and generate revenues, which contribute to your website profits.

According to an *eMarketer* report, acquiring a new customer costs five to ten times more than retaining an existing one. Therefore, every effort must be made to keep customers. Some companies use the recovery approach to increase customer retention and minimize product returns. A software company sends out the following e-mail to those who want to return a product:

> Dear [name of customer],
>
> Thank you for your recent order of [*name of software*]. I'm sorry to hear that you've found it necessary to return the software for a refund.

We've gone to great lengths to make sure that [*name of software*] meets the needs, and exceeds the expectations, of entrepreneurs like you. Therefore, unless you're dissatisfied with the way [*name of software*] performs, we'd like you to continue enjoying the benefits and convenience of owning it. In this regard, we'd like to offer you the rebate of $68.50— that's 50% of the price you originally paid for it. We're offering you this special accommodation because we certainly don't want to lose you as a customer, and look forward to serving you for years to come.

Simply reply to this e-mail, and a check in the amount of $68.50 will be mailed to you immediately. Please understand that your acceptance of this rebate signifies your decision not to return [*name of software*] at some future date. Should you not wish to accept this rebate offer, and choose to return [*name of software*], please place it in the original packaging (or another appropriately sized box), send it back to us insured (for your protection), and we will issue a full refund of your purchase price within 4 weeks of receiving the product.

Sincerely,

Name of customer service representative:

Marketing communications such as this one go a long way toward retaining customers, as well as recovering the effort and cost of getting them to buy in the first place. AOL uses a similar recovery approach when its "free trial" members call in to cancel their memberships. Instead of just letting potential customers go without a fight, AOL offers every member wishing to cancel the opportunity to continue enjoying AOL at no charge for another month—sometimes two or more. The company is justified in thinking that if members become accustomed to using AOL, eventually they won't want to cancel.

The key to the recovery principle is that no offer has to be static. Any of its parts—the price, the duration, the warranty, the privileges—should be flexible enough to meet the needs of customers.

Even if the profit margins from the downsell are considerably less than the standard margins, every unit of sale adds to the company's bottom line, helps to recover costs, and keeps customers in the company's income stream. When you consider that repeat customers spend 67 percent more—and after ten purchases, the average customer has referred seven people—every attempt to exercise the recovery principle is well worth the effort.

Online Marketing Communications

It's What You Do After People Visit Your Website That Counts

If you advance confidently in the direction of your dreams and endeavor to live the life which you have imagined, you will meet with a success unexpected in common hours.
—Henry David Thoreau

Online marketing communications play a low-profile but nonetheless pivotal role in the Internet marketing arena. Principal among these communications is the opt-in offer, the crafting of which is often more important than website copy for reasons that will become clear as you progress through this chapter. Irresistible autoresponder e-mails are yet another essential aspect of online marketing communications, because effective follow-up frequently spells the difference between mediocre and outstanding sales. Finally, learning how to write free reports, promotional articles, newsletters, e-zines, online ads, signature files, and banner copy enables you to complete the basic components that constitute the web marketing mix. This chapter looks at each of these marketing communications and how to create killer copy for each.

THE OPT-IN OFFER: YOUR MOST IMPORTANT ASSET

▼

Converting web visitors into customers is rarely completed during the website visit, but by crafting an irresistible opt-in offer and following up with e-mail messages designed to build rapport and a relationship with the prospects conversion rates of 15 to 25 percent (and sometimes greater) can be achieved.

My friend and fellow copywriter Alex Mandossian created a website (www.marketingwithpostcards.com) that attracts only about 100 unique visitors per day, but as many as 23 percent of his web visitors take him up on his opt-in offer to download three free chapters of his course. Because he has constructed his follow-up autoresponder e-mails effectively, he averages about $27,298 per month in revenue from his website. That results from just 100 unique visitors per day.

Capturing contact information is fundamental to the success of any business enterprise. As web marketer, entrepreneur, or copywriter, your primary goal, at the very least, should be capturing your web visitors' e-mail addresses. Without this information, you have, in effect, wasted all the time, money, and effort it took to get them to your website. For this reason, I can't overemphasize that constructing your opt-in offer is infinitely more important than crafting the offer for your primary product.

It's apparent, therefore, that you need to make your opt-in-offer copy as compelling as possible in order to convince visitors to give you this personal information. A good way to do this is by providing a benefit that gives visitors an incentive to give you their e-mail address. One method is to ask them to sign up for a free report (with an irresistible title), a free newsletter, a free course, free product, free chapters of your book—in other words, something that requires no financial commitment.

The following opt-in offer was designed as an exit pop-up (a window that pops up when the visitor leaves the site). The objective of this opt-in offer is to capture the contact information of as many web visitors as possible so that, through a series of follow-up autoresponder e-mails, prospects can be encouraged to sign up for a DHS Club discount buying membership. (See Figure 8.1.)

"How to Pay Less for Almost Everything" is a title that appeals to the target audience of the DHS Club website, which consists of people who like to save money on everything they purchase. The opt-in offer is designed to prequalify prospects. In this case, it means that

Figure 8.1 Opt-in offer.

anyone who signs up to receive this free report is interested in getting discounts and saving money on purchases and therefore is someone who might also be interested in signing up for a paid membership to the discount buying club to get even more discounts on a wider variety of products and services.

Five Keys to an Opt-In Offer That's Impossible to Refuse

In addition to creating an offer that prequalifies prospects, there are five elements that winning opt-in offers contain:

1. Compelling title that speaks to the needs of your target audience
2. Appealing benefits
3. Instant gratification
4. Assurance of privacy
5. Form for obtaining an e-mail address and, at least, a first name

Notice that the opt-in offer for the DHS Club satisfies all of these:

1. It has a compelling title ("How to Pay Less for Almost Everything") that speaks to the needs of the target audience (people who like saving money on all their purchases).
2. It offers appealing benefits the recipients will receive (secrets for easily finding the lowest prices on things they buy every day).
3. It offers instant gratification. (The valuable report will be sent to their e-mail in-boxes automatically within minutes.)
4. It offers an assurance of privacy. (Their contact information will be handled with the strictest confidence and will never be sold or shared with third parties.)

5. It includes a form that captures the e-mail address and the first name.

A free subscription to a newsletter or e-zine is the most common item featured in online opt-in offers. There was a time when free subscriptions were desirable, but because practically everyone is offering a free newsletter or e-zine nowadays, people are not as eager as they once were to sign up for them. A growing number of people regard free newsletters and e-zines as contributors to their already cluttered e-mail in-boxes, particularly since the content of most leaves a lot to be desired.

Since the objective of an opt-in offer is to get as many web visitors as possible to sign up, you must offer something irresistible that people can't wait to get their hands on right away, something that offers instant gratification instead of a promise of monthly (or weekly) issues of publications of dubious value. Examples of these are a must-have free report, a free software download, or a free e-book. Here are examples of Mark Joyner's most successful opt-in offers:

Free report: "How I Made $4 Million on a $0 Ad Budget" (a four-page 1,267-word article)

Free software download: EzineAssistant—software that formats outgoing e-mail copy to ensure that it looks professional (i.e., without line breaks in all the wrong places) for every type of e-mail program

Free e-book: Search Engine Tactics (this was downloaded more than a million times and captured as many e-mail addresses)

You conceivably could offer a free newsletter that presents irresistible content, but I don't recommend it as the primary opt-in offer. I don't mean to imply that newsletters and e-zines are no longer viable marketing vehicles. On the contrary, when written effectively, they're still a major marketing communication by which companies stay connected to their prospects and customers. However, for the purpose of capturing the contact information of as many web visitors as possible, they should be regarded as secondary opt-in vehicles.

Presenting the Offer

An opt-in offer doesn't have to be in the form of a pop-up window. It can appear as part of a webpage. An abbreviated form of it can even be featured in an online ad, embedded in an e-mail signature file, or announced in discussion boards and forums. Here is an example of an online ad designed for tax preparers that incorporates an opt-in offer:

> Discover *The Best Tax Break* that can give your small business and Schedule C clients a net tax savings of $1,800 to $2,125 every year. Send for the Free Report that reveals this secret by sending a blank e-mail to report@domain.com.

HOW TO WRITE IRRESISTIBLE AUTORESPONDER E-MAILS

Once you have captured the names of those people you enticed with the free report and confirmed their desire to subscribe to your list via a double opt-in procedure (see Chapter 4), if possible, what do you send them via e-mail? Send a series of follow-up e-mails using the autoresponder mechanism.

Quick Primer on Autoresponders

Most web hosts allow you to use e-mail addresses that automatically call up a prewritten e-mail that you upload to their server. When someone sends an e-mail to that address, your web host's server automatically sends out the prewritten e-mail that you uploaded. For example, if you send a blank e-mail to freelance@webcopywriting university.com, you will automatically receive my report entitled The Internet's Richest Source of Freelance Writing Opportunities. That, in a nutshell, is the concept of an autoresponder.

Taking this a step further, there are web hosts, e-mail programs, shopping cart programs, and services that allow you to send a series of prewritten e-mails to your opt-in list at predetermined intervals, say, every three days. This automates the follow-up system for you.

Marketers often use the rule of seven, which has its roots in radio and television advertising. The rule states that prospects must see or hear your message seven times before they consider buying. It's not a hard-and-fast rule, just a rule of thumb. It applies not only to radio and television advertising, but to online advertising as well. When you use autoresponders to send out seven or more marketing e-mails at predetermined intervals, you increase the chances of the prospect buying from you.

Crafting Autoresponder E-Mails to Your Opt-In Prospects

Step 1: Get recipients to consume what you just gave them for free. What's the use of getting them to download three free chapters, receive a free report, or download free software if you don't get them to read or use it? Most people don't read or use what they send for. If you don't get them to read the free chapters, they'll never buy the entire course. If you don't get them to read the free report that shows them how to save money, you'll never get them to sign up to join the discount buying club.

In the first autoresponse I developed to send to those who signed up to receive "How to Pay Less for Almost Everything," I wrote:

> Somewhere in the free report you received is the "best-kept secret" for amazing savings that is truly simple and effortless.
>
> Most people miss it altogether because they skim through the report too fast—and yet it's probably the most important

> thing you can do in *1 minute flat* that can give you cash
> back on all your purchases at hundreds of major stores. Well,
> I won't keep you in suspense any longer. I'll point out exactly
> where that best-kept secret is hidden. It's in the 11th para-
> graph of the report.

Later in the e-mail, I wrote:

> To save you the trouble of having to find your free report, I've
> made it easy for you and given you the link below. Click on
> the link and check it out to see how simple it is for you to get
> similar savings on your purchases.
> http://www.domain.com

Step 2: With every subsequent e-mail, highlight a different benefit of
your product(s) or service(s) and explore a different angle that slides
smoothly into a compelling reason why the recipient needs to buy
what you're selling.

The succeeding autoresponses in the "How to Pay Less for Almost
Everything" series extolled different virtues of the shopper's club.
Autoresponse number two reminded prospects that they could receive
30 to 70 percent discounts on the things they bought that week or
month and, in addition, they would receive free shipping. The third
reminded them that they would receive rebates on all the purchases
made by friends and family whom they bring into the club. The fourth
stressed that they were losing money each day they were not a member. Autoresponse number five told the engaging story of how the
shopper's club started out in a small apartment above a garage, how its
membership grew to more than 3 million, and how the combined buying power of its members means more savings to the prospect.

Crafting Autoresponder E-Mails to Customers

Autoresponder e-mails are not only for prospects. You can create a
series specifically for purchasers of your product or service to help

multiply one sale into a stream of ongoing back-end sales at the same time it reinforces the sale and minimizes buyer's remorse (and returns).

The autoresponse series that I wrote to purchasers of a $995 program for starting a promotional products distributorship consisted of seven e-mails. The first reinforces the sale by featuring the success story of the owner of a printing business who bought the program, relating how he used what he learned in the program to earn a six-figure income after only seven months and how he eventually closed down his printing business to concentrate on promotional products full-time. The e-mail also suggests a quick, three-step action plan for the customer to follow to get his or her promotional business or profit center up and running quickly.

The second e-mail starts with yet another success story—this time, the story of a woman who used the program to obtain her first order, amounting to $13,000. To learn her strategy, the reader is told to listen to the first tape of the two-tape course that came with the program. The remaining three autoresponse e-mails continue in a similar vein, each offering another success strategy and reinforcing the advantages of the program.

How to Format Your E-Mails for Optimum Readability

The readability of your e-mails is of utmost importance if your e-mails are to achieve their purpose of leading prospects down the intended sales path. There's nothing worse than sending an e-mail with jagged, uneven lines (a long line, followed by a short line, then another long line followed by another short line, and so on). This occurs when your e-mail is in one format and your recipient's is in another.

To avoid this, you should format your outgoing e-mail so that it is readable by all e-mail programs. Set your line lengths to 60 characters (including spaces) per line so that the lines don't automatically wrap. Don't panic. You don't have to waste time counting characters and manually adding hard returns when a line reaches 60 characters. Instead, you can use a free utility I've made available at the Web Copywriting University website. Go to http://www.webcopywritinguniversity.com/formatter/index.php, type into the Length box the number of characters per line that you want your e-mail to have, paste the text of your e-mail in the text box, and click on the Format Text button. Your e-mail will be automatically formatted for you with your desired line length.

HOW TO WRITE FREE REPORTS AND PROMOTIONAL ARTICLES

Writing free reports or promotional articles can be one of the most profitable things you do to promote the product or service you're selling on your website. When you write a free report or promotional article, not only can you use it as your opt-in offer, but you can also offer its content to websites, newsletters, and e-zines. The more it is picked up, the more traffic it will pump to your website.

Information is the Internet's main commodity, so when you have good content to offer, you'll find many takers. A promotional article entitled "Warning: Do Not Buy a Computer Until You Read This— Or You Might Get Ripped Off" offered compelling reasons for consumers to be wary when buying a computer. It listed six of the sneakiest—and even illegal—schemes employed by unscrupulous computer vendors to take advantage of unsuspecting buyers. Nowhere in the article was there a commercial slant; it consisted of only solid, informative content. The author's byline, however, provided the opportunity to plug her book about how to save $500 or more on a computer purchase.

To achieve its goals, a free report or promotional article must:

▶ Provide useful, bona fide content related to the product or service you're offering

▶ Be written in a way that positions you as an expert in your field

▶ Include a byline or a link that points back to your website

The important thing to remember is that the body of the report or article must contain information of value to your target audience. The sales pitch is introduced only after identifying the author (you) in the byline or resource box. Most e-zine and newsletter publishers are looking for articles of between 500 and 800 words. Some publishers are very strict about your article not being a sales pitch in disguise.

I've seen an article entitled "Nobel Prize Winner Discovers the Cause of Cancer—and How to Cure It" employed as a promotional piece by a website owner who sells a book. It starts by stating that Dr. Otto Warburg won two Nobel Prizes for discovering the cause of cancer and goes on to explain his theory. Only at the end does the vendor conclude that its product (the book) contains the necessary information that enables you to use Dr. Warburg's discoveries in order to not only prevent but also cure cancer and virtually all diseases. The one-page article is an example of a promotional piece that provides information of value to its target audience without appearing commercially slanted. It's the kind of article that would be accepted for publication by e-zine and newsletter publishers looking for content relating to health, antiaging, or longevity.

The key to writing successful free reports or promotional articles is to keep them factual, unbiased, informative, and, most important, engaging. Make them revelatory, if that's possible with your subject matter. Avoid making a sales pitch, no matter how skillfully you think you can disguise it, and, above all, never identify the name of your product or service in the article. That's a telltale sign of self-promotion. Finally, don't use superlative adjectives and phrases (*amazing, incredible, world's best, taking the world by storm, spreading like wildfire, causing quite a stir,* etc.), which will expose your commercial intent.

GUIDELINES FOR WRITING NEWSLETTERS AND E-ZINES

▼

For the following reasons, publishing your own newsletter or e-zine is one of the best and most economical ways to build traffic (and sales):

1. *It's free.* Anyway, it's almost free. It costs little or no money to produce and deliver a newsletter or e-zine no matter how many people you send it to.

2. *It's profitable.* You can easily build rapport and credibility with your subscribers and quickly be acknowledged as an expert in your field through your newsletter or e-zine. In turn, anything you promote or endorse will have a greater impact than any advertisement.

3. *You have a captive audience.* One thing that people consistently do online is check their e-mail. In June 2008, AOL Mail, in partnership with Beta Research, conducted an online E-mail Addiction Survey of 4,000 e-mail users and found that 51 percent check their e-mail four or more times a day and 20 percent check it more than ten times a day. People may not have time to visit the millions of websites that are out there, but most people do check their e-mail regularly and read selected items in their e-mail in-boxes. Your e-zine would therefore be more likely to have the undivided attention of your audience than would your website.

4. *It keeps you in touch.* Your newsletter or e-zine enables you to stay in constant contact with your audience, and it constantly puts your business in front of your prospects. It is a great way to remind people to do business with you or to visit your website, without sounding like an ad. Since newsletters and e-zines are all over the web, make sure you offer one that has

unique content of great interest to your target audience. More important, to attract the most subscribers your offer must have a compelling promise but at the same time be able to deliver on that promise.

The newsletter offer of AffirmWare reads:

Join the millions of people around the world who have discovered the power of affirmations. Send for your FREE SUBSCRIPTION to *"Affirmations of the Mind" Tips and Techniques Self-Help Newsletter,* the premier publication for self-improvement and personal growth. Each issue contains powerful sample affirmations that have been tested and proven to get results.

As with all e-mail writing, don't be tempted to put the whole kitchen sink in your newsletter or e-zine. While providing value is something to strive for, don't be tempted to litter your publication with a multitude of subjects and topics. It may not always be easy to stick to a single message in a multipart publication, so the best thing to do is to have a cohesive theme that enables you to lead your readers down your intended sales path.

Needless to say, the content you offer in your newsletter or e-zine must be related to the products or services that you are selling. Make sure you always provide bona fide content. Give your subscribers something worthy of their devotion, not just some disguised sales pitch, in return for giving you their undivided attention. This could be useful information, something free or discounted, or a special offer.

The trend I've been seeing is newsletters that are a quick read—brief and to the point. I've adopted the practice of including, right after the opening remarks of my e-mail, a line such as,"Estimated Reading Time: 2.31 minutes." That way, readers know what to expect. I believe that, as people lead increasingly busy lives, the estimated reading time for newsletters and e-zines will be well under five minutes.

GUIDELINES FOR WRITING ONLINE ADS, SIGNATURE FILES, AND BANNER COPY ▼

Writing online classified ads, e-zine and newsletter ads, signature files, banner copy, and other advertising copy for use on the web requires strategies a little different from offline ad writing. Where an offline ad might feature a strong benefit-laden headline or give the product's or service's unique selling proposition, writing your online ad requires a different kind of discipline—the same kind required to create an editorial as opposed to an advertisement. It's so easy to use short, punchy copy reminiscent of classified ads in the offline world, such as "Lose weight while you sleep. Click here to learn more" or "Learn a foreign language in 30 days. Click here for more information."

When you have only two to five lines in which to generate a response (such as in an online classified ad, advertising banner, or e-zine ad), it's tempting to resort to the tried-and-true techniques of advertising language. But do you really want your ad to say "I'm an ad—read me?" No! On the Internet, you'll probably be ignored. The trick is to stand out from the other ads in the medium in which your ad is placed. This is accomplished not by screaming the loudest or using hype, exclamation points, capital letters, and so forth, but by featuring something newsworthy in your ad. Many editorial-style headlines could double as copy for online ads, with a bit of retooling, as necessary. For example:

> $2 Million Scientific Project Unlocks the Secret of Aging: How You Can Become Biologically Younger!" You can turn back your body's aging clock and be able to prove it with a simple at-home test. Read entire article here: http://www.domain.com.

You might think that getting someone to click on a link should be relatively easy. After all, clicking on a mouse seems like a virtually effortless task, doesn't it? It may appear so, but not when you consider that every commercial enterprise on the Internet is asking your prospects to do the same thing. The web population has learned to become selective about what they click on, particularly in view of the endless choices and the limited time at their disposal. You have to give them a compelling reason to click. Here is another example of an editorial-style ad.

> 9 Facts You Must Know Before You Buy Any Product That Promises to Grow Hair or Stop Hair Loss
> Protect yourself from hair fallout and other horrors—and learn how to choose the right hair restoration product for your needs. Send a blank e-mail to 9facts@domain.com to receive free report.

The same applies to writing copy for banners, search engine listings, or SIG files.

Three Tips for Writing Online Ads

1. Make your ad look different, and articulate it differently from the rest of the ads in the medium where it runs so that yours will stand a chance at grabbing your audience's attention. Don't blend in with the rest.

2. Inject an element that will spark curiosity to get your audience to click.

3. Get prospects to opt in, if possible, instead of trying to sell in the ad. In the offline world, this is called the two-step approach. Only amateurs and fools run three- to five-line classifieds and try to make a sale from that one ad. There's just not enough space in a few lines to make the sale. Use the ad as a lead generator to get people to opt in to receive a free report, a free course, or a free e-book. That way, you acquire another qualified prospect to add to your mailing list.

Figure 8.2

Figure 8.2 is a SIG file I developed when I was working at Aesop Marketing Corporation. We ran it in both html and text versions. Both pulled robust click-through rates.

After a few seconds, the html version (Figure 8.2) morphs into Figure 8.3, which simply has the wording.

Figure 8.3

You may go to www.WebCopywritingUniversity.com/sig.htm to view the two-image signature file in action.

The text version reads as follows:

```
]=====================
"How did over a million people get free money grants
last year for their businesses?" Click on the link
below to find out how you, too, can be the recipient
of free money.
http://www.freestuffforentrepreneursontheinternet.com
]=====================
```

Here's another example of a SIG file that has a high clickthrough rate:

```
=====================
Did you know . . . that there's a simple
formula that has been *scientifically proven*
```

```
to prevent and CURE virtually all diseases?
Find out why this one-minute therapy is being
suppressed in the U.S. while more than
15,000 European doctors have been using it
to heal millions of patients—and how you can
use it, too. http://www.OneMinuteCureForAllDiseases.com
]====================
```

My own SIG file says simply:

```
Download your *free* eBook: "Frame-of-Mind
Marketing: How to Convert Your Online Prospects into
Customers" at
http://www.webCopywritingUniversity.com/download.htm
```

The title of my e-book doubles as my sales pitch because it contains the entire benefit right there in the title. When people click on the link, they arrive at the download page, where I first collect their contact information and then allow them to start downloading. A captured name and e-mail address is more important than a site visit.

If you write an ad where readers must click on a link to go to your webpage, they might choose to ignore it, and then you'll have nothing. On the other hand, if you offer to give readers something for free, if they do not visit your website you at least have their contact information. This is gold on the Internet because you can be in constant communication with them until they finally buy your product—and, more important, buy many other products from you.

Instead of directing readers to a download location as I did in my SIG file, you can opt to have them send a blank e-mail to your autoresponder to get the freebie. Either way, you will capture their e-mail addresses, because your web host sends you the e-mail address of everyone who sends a message to your autoresponder. The disadvantage here is that you don't get the person's first name—just an e-mail address—so you won't be able to personalize subsequent e-mails. However, the "send-a-blank-e-mail" method should not be discounted, because in online ads, SIG files, and bylines at the end of promotional articles, it is often easier to get people to send a blank e-mail to receive a freebie than to get them to click through to your website (where you can capture their first name and e-mail address via a form).

So much of your success depends on what you do after people visit your website. I estimate that up to 90 percent of your total sales will come from the skillful application of these follow-up marketing communications, combined with the e-mail strategies discussed in Chapter 4. Only a small number of visitors will become customers on their first visit to your website, but when you have mechanisms in place to capture the contact information of as many prospects as you can and start an e-mail relationship with them, that's when the real selling begins.

9

The Special Rules for Web Copywriting to the Business-to-Business (B2B) Market

A book about web copywriting would not be complete unless it included a section on how to write web copy that helps businesses sell their products and services *to other businesses* (i.e., business-to-business, also called B2B). Up until this point, the emphasis of this book has been on web copywriting for businesses whose major customers are consumers (business-to-consumer, also called B2C).

B2B marketing is the often ignored branch of marketing and has always taken a backseat to B2C marketing, so much so that whenever people talk about marketing—either online or offline—it's usually assumed they mean marketing to consumers, never B2B. In actuality, B2B marketing constitutes a significant percentage of overall marketing activity. More than half of Google's target advertisers and 38 percent of Yahoo!'s are B2B, and approximately one-third of all commercial searches on Google are B2B in nature.

As much as B2B marketing is ignored, even more so is the art of writing copy for B2B markets, especially online. B2B websites require a style of copywriting similar to the B2C web copywriting discussed in this book—with a few important distinctions. This chapter will prove beneficial not only to businesses and companies that own a B2B website, but also to copywriters who are seeking to specialize in the high-paying but often overlooked B2B web copywriting niche.

The material in this chapter was compiled largely from interviews I conducted with a fellow copywriter named Steve Slaunwhite, whose work and insight have been profiled in *The Wall Street Journal, Sales & Marketing* journal, *Marketing* magazine, *DMNews,* and more. In 2001, Steve wrote a copy piece for Hewlett-Packard that won the Business-to-Business Gold at the Promo Marketing Awards. He also wrote copy for five websites that were listed in *BtoB* magazine's Top 100. Steve is the author of several books, including *Writing for the Business to Business Market.*

The best way to illustrate the differences between writing copy for the B2B and B2C markets is by comparing how one would write two versions of copy for the same product but speaking to the two different audiences. If you were to write the copy to promote a new brand of house paint, for instance, the first version targeting homeowners (consumer audience) and the second version targeting professional painting contractors (business-to-business audience), would you write the first web page *exactly* the same way you would the second? Would you focus on the same features, dramatize the benefits in a similar way, and use the same writing style and tone to get your messages across?

Obviously not.

Why? Because a professional painting contractor's needs, interests, and criteria differ significantly from those of a homeowner when it comes to choosing a brand of paint. A painting contractor would not be motivated by quaint descriptions of family dinners against the backdrop of a beautifully painted dining room. Instead,

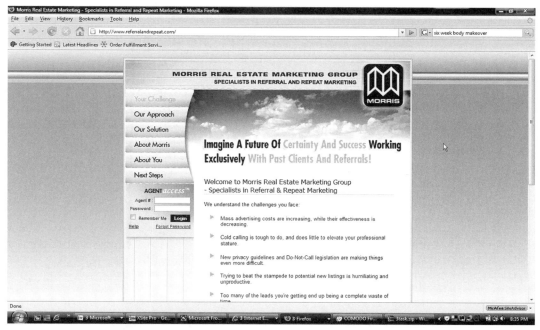

Figure 9.1 Sample of B2B website.

he would want to know about the square-foot-yield per gallon and the drying time required between coats—both features having a direct impact on how much money he'll make on a paint job.

Therefore, with only a few exceptions, writing web copy for the B2B market follows the same general rules and guidelines as writing for the B2C market, except that you're catering to a different set of needs. (See Figure 9.1.)

There are also a few other differences between the mind-set of business buyers and that of consumers that you need to be aware of in order to know exactly what it takes to persuade them to buy what you're selling. You must take these differences into account in order to create profitable landing pages, e-mail, online advertisements, or social media messages for the B2B audiences. Those differences can be summed up in the following five essentials.

1. Business Buyers Have a Split Personality

The split personality that business buyers possess has nothing to do with having some kind of dissociative neurosis, but rather it refers to having two personas that enact a virtual prize fight in their minds when they're making a buying decision. In one corner of the ring is the business buyer's persona that wants to address the needs of the business. In the other corner is the persona that cares about personal wants and preferences. Each enters the ring intending to do battle with the other.

For example, a warehouse manager who is considering the purchase of a new fleet of forklift trucks obviously wants the best in quality and performance for the company. However, he may also be concerned about the learning curve. "I don't want to work too many late nights training my operators," he may be thinking as he browses the web page. "My wife is already complaining that I don't come home for dinner often enough." If your web copy doesn't address that issue, he may decide against your product and opt for forklift trucks with a shorter learning curve instead, even if yours is clearly the superior choice!

When writing business-to-business web copy you must first highlight the *business* benefits. Show how your product or service will reduce costs, increase sales, avoid liabilities, gain a competitive advantage, improve quality, boost productivity, accelerate cash flow, and so on.

Second, you must highlight the *personal* benefits. Your web copy must also emphasize how your product or service will save buyers time, make their jobs easier, make them look good to their staff and superiors, help get them promoted, alleviate their fears, and get them home in time for dinner more often!

To identify your buyers' personal benefits, simply put yourself in a buyer's shoes and ask yourself: "How will buying this product for my company affect me personally?"

2. Business Buyers Care About Features

Just as it is important to highlight benefits when writing B2C web copy, highlighting benefits is also an important ingredient in creating winning B2B web copy. However, unlike B2C web copy wherein features need to be translated to benefits, in B2B web copy features in and of themselves are just as important as benefits—and in some cases, even more so.

For example, if you're writing the copy for a landing page to generate interest in a new air-conditioning system and the target market is HVAC contractors, the benefits of a cool, climate-controlled home won't win you buyers. HVAC contractors want to know every conceivable specification and technical detail about the product before they'll consider buying it—from CFUs and other performance statistics to sizes, weights, and installation procedures. If you fail to provide that information in your web copy clearly and accurately, you won't gain their interest or make the sale, no matter how desirable your presentation of the benefits may be.

The rule of thumb to follow is this: When in doubt, give equal attention to both benefits *and* features.

3. There Is Usually More Than One Business Buyer to Persuade

When your online marketing targets consumers, there is usually just one person who makes the buying decision. For example, if you have a website that sells running shoes and equipment, then your target audience—runners—is clear-cut, and speaking to the needs of runners is a fairly simple task.

However, when you're selling to business buyers, there can be several people involved in the buying decision. The individual needs, interests, and buying criteria of each of the decision makers can be quite diverse.

For example, if you're marketing a subscription-based online contact management system for salespeople priced at $250 per year per user and there are 75 people on the sales staff, that represents an annual company expenditure of $18,750. Since that constitutes a major expense, it is very likely that several people will be involved in the buying decision. The sales manager will want to know how the system will help her staff meet quota. The marketing manager will be interested in market statistics and reports. The CFO will demand a rapid return on investment. And the CEO will insist on more revenues and profits.

The challenge of the B2B copywriter is to speak to the needs of each of these decision makers and satisfy all of them as much as possible. You can accomplish this by creating different web pages and e-mails for each subgroup in your target audience. When doing this is not possible, you have to get creative and think of ways that you can address the needs of each of the buyers within a single piece of communication. Those ways might include a sidebar or a special text box where you can convey a specific message to a key member of the target audience.

4. The Offer Is Not the Same

In B2C online marketing, the buying process is usually accomplished in a single step—that is, the buyer clicks on the Order button, picks up the phone, or sends an e-mail.

By contrast, B2B online marketing usually involves a multistep process. That means that buyers are likely to have requested information beforehand, attended an event where they obtained some familiarization with the product or service, or viewed an online demonstration before making the commitment to buy.

If you're a warehouse manager, for instance, it's unlikely that you would simply visit a website, read some copy, and then click an Order button to purchase a $175,000 fleet of forklift trucks. You wouldn't do that if you wanted to keep your job! Instead, you would want to learn as much as you could about those forklift trucks first so that you could make an informed decision. After all, you might have to justify your purchase decision to a superior or to a committee when the time comes. Therefore, the offer you'd want to make in business-to-business is not the offer to buy your product or service but an offer of free information of some kind.

Here are some examples of free information offers that work well in B2B markets:

- ► Information kit
- ► Webinar
- ► Case study (aka product success story)
- ► Product brochure (downloadable, in PDF format)
- ► Online demonstration
- ► Consultation with a technical expert
- ► White paper
- ► Custom quotation

Giving away free information is one of the principal lead generation methods employed by business-to-business marketers. While it might not seem like a challenging task to get someone to send for a freebie, getting that lead can actually be just as challenging as getting the sale. That's because you should have already laid some effective groundwork about your product or service in order to motivate prospects to send for information about it in the first place. And you should have already succeeded in positioning your company as one that is capable of providing reliable information.

When writing *lead generation copy* for the web, here's a strategy that will dramatically increase your click-throughs and conversion rates: *Sell the free offer, not the product.* In other words, if your product is contact management software, for instance, and your lead generation offer is a free white paper, then sell the benefits of the white paper—as if that were the product. This one technique alone will usually double your results.

This strategy actually coincides with the advice I routinely dispense for B2C selling that crafting your opt-in offer is far more important than crafting the offer to sell the product or service itself. That's because no matter how skillful a web copywriter you are, it is more than likely that less than 5 percent of your website visitors will ever buy your product upon their first visit to your website. In B2B selling, that percentage may be even less, and sometimes it's even 0 percent because the actual sale could actually occur offline (such as fleet sales) and not online—even if the lead was generated online. Suffice it to say that in B2B, as well as B2C selling, the majority of the business tends to come from the relationship that is developed after the prospect has sent for the free information. That's why a copywriter's emphasis should be on selling the free offer, not the product.

5. Business Buyers Are Embracing Web 2.0

Business buyers are relying increasingly on blogs, discussion forums, social networking sites like LinkedIn®, and other Web 2.0 strategies in an effort to make better buying decisions. They are chatting with colleagues online about the latest products and services, exchanging success stories, making new contacts, and forming a myriad of special interest groups. A case in point: LinkedIn, an online network of more than 8.5 million experienced professionals from around the world, representing 130 industries, has, at the time of this writing, over 52,000 product managers as registered members.

At its basic level, *social media* refers to the online communities and technologies that enable people to share opinions, experiences, perspectives, and insights with each other. From a B2B marketer's perspective, it's about having great conversations with prospects and customers. Imagine yourself at a cocktail reception mingling with a group of your prospects and customers. It's a social gathering and yet the talk is about business. What might you glean from listening to those conversations, asking questions, and getting your questions answered? What you'll get is an intimate glimpse into the culture of your prospects' industry, as well as your specific prospect's company culture. You'll also get to hear their opinions, their concerns, what they want and don't want in the kind of product or service you offer, how they speak, and the terminology they use, and before long you'll know how to speak their language. That's the key to writing brilliant B2B web copy and crafting effective blog posts and social networking profiles—knowing what to say and how to say it in a way that resonates with your target audience.

Social media gives new meaning to what Robert Collier once wrote: "You must *enter* the *conversation* that's *already* happening in your *prospect's mind.*" Joining the conversations afforded by social media will put you well on your way to writing effective B2B copy.

Lose the Corporatespeak!

Because B2B copywriting speaks to the needs of businesses, companies, or corporations rather than consumers, copywriters often make the mistake of writing with stiff formality. That may be because they erroneously believe stiff and formal writing is expected in the business world. Here's an example of an actual headline used by a B2B website:

Sales Performance Optimization Solutions for
Enterprise Class Companies

The writer of this headline made the classic mistake of trying to *impress* rather than *express* effectively. Unfortunately, he failed on both counts. Although most B2B marketing communications, including web copy, tend to suffer from corporatespeak, that's not the most compelling way of articulating a sales proposition that wins the hearts of businesses. In actuality, stiff formality keeps prospects at arm's length and reinforces the barrier between you, the marketer, and them, the prospective clients.

The best way to discover the best writing style and tone for B2B web copy is to find out what your target audience reads online, what blogs they frequent, which websites they visit, which publications they subscribe to. This, then, again highlights the importance of becoming involved in social media. When you familiarize yourself with natural conversations that occur in your prospects' industry, you'll quickly discover that even technically oriented engineers prefer to read material that is clear, informative, and conversational rather than stiff and formal. Conversational copy draws your prospects closer and makes them more likely to want to do business with you.

10

Web Copywriting in the Age of Web 2.0

What is Web 2.0? Its concept is vast and multifaceted, holds various meanings to Internet users depending on their respective vantage points, and is the source of much disagreement about just what it means exactly. Most people toss the buzzword around without really understanding its implications, and they believe it represents little more than "a new and improved World Wide Web." This chapter covers the broad definition of Web 2.0, which is far from exhaustive and focuses only on aspects that are related to Internet marketing and copywriting.

The term *Web 2.0* was originally coined by Tim O'Reilly, founder of O'Reilly Media. It entered the Internet lexicon after the first O'Reilly Media Web 2.0 conference in 2004, although its seed components had been in existence many years before then.

Web 2.0 "describes the trend in the use of World Wide Web technology and web design that aims to enhance creativity, information sharing, and, most notably, collaboration among users," according to Wikipedia's definition. Examples of companies and products that embody the principles of Web 2.0 are user-generated sites such as Flickr.com, Scribd.com, Wikipedia, and YouTube.com, where users upload and share photos, videos, and information. Other examples are Skype, Digg, Google Maps, eBay, craigslist, AdSense, and MapQuest.

Under the overarching infrastructure of Web 2.0 exists social dynamics that a marketer can exploit in order to market much more effectively on the Web. Before we can develop a strategy for marketing on Web 2.0, we first have to identify its relevant components, which include, but are not limited to, those discussed in the following sections.

BLOGS

A *blog* is a website that is usually maintained by an individual who posts entries regularly, consisting of personal opinions, views, descriptions of events, or other material such as pictures, audio, or video. Many blogs function as online diaries, and others provide news, updates, and commentary about a specific subject. Blogging has become such a phenomenon that as of June 2008, Technorati, the leading blog search engine, was tracking over 112.8 million blogs.

Blogs, as a self-publishing platform, now collectively command a significant mind share of the Internet population and have diminished some of the clout and power of the giant publishing conglomerates. According to Michael Malone of ABC News, "[M]any blogs enjoy readerships larger than some major metropolitan newspapers." The popularity of blogs is attributed to a number of factors: (1) Several popular bloggers have outscooped many of the major newspapers, landing the top stories of the day at speeds faster than news publications can turn around and sell a single issue; (2) many readers tend to rely on blogs because the major newspapers and magazines tend to lack balanced coverage, and bloggers shine the light on issues that mainstream media try to obfuscate, sugarcoat, or sanitize for the sake of political correctness or their advertisers' demands; (3) bloggers provide the benefit of their personality, something that mainstream media lack. They're independent thinkers, and they can be cantankerous rabble-rousers, muckraking journalists, or peace-loving hippies, and the public loves them because they're real; (4) readers of blogs gain a sense of community and belonging that they can't get from reading newspapers and magazines—not to mention the advantages of having human interaction and instant feedback and the opportunity to have one's opinions heard.

SOCIAL BOOKMARKING SITES   ▼

These are sites that provide their users with a platform to save links to bookmarked webpages that they want to remember or share with other users. The bookmarks are usually public, but they can also be saved privately or shared only with specific people, groups, or networks. There are hundreds of dedicated social bookmarking sites in existence, each representing a specialized view of the World Wide Web. The original social bookmarking site, Delicious (formerly del.icio.us), which is now owned by Yahoo! and has just relaunched to version 2.0 in 2008, has more than 5 million users and 150 million bookmarked URLs at the time of this writing. Other dedicated social bookmarking sites include StumbleUpon, Reddit, and Google Bookmarks. Surprisingly enough, the social networking sites Facebook and MySpace have emerged as enormously popular ways of social bookmarking—overtaking dedicated social bookmarking sites like Delicious, StumbleUpon, Reddit, and Google Bookmarks. According to a 2008 report by ShareThis.com, the top three vehicles for sharing social bookmarks (next to e-mail) are Facebook (10 percent), Digg (7 percent), and MySpace (6 percent). Software giant Microsoft also jumped on the bandwagon and launched a social bookmarking product of its own called Social Bookmarks in September 2008.

Just as blogs have shifted some of the power away from traditional publishers, social bookmarking sites have likewise taken some of the authority away from search engines, which used to be the only way for the Internet population to know which websites are relevant and important. Whereas search engines use software, which algorithmically determines the meaning of a Web resource, social bookmarking sites have human beings who qualitatively identify the importance and relevance of those Web resources.

SOCIAL NETWORKING SITES

These are online communities, the most notable of which are MySpace (242 million members), LinkedIn (24 million professionals spanning 150 industries), and Facebook (100 million members), that bring together people who share interests and activities or who are interested in exploring the interests and activities of others. They facilitate the process of being in contact with like-minded people through a variety of methods such as messaging, chat, e-mail, file sharing, video, blogging, and discussion groups.

AUTHORITY SITES

Because of their popularity for certain subjects, topics, or search terms, these sites are recognized as "authorities" by search engines. These sites usually contain very high quality and accurate content, and people often search for them. Most search engines like Google, for instance, have an algorithm that deems a website as being of a higher quality based on the number of high-quality websites linking to it (backlinks). When it comes to giving a website "authority site" status, however, Google not only makes use of backlinks to determine popularity but also observes how often people click on a specific website for those particular terms—and sometimes a careful manual review is warranted. Quality content and useful information are the key components that set authority sites apart from the rest.

When you reflect on these components that constitute the emerging social dynamics on the Web, it's easy to see that the undercurrent they all share is *interactivity*. They also point to the online population's need to be heard, to express themselves, to contribute, and to matter. From the staggering numbers of people who are members of MySpace, Facebook, and LinkedIn, not to mention the countless other social networks, it is plain to see that social networks have become an integral part of the fabric of Internet society. From a marketing perspective, the social media of Web 2.0 present the concept of marketing as a *conversation* between and among people.

Several key factors have contributed to the growth of Web 2.0:

1. Computer hardware has continued to get cheaper and faster, with memory capacities increasing rapidly.

2. Broadband Internet use has become more common, as well as affordable, in recent years. Forty-two percent of American adults had high-speed Internet in their homes as of March 2006, according to a Pew Internet study. In the early days of the Internet, when dial-up service was the norm, uploading and downloading of digital media online (at sites like YouTube, Flickr, and iTunes) would not have been possible.

3. The availability of abundant open source software has resulted in cheaper (and often free) customizable software options.

4. There are now many easy-to-implement models for monetizing Web 2.0 businesses that weren't previously available.

What does all this mean to a marketer, advertiser, or copywriter? The enhanced interactivity afforded by Web 2.0 enables us to forge better relationships with our prospects and customers, and it also means that the Web now has an organized feedback mechanism that lets marketers feel the pulse of their target audiences more than they ever have before.

During the mid-1990s, when the Web was still largely a text-driven medium, websites were patterned after documents designed for print media. As such, online news websites were modeled after their physical counterparts (newspapers), and much of our direct-response web copy (e.g., the sales letter) was modeled after direct-mail sales letters. Years later, studies employing eye-tracking equipment gave valuable feedback about the way Internet users actually read a news webpage—and this has revamped the format and style in which news websites are designed. In the direct-response arena, however, no feedback channels were available except some scattered chat rooms and forums. Therefore, sales letters continued to be the choice format for direct-response websites, even though sales letters were suitable for the printed page, not the web.

Over the last eight years, I've taught a signature model of web copywriting that resembles editorial writing more than it does sales copy. I've also been predicting that one day, whenever a website uses the mere salutation "Dear Friend" (which is the hallmark of the sales letter style of copywriting), it is likely to cause prospects neither to read the sales letter nor to buy whatever one is selling. The reasons I made such a prediction are threefold: (1) The words "Dear Friend" and any other telltale signs of a sales letter are cues that cause prospects' resistance to go way up because they know from the get-go that you're trying to sell them something. In fact, as far back as five years ago the words "Dear Friend," when used in the body of an e-mail, caused spam filters to flag the e-mail as spam. (2) I was fortunate enough to have witnessed firsthand the results of scientific testing at Aesop that made it perfectly clear that editorial-style web copy out-pulls sales letter–style web copy. (3) I ran a promotional campaign for a very well-known direct marketer, who was quite possibly the best direct-mail copywriter in the world. He and his partner asked us to run a 13-page sales letter that pulled an amazing 7.1 percent conversion rate when sent to a million people via direct mail. But when we ran the same piece word for word on the web and drove a million people to the website, we got only 15 orders—a dismal 0.0015 percent conversion.

Now in the days of Web 2.0, my prediction is coming true. Even a colleague of mine, Michel Fortin, a leading online copywriter who has written top-producing sales letters for the most successful Internet marketers, has seen the progressive decline in the effectiveness of the sales letter. He has even written a 51-page report entitled *The Death of the Salesletter: Web 2.0 and Its Impact on the Future of Internet Copy,* wherein he calls for a move toward writing more editorial-like copy that gives more content, turning the sales process into an experience, and cutting down the length of copy to be stronger, pithier, and more to the point. In the report, Michel confides that most of the other top Internet marketers agree that sales letters are falling out of favor, and they are also predicting the demise of what they call "ugly websites," describing sales letters as "cartoonish."

This gradual departure from the sales letter style of web copywriting makes sense from the standpoint that the web is now littered with template-based, cookie-cutter sales letters, a parade of wearisome product launches, and lackluster opt-in and name squeeze pages. It also makes sense because Web 2.0 offers a plethora of alternatives to the overused marketing and copywriting tactics that no longer work.

Web 2.0 has given rise to new tools and resources that enable marketers and copywriters to relate to their prospects and customers in a whole new way. The emergence of social networks, for instance, now gives us the opportunity to start a dialogue with our prospects and customers in online social environments that feel comfortable and nonintrusive to them. We also now have continuing conversations with them in these "social" settings that enable us to anticipate their needs, serve them better, gain their trust, and demonstrate to them what it would be like to do business with us.

Isn't this infinitely better than force-feeding your offer to them when they arrive at your website and asking them to buy something they haven't told you they need?

Never has there been a better time to be a skilled web copywriter than during this era of Web 2.0, which requires a unique and impactful way of communicating. For example, learning how to craft powerful cyber bites (see Chapter 6) enables you to write effective blog posts about your product or service that don't come across as marketese. Telling a story (which is germane to social networking) and making sure the story has the Trifecta Neuro-Affective Principle installed in it will go a long way toward causing the bloggers and the social networking population to "feel right" about your product or service, decide it's a "good fit" for their particular situation, and convince them that they need look no further than your product or service to fulfill their needs.

I liken Web 2.0 to the workings of the billions of neurons in the brain. Neurons have the amazing ability to gather and transmit electrochemical signals and pass messages to each other. This is not unlike the deep-linking architecture of Web 2.0. The 112.8 million blogs and their participants, the hundreds of social bookmarking sites and their users, the dozens of social networking sites and their millions of members, and the numerous authority sites are interconnected in an intricate lacework of branches resembling the treelike projections of a neuron, called dendrites. When a thought enters the brain, it causes a cascade of electrochemical signals in the neural network that are transmitted through the dendrites to other neurons at lightning speed. Likewise, when information is strategically placed into the Web 2.0 architecture such as a blog, for instance, that information gets transmitted throughout the intricate sharing, trading, and collaborating network of Web 2.0 at an astounding speed.

The deep-linking interactivity of Web 2.0 is facilitated by sharing utilities (such as ShareThis, AddThis, and Digg This), which make it easy to distribute information to social media and allow a message, article, or story to be shared across the social web with the click of a single button or link. (See discussion later in this chapter for details about sharing utilities.)

The mechanics of Web 2.0 may seem complex to you at first, but you don't have to thoroughly understand everything about it in order to reap the benefits of marketing on the Web 2.0 frontier. Let's take a look at an example that shows the power of Web 2.0 in action. Suppose you posted a cyber bite or story on a blog that has 3,686 avid subscribers, with a prominent link to your website and a ShareThis button. How many people do you think would most likely click through to your website, not just out of curiosity but as hot prospects who are ready and willing to buy what you're selling? Wouldn't that be infinitely better than selling to website-hopping Internet searchers who happen to click on your pay-per-click ad? Provided your post is geared to the interests of the blog's subscribers, wouldn't a website visitor coming from a blog or an authority site be in a better frame of mind to buy from you (especially since they've read your well-crafted post) compared to the cold prospects clicking through to your website from traditional outbound Internet marketing campaigns?

Extending this scenario a little further, if you used relevant keywords in your blog post, it would have a high likelihood of getting a prominent position on search engines for those keywords—not just on the day you post, but for as long as the blog exists. So that will then give you permanent search engine exposure because blog posts don't get taken down.

Now suppose you got 50 sales from your blogging efforts, and customers are beginning to recommend your product or service to others and posting their positive reviews on blogs. Since you spent the time earlier to craft the cyber bite or story (based on the Trifecta Neuro-Affective Principle), you've given the bloggers a digestible nugget (or meme) that made it easy for them to spread the word—so that meme gets broadcast throughout the blogosphere. On the blogosphere, good news travels extremely fast. So now how many more people are going to be exposed to your message and persuaded to try your product or service?

Nice going, but what else can you do with those wonderful reviews within the Web 2.0 infrastructure? You can circulate the best reviews on various authority sites such as www.ILikeTotallyLoveIt.com, which is an authority site for online products. Circulating your reviews among authority sites is an excellent and fast way of not only generating increased sales but also having the reviews picked up by the search engines.

Now you see how using the social dynamics on Web 2.0 can create a cascade of interconnected benefits. So what's next? Since your cyber bite, story, or video has turned into a meme and you now have sales coming from multiple blogs, and you also now have a handful of great reviews, what else can you do in Web 2.0? You can turn your message into a genuine news story (one that, again, uses the Trifecta Neuro-Affective Principle), do an audio recording of it, and convert it into a podcast. There are many podcasting guides available online that show you how to do this. Provided your podcast offers great content, word travels extremely fast when your podcast hits iTunes and rave reviews come pouring in.

What else can you do with the news story you've written? You can submit it to social bookmarking sites and get free publicity without hiring a PR firm or sending out press releases via the online press release services. Social bookmarking sites are always hungry for newsworthy stories, and if you have an incredible story to tell that's related to your product or service (such as the story of Dr. Lorne Thomas—see Chapter 6), a story that emphasizes the unique angle of your product or service, or a story about how your revolutionary product or service came into being, your story is likely to be picked up and distributed quickly throughout the entire blogosphere. When that happens, your story could also be spotted by Tailrank, a meme-tracker that finds the hottest posts from millions of blogs. And if all goes well, you might even land on megapopular authority sites like Digg or Slashdot. Stories picked up by an authority site like Digg (which boasts of its social and democratic voting system that determines which stories are featured on its front page) are regarded highly by search engines and are consequently given high rankings in search results for relevant keywords and phrases.

You can also turn your news story into a two- to three-minute video, give it a great title, keyword-load it, and submit it to social bookmarking sites, video-sharing websites, and vlogs—and watch the video appear on Page 1, 2, or 3 of Google's organic search results for your keywords practically overnight.

Are you beginning to see how one simple marketing message can snowball into an unstoppable flow of traffic and sales on Web 2.0? And that's with no cost except the time it takes to craft your cyber bite, blog post, article, story, or video.

The scenarios I've presented here don't even encompass a small fraction of the possibilities of marketing via Web 2.0. I haven't even touched on social networking sites, which are an entire universe of marketing possibilities on their own. MySpace, for instance, has the potential to pluck a product or service out of obscurity and put it at center stage on the Web, the way it "discovered" over 8 million unknown artists and gave them the kind of international visibility they wouldn't have otherwise had without this networking site. Most people tend to think MySpace has a younger demographic that ranges from ages 12 to 24, but in actuality, according to an October 2006 report from comScore, more than half of MySpace visitors are now age 35 or older. The site's demographic composition continues to shift toward dramatically fewer users in the 12-to-24 age bracket, the highest growth in the 35-to-54 age bracket, and modest growth in the 55+ age group.

Facebook, another popular social network and the fourth-most-trafficked website in the world (according to comScore), also represents significant implications for business owners, marketers, and entrepreneurs. People likewise assume that the majority of Facebook's users belong in the 12-to-24 age group, but Facebook posts actual statistics on its site stating that its fastest-growing demographic consists of those 25 years old and older, and that more than half of its users are beyond college age.

Social Networking Sites for Prospective Customers

It's easy to mine the social networking sites for prospective customers for your business, if you know how. For instance, you can join selected groups in each social networking site in order to market your product or yourself in various niches. To give you an idea of how rich a source of connections MySpace is, for instance, go to www .MySpace.com and click on the Groups link under the More tab—you'll find 34 categories of groups including Health/Wellness/Fitness, Hobbies & Crafts, Money & Investing, Romance & Relationships, Automotive, Computers & Internet, Recreation & Sports, Games, and Family & Home. What's incredible is the huge numbers of groups there are in each of the categories. If you're marketing a health product or service, for instance, there are 31,993 groups in the Health/Wellness/Fitness category you can market to; if you're selling a relationship book, there are 74,548 groups in the Romance & Relationships category; if you're selling an automotive product, you can market to the 57,573 groups in the Automotive category. These are the numbers of groups, of course, and each group has its own corresponding number of users. A single group in the Health/Wellness/Fitness category called Natural Cures, for instance, has 19,244 members, a Body Building group has 149,871 members, and a Yoga group has 13,748 members. Groups in other categories have similarly staggering numbers of members. Perusing the groups enables you to mine MySpace for profitable niches for your product or service. You can sign up to join these groups, and that will give you an opportunity to market to these groups if you know the correct and appropriate way to do it. (This chapter gives you guidelines.)

How to Dramatically Expand Your Existing Network of Business Connections

As far as making unlimited business contacts is concerned, LinkedIn is far and away the social network of choice. Whether you're a web copywriter who's looking to obtain new clients or a businessperson or entrepreneur looking for more customers, LinkedIn provides the platform for getting an astounding number of targeted business connections without your ever having to leave your home or office. LinkedIn offers a totally different networking ballpark with undeniable business-building benefits that even reluctant businesses and technophobic entrepreneurs are being enticed to join because of the unparalleled opportunities it presents. Among the countless benefits of being a registered member of LinkedIn are the following:

▶ LinkedIn profiles get a fairly high positioning on Google. Therefore, when you craft your LinkedIn profile (using the Trifecta Neuro-Affective Principle and other copywriting strategies in this book), you influence what people see when they search for you and cause them to visit your website or do business with you.

▶ Your LinkedIn profile allows you to publicize not just your website or your company but also your blog, if you have one, by selecting "Other." You can then modify the name on the link to your name, add a keyword-rich description, and set your public profile to Full View. Your blog will then be automatically search engine optimized and is likely to be picked up by Google, Yahoo!, and the other search engines.

▶ The more connections you add on LinkedIn, the higher the likelihood that your profile will appear at the top of search results when people use search engines to look for someone to hire or do business with. The countless ways that online marketers and web copywriters can use LinkedIn could fill an entire volume, but you can easily do a search on any search engine for "ways to use LinkedIn" and you'll find plenty of ideas to get you started.

This brings us back to the importance of web copywriting skills if you want to set yourself apart from your competitors and cause people to buy your product or service or do business with you within the Web 2.0 social communities.

The important thing to remember is that all the success you can have on Web 2.0 comes down to honing the priceless skill of writing web copy. With this skill, anyone can create a breakthrough brand on the Internet and plug it into the key components of Web 2.0 such as blogs, social networking sites, or even videos on YouTube, to become famous on the Web, become an authority in one's field, or become a subject matter expert in as little as 14 days. Web 2.0 requires a new kind of marketing communication—one that is cognizant of the fact that practically everyone is well connected nowadays, including your prospects and customers. To learn more about how to use Web 2.0 for marketing purposes, go to http://www.MarketingWeb2–0.com.

GUIDELINES FOR WRITING COPY FOR DISSEMINATION IN SOCIAL MEDIA

As with any marketing campaign, it's unrealistic to just plug your marketing content into the key components of Web 2.0 and expect a flood of sales and profits to beat a path to your website. I've seen numerous entrepreneurs, authors, and performing artists try their hand at various aspects of Web 2.0, such as blogs and social networking sites, and scratch their heads when they fail to produce results of any significance. It's not just about creating a blog or having a presence on MySpace, Facebook, or LinkedIn. You need to have a strategy for engaging as many of the components of Web 2.0 as possible. You also have to carry on conversations with people in social media. Most important, you must learn how to communicate within the parameters of social media, because if you do it the wrong way you could jeopardize your own marketing efforts or, worse, you could quickly degrade your online reputation.

Like all forms of marketing, familiarizing yourself with the Web 2.0 climate, its culture, and the appropriate way of writing copy that gets results requires a bit of time. This is the cornerstone of success in Web 2.0, which eludes so many commercial aspirants. Once again, it all comes down to marketing to the frame of mind of your prospects.

Here are fundamental guidelines for writing copy for dissemination within the social media of Web 2.0:

1. Exercise subtlety in your marketing efforts. The social media entity as a whole disapproves of blatant self-promotion—whether it be in the form of a blog post, a YouTube video, or a message on a group discussion thread. Ninety percent of your messages should consist of content, and 10 percent (at most) advertising. This also applies to posts on Twitter.com, a free social networking and microblogging service that allows its users to send and read other text-based posts of up to 140 characters in length (otherwise known as *tweets*). Refrain from making your microblogging posts nothing but press releases. Engage your readers or followers in conversation (sometimes unrelated to your product or service) instead of "talking at" them in a monologue, especially one that is replete with overpromotion.

   Both blogging and microblogging must be characterized by transparency and authenticity in order to give your readers and followers the feeling that they know you. That familiarity goes a long way toward deepening trust and making them more likely to want to do business with you. When you temper your advertising messages thus and keep your posts from being too commercially slanted, they have a higher probability of being shared throughout the intricate lacework of social media.

2. Research the interests of your target audience (e.g., the blog subscribers and social networking group members) and find quality information that you can share with them. There are usually numerous topics of interest to any niche that you could post on appropriate blogs or disseminate throughout social media. If you sell a skin care product, for instance, you can write about exciting scientific breakthroughs in antiaging or acne control (especially if you can tie the breakthrough to an ingredient or benefit of your product), or you can write a

review of the top skin care products (including the one you sell) or give unique and valuable tips that skin care seekers want to know.

3. You have the option of either contributing blog posts on other people's blogs or creating your own blog—or both. Nowadays, it's easy to create your own blog in a matter of minutes with Google's free, easy-to-use, full hosted Blogger tool (Blogger.com) or through a paid blogging service like TypePad. When you post messages, articles, or stories on your own blog, you enjoy greater creative liberty, of course, and your blog posts aren't subject to the whims of a blog owner who can choose to retain or delete your post.

For marketing purposes, the importance of having your own blog or submitting blog posts on other people's blogs is the search engine exposure you can potentially get. Search engines frequently crawl blogs, especially those that are regularly updated, and often reward them with high rankings when they have topical relevance. Therefore, when writing blog posts, in addition to giving topical content that your target audience wants you should also sprinkle relevant keywords strategically in order to attract the right kind of traffic—and make sure you have prominent links to your website.

Familiarize yourself with the mechanics of the sharing utilities (such as ShareThis, Digg This, or AddThis) so that, whenever possible, you can use them on the sidebar, in the footer, or underneath the headline of your posts. When you do this, you make your messages much more likely to (a) be voted on by readers on authority sites like Digg; (b) be followed by memetracking websites like Techmeme and Poly-Meme, which analyze blog posts to determine what webpages are being discussed or cited most often; (c) capitalize on the deep-linking architecture of Web 2.0; and (d) get high-quality traffic to your website.

The ShareThis utility (ShareThis.com), for instance, makes it easy to share your articles across the social web with the inclusion of just a single widget. This eliminates the need to install separate buttons for submitting to Digg, Newsvine, Reddit, and other social media websites. Using a sharing utility like ShareThis enables you to add bookmark invitations to blogs or webpages, and this then turns into a productive, passive bookmarking strategy. The cumulative effect of dozens, if not hundreds or thousands, of your blog pages, each with a bookmark invitation to save and share, can potentially allow your blog to dominate the blogosphere and drive traffic to your website 24/7.

You can also take a more aggressive role in disseminating your messages than just waiting for visitors to find and bookmark your content. You can do this by first building networks of associates and friends to introduce and share your content with. Then you can implement an active bookmarking strategy whereby you create content and systematically share and promote it with like-minded networks, thereby providing value to the community and facilitating distribution of your content.

Does having a blog produce any sales benefit for you if you don't have many visitors or subscribers to your blog? This is the question that crosses the mind of marketers who are considering the possibility of starting a blog but are unsure of whether the time they spend creating content for their blog could pay dividends in terms of website sales. The number of readers or viewers you attract to your blog post—or your social bookmarks or YouTube videos, for that matter—is only one of the contributors to the marketing power of your Web 2.0 activities. Another essential aspect of marketing on Web 2.0 is the search engine ranking you get by just having those blog posts, videos, or links in cyberspace to begin with. A well-crafted blog post that uses keywords (especially "long tail" keywords and niche phrases discussed in Chapter 11) in its headline and body content is likely to rank high in the search engines. Search engines aim to deliver relevant content in their search results, so the more you use keywords strategically in your blog posts, the more you attract readers, links, Diggs, social bookmarks, and relevant search traffic. Likewise, a well-made online video uploaded to YouTube and the other video-sharing websites, if loaded with relevant keywords, has the potential to land on Page 1 or 2 of Google's search results for those keywords within as little as 24 to 48 hours. (See the case study in the subsection entitled "Marketing via Online Videos" later in this chapter.) That's because social media such as online videos and blogs are regarded as high-priority content by search engines and are favored for high search engine rankings. The value of a high search engine ranking alone, and the accompanying web traffic and sales it brings to any online business, makes it worthwhile to start a blog.

4. Inject a unique and likable personality into the messages or posts you plant on the fertile ground of Web 2.0. Consumers of social media like knowing the person behind the blog, the article, the profile, or the group discussion thread. Engage them with relevant stories that capture their imagination (and emotions), and put your human and social aspects on display. Ultimately, your objective is to create a distinctive personal brand that distinguishes you from the rest of the business entities on Web 2.0.

5. Pictures are an intrinsic part of the social media landscape, particularly social networking websites. Therefore, whenever possible, include a picture that captures the interest or curiosity of your audience. The picture you choose should, in conjunction with your message, give a compelling reason why someone should click on the link to visit your website. Many members of social networking sites who are performing artists (such as bands, actors, stand-up comedians, and

recording artists) lament the fact that because their social networking webpages are on MySpace, Facebook, or other social networking websites, no one seems to be clicking through to check out their official websites. The reason for this is almost always because they've put the proverbial entire kitchen sink on their social networking webpage so that readers don't feel compelled to visit their website to learn more.

Whether you're a promoter of a rock band or a marketer of consumer products, you must view your social networking webpage as a first encounter with someone you would meet in real life. When you first meet someone, it's never advisable for you to tell them everything there is to know about you because, otherwise, where's the mystery? Instead, you should instill a sense of incompletion (see the discussions of the Zeigarnik effect and the cliffhanger principle in Chapter 5)—create that "brain itch" I referred to earlier—so that they'll feel an irresistible urge to click through to your website, where you can make a proper pitch for your business. Most of the other psychological devices discussed in Chapter 5 can be successfully applied to the About Me part of your social networking webpage, as well as any bulletins and other messages you post on social networking sites.

6. Online videos have become the choice vehicle for consuming information in social media these days. According to a November 2006 report in *Marketing Experiments Journal*®, Internet surfing has overtaken television as the most popular recreational activity. On average, people spent 3.6 hours a day on recreational Internet surfing, compared to 2.5 hours watching television and 1 hour participating in online chat. Of the many forms of recreational Internet surfing, watching online videos is the number one activity because video is deemed an entertaining way of obtaining information and people are able to watch their videos in a variety of ways, including via wireless devices. The popularity of online videos is underscored by the fact that YouTube even has its own ded-

icated icon on the home screen of iPhone, the world's most popular mobile phone, allowing users access to YouTube videos in a single click.

Although the majority of videos on YouTube and other video-sharing sites are produced for fun and notoriety, marketing professionals produce them for the purpose of driving traffic to their websites and selling more of their products or services. The key to a successful video designed for marketing purposes is to avoid creating a glossy, overproduced video that an advertising agency might produce. Instead, make it look as though it was created by average individuals, and make it as entertaining as possible. The video should either be humorous or have shock value, and ideally it should have no overt promotional language, no sales pitch, and no product placement—but it does need to have a covert call to action, such as a URL embedded strategically throughout the video. Additional strategies for using online videos to trigger the social networking aspect of Web 2.0 are detailed in the next section, entitled "Marketing via Online Videos."

7. Under no circumstances should you spam the blogosphere—that is, don't litter blogs with blatant advertising messages offering no relevant content. Neither should you create spam blogs. Spam blogs, sometimes referred to as *splogs,* are blog sites that their creators use solely to promote an affiliated website(s) or to artificially increase the search engine rankings of such associated site(s) in an effort to increase the page rank or backlink portfolio of those websites. As is discussed in the next section, it makes no sense to obtain a high Google ranking if your indexed listing is ignored or your prospects don't do what you want them to do, which is to visit your website and eventually want to do business with you. Spamming the blogosphere paints you as a disreputable blogger who offers worthless content. Furthermore, not targeting your audience and just sending out messages into the blogosphere using a shotgun approach could result in the

deletion of your posts or the deletion of your profile, if you conduct those spamming activities on social networking sites.

Instead, take the time to familiarize yourself with blog protocols and the appropriate way of communicating in specific blogs, and whenever possible observe what successful marketers are doing to break the ice, attract appropriate attention, and deliver compelling invitations to visit their websites.

MARKETING VIA ONLINE VIDEOS
▼

In February 2005, a fledgling company called YouTube opened for business and provided an online space where users could upload, view, and share video clips. YouTube wasn't the first video-sharing site in cyberspace—the first one was ShareYourWorld.com (now defunct) dating back to 1998—but it was the one that sparked the Internet video revolution and spawned hundreds of imitators.

The collective impact that YouTube and other video-sharing websites have made in the lives of Internet users is staggering, and online video-watching has reached epidemic proportions, encompassing 46 percent of all broadband traffic. Now its effect on the way we do marketing on the Web is also becoming evident. Consider these statistics:

► Ten percent of all North American Internet traffic is going to YouTube (according to a report by Ellacoya Networks, June 2007)—this percentage is growing steadily as YouTube grows in popularity, and it becomes even more accessible on wireless devices such as the iPhone.

► The average Internet user spent 194.3 minutes watching online videos in the month of October 2007. (This weighted average was extrapolated from findings of a study by comScore and Media Contacts.)

▶ The average YouTube visitor spends 27 minutes on YouTube videos per visit.

▶ Over 52 percent of web traffic consists of video content.

▶ Seventy percent of all U.S.-based Internet users watched videos on the Internet as of March 2007—and this usage is growing every month (Source: *The New York Times*).

▶ An *eMarketer* report forecast that more than 154 million Americans would watch online videos in 2008—that's a 12.1 percent increase from 2007.

When you consider these trends, it's easy to see why videos have become high-priority content on the Web. Because of the popularity of online videos, the search engines now crawl video sites every few minutes looking for videos. That's why video links and clips often show up in Google, Yahoo!, and MSN search results even before other types of content do, sometimes in as little as minutes after a video is uploaded. Case in point: The owner of www.OneMinuteCureForAllDiseases .com created a five-minute video at a cost of only $196, uploaded it to YouTube (http://www.youtube.com/watch?v=y3bAl9lSHg0) at 11:43 A.M. on September 3, 2008—and two minutes later, Google had already listed the video on Page 2 of its search results for the key phrase "one-minute cure for cancer."

This kind of immediate search engine visibility has never been possible before, especially for a brand-new website. It usually takes up to a year or longer for a website with a newly registered domain name to gain any kind of search engine ranking for main keywords, typically showing up in search engine results only for keywords that are not competitive.

The online video boom represents a golden opportunity for all commercial enterprises on the Web. YouTube, in particular, has been hailed as the advertising medium of the future by one of the world's biggest advertising agencies, Leo Burnett. Clearly, the viral, interactive, and community-led nature of YouTube makes it the ideal platform for advertising and marketing.

One might be tempted to assume that marketing via YouTube would work only when targeting the younger, more computer-savvy population that characterizes YouTube uploaders (average age: 26.57 years old—see the list of statistics that follow this discussion). This is most certainly an erroneous assumption because even though the average age of video *uploaders* is 26.57, the video *viewers* encompass practically everyone who has Internet access. That includes almost all ages and demographics except perhaps senior citizens over the age of 76 and children under the age of 12. Consider the fact that over 4 million of the original iPhones had been sold as of January 2008 (according to Steve Jobs's Macworld keynote on January 15, 2008), and another 3 million of the iPhone 3Gs were sold as of the time of this writing, before they were rolled out in all countries. According to *Podcasting News,* iPhone users are "30 times more likely to watch YouTube videos" because each iPhone has the YouTube icon on its home screen, making online videos just a touch of the screen away. Only half of iPhone users are under the age of 30, according to a 2008 survey conducted by Rubicon Consulting. The other half consists of baby boomers (born between 1946 and 1964) and Generation X (born between 1965 and 1981). Online video usage among iPhone users gives only a glimpse of the trend in online video viewing. Entrepreneurs are, therefore, able to use online video as a complement to their other online or traditional marketing campaigns, to market to practically any Internet users from age 12 to 76 in a wide variety of markets. While some products and services do lend themselves to online video marketing more than others, practically any company that has a commercial website can use online videos to drive traffic to their website, where they can make a proper sales presentation. At the very least, the high search engine rankings alone that online videos produce (as a result of keyword loading) make online video marketing well worth the effort.

It therefore behooves all Internet entrepreneurs, copywriters, and companies that do any kind of marketing on the Web to learn the subculture of the video-viewing public. The commercial content uploaded to YouTube as a percentage of total uploads is only 4.7 percent as of March 2008 (see "YouTube Statistics"), but that figure will grow significantly as marketers and commercial enterprises awaken to the opportunities afforded by the advertising medium that is online video.

YouTube Statistics

Courtesy of Michael Wesch

Assistant Professor of Cultural Anthropology

Kansas State University

Average YouTube video length: 2 minutes, 46.17 seconds

Average age of uploader: 26.57

(Note: This is not the average age of anybody who has ever uploaded a video, but the average age of active uploading.)

Unambiguously user-generated (amateur): 80.3%

Professional: 14.7%

Commercial content uploaded as a percentage of total uploads: 4.7%

Vlogs uploaded as a percentage of total uploads: 4.7%

Percentage of videos that are probably in violation of copyright: 12%

If you're an online marketer or entrepreneur, an advertising professional, or a marketing executive who wants to take advantage of the benefits that online videos have to offer but don't have the time, budget, expertise, or resources that you think are required to create an Internet video, I'll show you useful resources in the latter part of this chapter. These resources will enable you to create an effective video in as little as a day and spend less than $100—without having to appear in front of the camera, hiring actors, or even owning a video camera. I'll also provide you with resources for having your video produced from start to finish for as little as a few hundred dollars.

How to Create an Online Video That Drives Massive Traffic to Your Website

Before you go about trying to create an online video (or having one created for you), and before writing a single word of copy (i.e., the script) for it, here are a few guidelines:

Limit the length. The video must necessarily be no more than three to four minutes long. Various tests were done on videos posted on Google Video (http://video.google.com) to track the length of time people were willing to watch an online video, and it was found that 3½ minutes is the optimum length. Another interesting finding is that video viewers generally pay attention to a video for 7 to 15 seconds before deciding to click away. Therefore, you have a 7- to 15-second window in which to grab their attention and get them to continue watching through to the end.

This is where many of the copywriting principles described in this book, especially the Trifecta Neuro-Affective Principle, can be put to good use. The discipline that you've learned for riveting the attention of website visitors in the eight seconds they give you before clicking away will serve you well in the medium of video. While video obviously has other components, such as visuals and music, that contribute to its commercial appeal, the words that are spoken or displayed on the screen (i.e., the script or the copy) are the glue that binds them all together into a cohesive whole.

Use inexpensive, "rough-around-the-edges" production. In order to harmonize with the culture that is present in video-sharing websites, your video must not look like a sleek, professionally produced piece. Doing so removes all doubt that it is nothing but a commercial. Companies invest huge production budgets in online video, but the ones that are successful in marketing via the video-sharing websites are the ones that cleverly disguise their videos to look like they were produced by amateur video buffs. With a little improvised acting, a script that uses natural language, deliberately sloppy camera moves, and poor production, a video can look consumer-generated and yet make a powerful commercial impact.

Remember that because we're bombarded with an average of 3,500 commercial messages per day (see Chapter 1), the last thing we want to see is yet another advertisement. No one will sit and watch your obvious commercial video any more than a TV viewer will watch just for the commercials.

Entertain, inspire, shock, or teach them—or make them laugh. The general Internet population has the mentality of not wanting to be "sold" (see Chapter 1, Morkes and Nielsen study), and the online video-watching subculture is just as averse to obvious attempts by marketers to sell them something via video. But they're not averse to being finessed into buying if you entertain, inspire, or shock them; teach them something; or make them laugh (13.4 percent of YouTube videos are categorized as comedy, according to the study conducted by Professor Michael Wesch). How-to videos, funny videos, and videos that explode a myth are just a few avenues for advertising a product or service via video.

A short video entitled *"The Secret" Exposed—Is the Law of Attraction a Hoax?* (http://www.youtube.com/watch?v=hLkvvpJ_pVQ) challenged the prevailing beliefs about a much-loved principle such that it got people to view the video and ultimately sold out the book's entire first print run of 5,000 copies. (See Figure 10.1.)

Another YouTube video shows the story of a young man who started a burger museum in his basement to show that, because of the chemicals and preservatives put into them, burgers bought at McDonald's don't go bad. The video went viral, garnering over a million views and generating $29,950 per month in membership revenues for the website that the video directed traffic to. The video cost less than $82 to produce. But the interesting part is this: The subject matter of the video had very little to do with the website it funneled traffic to, except that the website is a resource on health, nutrition, and longevity—which leads to the next guideline . . .

The Secret" Exposed" - Is the Law of Attraction a Hoax?

Figure 10.1 "The Secret" Exposed thumbnail.

Drive them to your website or sales page in the proper frame of mind. Most companies that do advertising via online video make the mistake of producing their videos as though they were extended adaptations of 60-second advertising commercials. That type of video might be appropriate for posting on a website, but if it's meant to be uploaded to video-sharing sites, it will rarely be effective. The most important job that your video needs to do is to get the viewer to your website or sales page in the proper frame of mind or, ideally, primed for the sale. It is the task of your website or sales page to do the selling.

In the first of the preceding examples ("The Secret"), the video doesn't do any selling whatsoever; it simply exposes the myths, inaccuracies, and hidden dangers surrounding the Law of Attraction as it is currently taught—and then hints at the missing secret that causes desires to necessarily manifest into existence. Curiosity is then incited in the viewer, and that mental tension caused by uncompleted tasks takes over. By the end of the video, the viewer has no recourse but to go to the website, whose URL is embedded strategically throughout the video.

In the second example, the video doesn't do any selling either. It just tells an interesting and thought-provoking story about the chemical composition of McDonald's burgers. By the end of the video, the viewers, if they happen to be health-conscious individuals, are compelled to learn more, so they visit the website, whose URL is (again) embedded in various frames of the video.

Sometimes, the preselling can be done well in a video by employing the Trifecta Neuro-Affective Principle creatively. Let's use the example from Chapter 6, with the headline that reads "I should already be dead." That entire web copy, which employs the Trifecta Neuro-Affective Principle and consists of only ten paragraphs, could conceivably be turned into a video that is three to four minutes long. It could be just simple on-camera footage of Dr. Lorne Thomas giving his dramatic first-person account of how he reversed the death sentence of Lou Gehrig's disease. By the end of the video, viewers who are in the target audience of the THC company won't be able to wait to hop over to the website that gives them all the information about the healing method Dr. Thomas talked about.

Embed your URL strategically.   One of the most important keys to promoting your website via online videos is embedding your URL (website address) throughout all frames of the video—except when the URL distracts from or competes with the content of the video. Your URL is likely to get imprinted into the brain of your viewer and be remembered long after the video has been viewed. Additionally, various video-sharing websites have their respective criteria for creating thumbnail representations of your video from the video stills that constitute it. YouTube, for instance, creates a thumbnail from the video still that is located at the exact halfway point of a video, and that thumbnail is used to represent your video in search results and other displays. Other video-sharing websites have other criteria for creating the representative thumbnail for your video. Therefore, if your URL is embedded in all the video's frames (which encompass all your video stills), all your thumbnails in all the video-sharing web-sites will be branded with your URL. One last advantage to embed-ding your URL is that even if your viewers don't reach the end of your video, where you invite them to visit your website, they would have already seen your website address. (See Figure 10.2.)

How to Optimize Your Video for Search Engine Purposes

Thus far, I've only touched on the content of the video as it relates to getting viewers to take the action that you want them to take, which is usually to visit your website. But just as great web copy would be pointless if a website didn't have the eyeballs (traffic) to read the web

Figure 10.2 URL embedded in video.

copy, a video with great content that gets viewers to visit your website won't mean much if there aren't enough people to view the video in the first place.

Of course, there are a variety of ways you can promote a video, such as sending the video link to your e-mail list, if you have one, and asking your e-mail recipients to pass it on to others or post the video on their websites. However, nothing you can do to promote the video is as good as getting the video to show up on Google and the other major search engines when surfers search for keywords and phrases that your target audience uses to find a product or service like yours. Just because you've uploaded your video to YouTube doesn't necessarily mean that your video will be found on the search engines. Just as websites have search engine optimization (SEO) strategies to make them rank well in the search engines for specific keywords and phrases, so, too, do online videos. However, the search engine optimization strategy for videos takes only a few minutes to perform, whereas SEO for websites can be time- and effort-intensive.

When uploading to a video-sharing website, you'll be asked for a few pieces of key information:

Media title: Create a compelling title of 64 characters (including spaces) or less. Load the title with your desired keywords or phrases. For example: *"The Secret" Exposed—Is the Law of Attraction a Hoax?*

Media author: Put the URL of your website here, such as http://www.GreatestManifestationPrinciple.com.

Description: Put the URL of your website first (that way, your URL will be the first thing that shows in search engine results), followed by a keyword-rich description that includes what the video is about and the benefit of watching it. The ideal length is 200 characters. For example: http://www.GreatestManifestationPrinciple.com—Why the Law of Attraction does NOT work for most people—but here's the missing principle whereby your desires CAN and MUST manifest—www.GreatestManifestationPrinciple.com.

Tags: Use "long tail" keywords (see Chapter 11 for discussion) whenever appropriate and do not duplicate tags. The ideal number of tags is six. For example: *Law of Attraction, the secret, manifest your desires, manifestation, manifesting, intentions.*

The search engines don't care much whether your video is professionally produced or consists merely of slides accompanied by audio—or if it's just footage of you walking your dog, for that matter—as long as it has the proper search engine optimization as described here.

But what good is being on Page 1 of Google's search results if your listing is ignored, your prospects don't click on it, they don't watch your video, and even if they do watch your video, they don't do what you want them to do, which is visit your website? There needs to be a seamless relay, or a chain, from the moment your prospect sees your video listed in Google's search results, clicks on the link to watch your video, and then visits your website and reads your web copy. At every stage of the relay, skillful web copywriting is of the essence so as not to break the chain. I'm sure you're familiar with the saying "A chain is only as strong as its weakest link." That is certainly the case when it comes to marketing your website through online videos. That's why you need to master the principles I've covered in this book to pull off the coup that online video marketing requires.

Uploading Your Video

After your video has been created and optimized using the guidelines delineated here, you can upload your video. While you could choose to upload it only to YouTube, that wouldn't be a sufficient strategy for maximizing the chances that your video will be found by the search engines. The secret to getting a high ranking on Google and the other search engines in as little as an hour is to submit your video to as many video-sharing websites (Google Video, Yahoo! Video, Flickr.com, iFilm, etc.), blogs, social bookmarking sites, and podcast directories as possible. That way, all those sites will have links point-ing to your website, and when the search engines find those inbound links they will deem your website relevant and important and rank it high in searches for your keywords and phrases.

Uploading your website to all those websites, blogs, and directo-ries, however, is a time-consuming process that could take approxi-mately two weeks, including the time it takes to set up accounts with each of the video-sharing sites, social bookmark communities, and podcast directories. There are software programs available that can automate certain portions of the video submission process, all with varying degrees of usefulness. One of the best resources I've found is Traffic Geyser, a subscription-based service that not only has an Auto Signup Tool that enables you to sign up for 40 accounts at the same time, but uploads your site to 35 video-sharing websites, 6 blogs, and 12 social bookmarking sites simultaneously. It also converts your video into a podcast feed and submits it to podcast directories. The other is Tube Mogul, which has an analytic technology that enables you to find out when, where, and how often your videos are watched, measure the impact of marketing campaigns, gather com-petitive intelligence, and share the data with colleagues or friends.

One of my client's videos for which I wrote every component of the chain, from search engine listing to video script to website copy, landed on Google's Page 1 results for his top keywords, *understand-ing husband,* within 24 hours. In fact, his video, which was uploaded to 35 video-sharing websites, 6 blogs, 12 social bookmarking sites, and a few podcast directories, landed in two positions on Page 1 of Google. The video uploaded to GoFish.com ranked number five, and the video uploaded to YouTube.com ranked number seven on the same page! (See Figure 10.3.)

The beauty of having your video listed in the organic search results (which costs you nothing) is that, unlike traditional paid advertising or pay-per-click advertising such as Google AdWords, your listings are permanent. They may not always have the exact same ranking, but they will stay up forever because no one is going to take down your videos.

understanding husband - Google Search   Page 1 of 2

Web Images Maps News Shopping Gmail more ▼   Sign in

Google

| understanding husband | | Search | Advanced Search |
| | | | Preferences |

Web   Results **1 - 10 of about 764,000** for understanding husband. (0.05 seconds)

Advice from a Caring and **Understanding Husband** -   Sponsored Links
Southern Maryland ... ⊘
May 9, 2006 ... Advice from a Caring and **Understanding Husband** Dear   Know Your Man? ⊘
Husbands: Please be aware that as your wives age, it is harder for them to Take This Quiz To Find Out.
maintain the ...   Browse Our Fun, Free Quizzes Now!
forums.somd.com/dating-marriage/73686-advice-caring-**understanding**-   www.LifeScript.com
husband.html - 45k - Cached - Similar pages

Divorce - **Understanding husband**? ⊘
Aug 29, 2006 ... My friend is always out of town because of her job. But her **husband** told her
it deosn't bother him. She felt she was lucky to have such an.
www.iwishisaidno.com/forum/2630-**understanding-husband**.html - 77k -
Cached - Similar pages

Marriage and the **Husband**-Wife Relationship: A non-**understanding** ... ⊘
Hi Sulakshana, Right now its not good for you and the baby to take too much pressure. Try
getting together with old friends and relatives, ...
en.allexperts.com/q/Questions-Marriage-**Husband**-864/non-**understanding-husband**.htm -
20k - Cached - Similar pages

REP-AM.COM Election NewsMichelle Obama vouches for **husband's** ... ⊘
Everywhere she goes, Michelle Obama, a native of Chicago's South Side and daughter of a
city pump operator, vouches for her **husband's understanding** of ...
www.rep-am.com/news/elections/334962.txt - 43k - Cached - Similar pages

Marriage Enrichment: How to Build a Bionic Wife - marriage ... ⊘
BionicWife.com - marriage enrichment, **understanding husband**, save my marriage,   ← RANK # 5
marriage counseling, bionic wife blueprint.
www.gofish.com/player.gfp?gfid=30-1209066 - 29k - Cached - Similar pages

Understanding Your **Husband's** Battle for Sexual Purity ⊘
Do you understand your **husband's** battle for sexual purity?
womentodaymagazine.com/relationships/understandmenbattle.html - 18k -
Cached - Similar pages

YouTube - Marriage Enrichment and **Understanding Husband** ⊘
http://www.BionicWife.comCounter-intuitive blueprint for marriage enrichment,   ← RANK # 7
understanding husband, marriage counseling, save my marriage http://www.
www.youtube.com/watch?v=w7DVOCKJDzc - 78k - Cached - Similar pages

The Key to **Understanding** The **Husband** of One Wife. :: Christian ... ⊘
Apr 27, 2006 ... 1 Timothy 5:3 "Honour widows that are widows indeed" precedes and sets up
the **understanding** for 1 Timothy 5:9 "wife of one **husband**" making ...
www.christianmarriage.com/home/index.php?name=News&file=article&sid=50 - 47k -
Cached - Similar pages

Breast Cancer - A **Husband's** Guide to **Understanding** Breast Cancer ... ⊘
Information on breast cancer: signs and symptoms, breast health, and breast cancer drugs
and treatments. Join a community of breast cancer support and ...
www.healthcentral.com/breast-cancer/c/5985/11957/guide-cancer/ - 41k -

http://www.google.com/search?hl=en&rlz=1T4TSHB_enUS212US212&q=understanding+...   5/4/2008

Figure 10.3 This video landed two positions on Page 1 of Google within 24 hours.

Resources for Creating Your Video

Clearly, online videos are the website traffic generator of choice, and the online video landscape is a level playing field where all business enterprises of any size have an equal chance at generating massive website traffic—whether they have a large budget or a shoestring budget. By mastering the principles in this book, you can utilize your web copywriting skills to write a compelling two- to three-minute script for your video, then employ easy-to-use video software like Pinnacle Studio or Magix Movie Edit Pro to put it together without even having to shoot actual video footage if you don't want to. Your entire video could consist of stock pictures, slides, or stock video clips that you can purchase online at a very low cost. If you don't have a microphone or recording equipment, or you don't like the sound of your voice, you could hire an inexpensive voice-over professional for as little as $30 for 30 seconds. If you prefer to have someone else do the entire video for you, from script to production to uploading, you could do that as well. Following are resources I have used to create videos for my clients as well as for my own business enterprises:

Stock photos: Dreamstime.com and iStockphoto.com.

Stock video clips: iStockvideo.com and Revostock.com.

Online voice talent companies: ProVoiceUSA.com and VoiceTalentNow.com.

Music: MusicBakery.com, BeatSuite.com, and RoyaltyFreeMusic.com.

Video editor: Post job on Elance.com or type "video editor" in craigslist.com searchbox.

One-stop shop for online video production: ViralVideoWizard.com. (This service provides everything including writing the script, assembling all photos and video clips, producing the video, and uploading it to 35 video-sharing sites, 12 social bookmarking sites, 6 blogs, and podcast directories.)

ONLINE MARKETING WITH AUDIO ▼

The use of audio for Internet marketing purposes has been steadily gaining steam for the last several years. Audio has been used for a plethora of applications: welcome messages on a website's home page, audio testimonials, talking sales letters, talking e-mails, audio postcards and e-zines or newsletters, audio sales tools for affiliate programs, audio learning, and a lot more. The use of audio offers a lot of advantages, but it also has its drawbacks.

Advantages

1. Audio offers an added dimension to websites, online marketing communications, and advertising campaigns. It brings the human touch to an otherwise impersonal, text-driven communication. People are inclined to think they know you and your company when they hear your voice or the voice of your spokesperson.

2. Audio tends to make you and your company more credible to your prospects because you become a "real" person to them, not just some unknown individual hiding behind a website. In the online world, where relationship marketing reigns supreme, people prefer to do business with a person, not just a faceless entity. And even if the company or enterprise comes across as a faceless entity, people want to be assured that they could actually reach a real person who could help them, should they have questions or problems. When testimonials are presented via audio, prospects tend to feel reassured that they are real and not fabricated, thereby affirming the credibility of product endorsements.

3. Social psychologists report that humans are more likely to trust you if they can hear you as well as see you. That's

because the spoken word represents an additional avenue of communication. On the Internet, where trust is a hard-earned commodity because of the high incidence of identity theft, scams, and frauds, any opportunity to gain people's trust online—especially that of our prospects and customers—is a welcomed opportunity.

4. The human voice has the power to influence, motivate, persuade, and create instant rapport or cause people to respond or take action.

5. Audio offers a refreshing alternative to text-based web marketing. Some people would rather listen to sales messages and marketing communications than read them. Some people are also more likely to obey calls to action (buy, order, call, sign up, etc.) when heard rather than written. Additionally, a percentage of the population comprehends and retains what they hear rather than what they read.

6. It's easier than ever to add streaming audio to your website without expensive equipment or technical knowledge with the use of services like *Audio Generator* and *Audio Acrobat*.

Disadvantages

1. According to a 1997 study conducted by the leading web usability engineers John Morkes and Jakob Nielsen, 79 percent of the Internet population skim webpages quickly (see Chapter 1), stopping only when something catches their eye. The finding that online surfers are scanners is corroborated by more recent eye-tracking tests conducted by the Poynter Institute for Media Studies in July 2007. Another study conducted by a search engine optimization organization shows that Internet surfers who conduct searches via search engines visit 25 websites in three to four minutes. The average mile-a-minute website-hopping surfers are not inclined to break their stride by stopping to listen to audio. They scan quickly,

ignore time-wasting distractions, and move on to the next website if nothing in the copy interests them.

2. While it's true that the human voice adds a personal touch and has the power to influence people, there also exists the probable reality that if the voice, the content, or the delivery of the audio message is less than ideal, people might get the wrong impression of you (and your product or service) or form an image of you that you don't wish to project. I've seen marketers with compelling website copy destroy their chances of making sales by installing audio that made website visitors not want to do business with them. People are easily turned off by a wide variety of vocal nuances of which we are unaware, including, but not limited to, accent, diction, inflection, and aggressiveness or timidity.

3. Audio messages, especially those that play automatically the moment visitors arrive at a website, tend to cause mental confusion because the prospects don't know whether to listen to the audio or read the copy. Since they can't listen and read at the same time, neither the web copy nor the audio makes the full impact on them that you would like them to have. When website visitors are bombarded with multiple messages simultaneously, the Zeigarnik effect kicks in (see Chapter 5); they tend to tune out and choose neither to read nor to listen at all, but instead click away.

4. It's a known fact that most people do not buy a product or service the first time they're presented with the sales message or marketing communication or the first time they visit your website. Sales usually happen after your repeated attempts to get prospects to revisit your website, take a closer look at your offer, and seriously consider buying. If most of your sales message (your sales letter, your testimonials, etc.) was delivered in audio, it is not likely that prospects will listen to your audio message(s) again, especially if they've already listened to it (or them) before. Furthermore, if they did listen to your audio message before and

found some compelling gems in it that are likely to make them buy now, when they do come back to your sales message a second time, third time, or beyond, they won't be able to easily zero in on those compelling gems unless they listen to the audio again and try to find them in the unsearchable medium that is audio. When your web copy is delivered via the written word, your prospects can be exposed to your entire sales presentation again; they have the option to skip to desired sections (and even use the search function) to get to it instead of clicking the Play and Fast Forward buttons to find what they're looking for.

5. While it may be true that some people are better listeners than readers, their particular learning style doesn't necessarily translate into a preference for audio over the written word when it comes to consuming marketing messages on the Web. Many other factors come into play, not the least of which is time. Most people online are busy and time-strapped, and that makes them want to get their information as fast as possible. Since they generally can skim through a lot more written information than they could by listening to an audio recording in the same amount of time, they would most likely choose to read rather than listen—even if they happen to be better listeners than readers.

6. There exists an array of circumstances wherein information delivered via audio isn't possible, let alone ideal. All circumstances that require Internet surfers to turn down their speakers or take the sound out altogether would naturally negate any benefits of having audio—for example, using the Internet at a quiet workplace or one that doesn't allow non-work-related sound, at night when users are within hearing distance of sleeping/working/studying spouses/roommates/partners, and times when users don't want others to hear what they're up to. These restrictions alone significantly reduce the percentage of people who can listen to your audio messages. Additionally, some audio files can take time to download, and this

can cause people to click on the web browser's Stop button to terminate the download and move on to other web content that is more convenient to consume.

The advantages and disadvantages listed here are far from exhaustive, but they do allow us to conclude that audio can be turned into a marketing advantage on the Web when used in the right way and under the right circumstances.

The most important guideline to bear in mind is that audio should generally be used as an option rather than a stand-alone vehicle for sales messages and marketing communications. For example, if you have a welcome message or sales pitch that you'd like to deliver via audio, don't let it play immediately upon a visitor's arrival at your site. Whenever possible, give your website visitors the choice of listening to your audio message or not, instead of just delivering it to them intrusively. Your website copy should not simply use the words "Click here to hear a Personal Message from [*Your Name/ Title/Company*]," however. That doesn't give them sufficient incentive to listen—it is like asking a TV viewer to switch channels to listen to your sales pitch. You need to give them a compelling reason why they should take the time to listen—how they will benefit, what they will learn, what's in it for them. If your message is short, it might also be a good idea to provide them with the approximate length of the audio so they can make an informed decision.

Want to find out how you, too, can have a 3-day workweek? Click the Play button below to listen to a 45-second message from Celine Stewart, CEO, MyVirtualAssistants.com

 Click Here Now! ▶ ❙❙ ◼

If you plan to offer your website visitors the option of either reading your copy or listening to the entire sales letter via audio, you could write copy as follows:

Want to make this website talk?
If you'd rather listen than read the contents of this
webpage, click on the Play button below.

In the preceding example, it is not necessary to include the length of the video, because if it is longer than the time visitors want to spend on your website they might be discouraged from listening to the audio and tempted to skip reading your web copy altogether.

If you're featuring audio testimonials on your website, don't make the mistake that so many website owners make, which is to display a picture of the testimonial giver(s) or the people giving the product endorsement, their name(s), and a quote taken from the audio testimonial—or sometimes no quote at all.

If you present your audio testimonial as shown in Figure 10.4,

John and Mary Smith – Bend, Oregon

"This has made a big difference in our lives!"

Figure 10.4 Audio testimonial with picture and quote.

chances are that your website visitors won't play the audio because you've given them no good reason to do so. Remember, they're probably just scanning your webpage, not reading it word for word, and they won't break their stride unless you give them sufficient reason to click. I recommend that you display an excerpt of the audio testimonial right next to the audio buttons and picture (if any)— preferably the most praise-filled quote that the testimonial giver said about your product or service. (See Figure 10.5.) Then give website visitors the opportunity to click on the Play button if they want to hear the testimonial in its entirety. When you do it this way, website visitors who are just scanning your website will see the praises people have given your product or service, even if they didn't have the time or inclination to listen to the audio.

When it comes to using audio on your website, remember that every time website visitors listen to audio, you run the risk of having them pry themselves loose from your sales process. To a certain extent, you could lose control of the sales process because your prospects could go into a slightly different frame of mind while listening to the audio component. And to the extent that audio successfully supports the sales flow or takes your prospects' focus away or even turns them off, your sales process could either advance or

"We saved our home from foreclosure – and saved

our marriage, too!

"We'd be homeless and divorced today if it weren't for the amazing

book, *How to Survive Foreclosure – or Avoid It Altogether!*"

-- **John & Mary Smith**, Bend, Oregon

▶ ❚❚ ■   ←Click the Play Button to read entire story.

Figure 10.5 Audio testimonial with excerpt.

come to a screeching halt. Internet surfers need only the slightest provocation for them to leave your website in favor of other websites. Their attention is fragile and can be shattered by factors like poor sound quality, vocal tone, or something seemingly inconsequential like the way a word is mispronounced. That's why it's the job of a skillful web copywriter to tighten the reins on prospects and direct their actions toward the desired response.

Always remember that if you're using audio to present any aspect of marketing, general web copywriting principles and rules still apply. Just because audio is a different medium of delivery doesn't mean you have the liberty to express yourself in an unfocused, uncompelling manner. If your prospects opt to listen to your audio, you must show that you respect their time and use it to state your case quickly.

Thus, what is said on audio should be scripted with as much care and skill as you would use to write web copy. Even though you're working from a script, you should also make sure that the delivery doesn't sound scripted. Very few things turn a listener off more than to hear audio delivered by someone who's obviously reading from a prewritten script. If you're using audio to give your website visitors an audio glimpse of who you are with the objective of creating instant rapport and making them feel that they know you, which ideally will make them want to do business with you, proceed with caution. If you have a great speaking voice, one that projects the kind of image you want your listeners to have of you or your company, and you can deliver the script with ease, then go ahead and do so. But if you have a voice that does not command attention or respect, or you have an accent, regional diction, or any other vocal peculiarities that might alienate people, consider hiring a voice-over professional to record your script. It would be better for people not to hear your real voice than to hear it and decide they don't want to do business with you. This happens more often than one might think.

If you consider that the average amount of time an Internet surfer stays on your website is eight seconds, you'll find you've wasted all the time you're given on a welcome audio that does not advance the sale. Just as you shouldn't waste the prime selling space of your website (the first screen) with unnecessary words of welcome, neither should you waste the first audio contact with pleasantries that make someone click away from your website before you've even had the chance to present your offer. I prefer the term *Welcome audio* to *Introductory audio,* and it should either (1) present what the website promises to deliver—that is, the solution to the prospect's problem, pain, or predicament; (2) incite curiosity about your product or service so as to cause the person to read the copy; or (3) cause the person to perform a specific activity, such as fill out an opt-in form to receive an e-course, report, or other freebie. Unless your product or service is one that sells itself after a brief description or cyber bite, don't attempt to do premature selling in the Welcome audio.

Whenever possible, use the Trifecta Neuro-Affective Principle (see Chapter 6) to plant cyber bites in your script. These go a long way toward changing your prospects' minds in favor of your product or service and maximize the probability that your prospects will believe your product or service is the right fit for them and that they should look no further.

If you're presenting an audio message, whenever possible offer your prospects the option to read the text version (or transcript) of the message as well. That way, you make your message accessible to those who prefer to read rather than listen or to those who are unable to listen because they're in environments where they're unable to do so.

Enhanced user experience is an important consideration when you offer audio or text versions of your marketing messages, or both. More important, however, when you enable your prospects to consume your marketing message in the way that's most comfortable for them, or in the way that has the greatest impact on them, it makes them more likely to consider buying the product or service you offer.

11

Last but Not Least
Tying It All Together

Nothing in the world can take the place of persistence. Talent will not. Nothing is more common than unsuccessful men with talent. Genius will not; unrewarded genius is almost a proverb. Education will not; the world is full of educated derelicts. Persistence and determination alone are omnipotent. The slogan "Press on" has solved and always will solve the problems of the human race.
—Calvin Coolidge

Success in any endeavor, particularly in selling, is part ambition, part observation, and part determination. Writing web copy that sells is no different. As with any discipline, some people who practice the principles discussed in this book will fail to meet their sales objectives. Barring unrealistic expectations, I wish to offer solutions that will prevent that from happening. This chapter examines tracking and testing, troubleshoots web copy that is not generating sales, and presents a four-step process to web copywriting success.

TRACK IT, FIX IT: WHAT TO DO WHEN WEB COPY IS *NOT* WORKING
▼

When I was creating offline copywriting, I learned one lesson I'll never forget. Do you remember those infomercials advertising contour pillows? In the original infomercials, the advertisers highlighted what they thought were the pillow's top two benefits: that they help you sleep better and that they make you more comfortable while you sleep.

When the pillows didn't sell too well, the advertisers phoned 100 actual buyers and asked them why they had purchased the pillows. Over half bought because of neck pain, the other half because of sleeplessness or because their spouse snored—benefits not even mentioned in the infomercial.

Based on these findings, they rewrote the pillow offer. Since 52 percent bought because of severe neck pain, the alleviation of neck pain became the lead benefit. Sales multiplied by more than ten times. Comfort Sleeper, the company that manufactures the pillows for Walmart and the largest retail foam manufacturer in the United States, reported that sales in the stores went up 1,000 percent. The packaging for the entire industry changed to emphasize these benefits, and, as a result, a dormant product became a hot item overnight.

The advertiser also phoned people who didn't purchase (those who called the order line but decided not to order) or who returned the pillows. Those who did not purchase were confused by certain things said in the infomercial, and they had objections or questions that weren't answered to their satisfaction. Those who returned them said the pillows made their neck hurt more.

Consequently, the ad company further refined the infomercial to remove the confusion and answer objections. Comfort Sleeper also put a note inside the package sent to pillow customers that forewarned them that their neck might hurt during the first few days of using the pillow because the neck was still adjusting to the contour, but that they could look forward to comfort after that (which was the truth). As a result, sales soared again, and this time returns were greatly reduced.

It all boils down to knowing your audience. Sometimes copywriters think they know their audience well, but, in actuality, they don't. In the case of the contour pillows, the ads overlooked key problems, pains, and predicaments (the three Ps) of their customers (neck pain, sleeplessness, and snoring spouses). Not until the phone survey provided feedback did the ad copy get it right.

Similarly, copywriters can guess what the target audience's hot buttons are, but if we don't know why people are buying the product or service, we won't know how to rewrite the copy if it isn't pulling in sales.

If you are the web copywriter hired to write the copy for a flat fee, you may not care much about this, except that you might not get repeat business. If, however, you're a web copywriter who is getting a percentage of the sales or an Internet marketer who writes web copy for your own products and services, this will matter a great deal.

Surveying customers is so much simpler on the Internet. You no longer have to phone 100 people. All you need do is send a well-designed e-mail to those who bought the product and ask the following questions:

- ▶ "What are the reasons you bought this product or service, or what motivated you to buy?"
- ▶ "Can you list the top benefits of the product or service that convinced you to act?" Alternatively, you may prefer to list the main benefits and say, "Here are a few of the benefits of our product or service. Please rank them in order of importance."

When the copy I wrote for a diet pill website didn't pull as well as I expected, I used these questions in a minisurvey that I created for free at www.freeonlinesurveys.com, which then added a link in my e-mails to purchasers of the pills. All the customers had to do was click on the link and a pop-up appeared, which enabled them to answer and submit their answers in a matter of seconds. Therefore, I was able to do my research easily (and at zero cost) and make the necessary changes to the copy based on the survey findings.

For those who don't buy but have left their contact information and for those who return the product they bought, try asking the following questions:

▶ "Why didn't you buy?"

▶ "What, if anything, was confusing about the offer?"

▶ "Why did you return the product?"

When you survey your customers, you often discover that the top benefit is something you buried somewhere in the middle of your web copy. Based on this information, you can restructure it accordingly. One of my clients, who sells a program that teaches people how to start their own promotional products (advertising specialties) business, used this headline on his website:

How to Get Your Share of the $18 Billion
Promotional Products Industry

When it didn't pull, we surveyed those who bought the program and learned that the main reason they bought was because they wanted to find the factories that manufacture the promotional products. We rewrote the headline to read:

Start a lucrative promotional products profit center or
distributorship easily with . . .

The Ultimate Resource for Finding Promotional
Product Factory Sources

The new headline boosted response by 23 percent, without changing a single word of the body copy. We would not have had those incremental sales had we not bothered to query the customers. The bottom line is that you must be willing to do what it takes to accomplish your objectives.

Another way to find out what people's opinions are about your product or service is doing a search on Google or other search engines to see what is being said about it in relevant forums, newsgroups, or blogs. A client of mine who markets a health book that discusses the merits of a natural oxygenating substance "eavesdropped" on the conversation threads in popular health forums and blogs. She found out that people had the mistaken notion that the book was about Miracle Mineral Solution (MMS), sodium dichloroacetate (DCA) or ozonated water, which it wasn't. She also found out that people had many unanswered questions that made them skeptical and kept them from buying her book. I suggested the addition of a prominently positioned Frequently Asked Questions (FAQs) section on her website to address all the objections people had voiced in the forums and blogs. This effectively quadrupled her sales even while her website traffic remained constant.

FOUR STEPS TO WEB COPYWRITING SUCCESS

▼

I learned a foolproof secret to success in any undertaking, and I've applied it to web copywriting, as follows:

> *Step 1: Understand exactly what you want your web copy to accomplish.* In other words, define your objective, but this time be more specific. If you can, quantify the results you want to get. It could be to convert 10 percent or more of your web visitors into customers, or to sell ten books per day, or to

generate $1,000 in sales per day. Write down exactly what you want to accomplish.

Step 2: Take action to fulfill your objective. This includes writing the best possible web copy and marketing communications and getting traffic to your website (using linking strategies, search engine optimization, a revenue-sharing [affiliate] program, pay-per-click search engine advertising, online video, or any other traffic-generating methods).

Step 3: Observe what's working and what isn't working. Track and test your results continually. Do more of what's working, and eliminate what's not working (including, but not limited to, key elements of your web copy).

Step 4: Keep adjusting your actions. Do this until you accomplish your desired objective.

When you do these four things, you'll never be without options. You'll never sit there and say, "Why does it work for others and not for me?" Probably the most important step is Step 3, "Observe what's working and what isn't working." That is how I developed my own unique model of web copywriting, and I did it through tracking and testing.

On the Internet, you have to be tracking results and testing continually. I'm fortunate to have come from a web copywriting environment in which we tested everything. We tested e-mail subject lines; we tested whether personalizing the subject line was better than not personalizing the subject line. We tested lead-ins, dissonance elements, and various formats of newsletters. We tested web copy headlines, web designs, sites with pictures, and those with no pictures. We even tested different prices, offers, guarantees, closes, and bullet points. You name it—we tested it.

However, as I mentioned earlier, things change so rapidly on the Internet that I cannot confidently say that what worked six months ago still works as effectively today. Search engines change their algorithms constantly, spam filters and pop-up blockers are becoming ever vigilant, and acceptable business practices on the Internet are being altered by regulations and sanctions. That's why nothing beats the practice of constant testing and tracking to obtain your own marketing intelligence for your particular audience.

The kinds of things you discover when you track and test are astounding, and they affect the profitability of the website not just for the here and now, but also for the long term. Testing and tracking are so fundamental in direct-response marketing that they are a given; yet most people on the web don't test anything. They write the web copy once, they launch the product or service, and when it doesn't pull, they wonder why. They don't realize that tracking and testing can significantly boost the sales of a website.

The concepts of tracking and testing would require another book to explain thoroughly, but here are some fundamental concepts that will help you get started.

Track Your Results

We've discussed a number of marketing methods, including writing a free report or promotional article and disseminating it in newsletters and e-zines, ads in e-zines, online classified ads, pay-per-click advertising, a great SIG file that your affiliates use every time they send out e-mail, and so on. Let's assume that this month you did all of these things and you received a decent number of orders. What do you do next month? Repeat all of the same things again, right? Wrong!

You find out which things worked and which didn't so that you can repeat more of what worked and none of what didn't. If, for instance, you determine that your free report that ran in an e-zine last month accounted for 93 percent of your sales and the online classified ads did not produce a single sale, then you would contact more e-zine and newsletter publishers to run your free report and you'd cancel your online classified ads.

The thing to remember is that it isn't you who decides what works, no matter how many years of experience you have in marketing, nor is it you who determines the best-performing headline, offer, guarantee, or price. Nothing works until the tests prove it works.

Marketing great Ted Nicholas, who reportedly spent over $500,000 testing and tracking copy elements, asserts that simply by changing the headline you can increase the pulling power of a direct-response ad by 1,700 percent, even when the rest of the ad is identical! The only way to learn this is through testing.

Let's say you are running an ad that's pulling a 2 percent click-to-sale conversion rate. You figure that since 2 percent is a decent response rate, you're earning a net profit of $1,000, and your advertising cost is $500, you can't complain. "Why, that's a 100 percent return on my investment," you say to yourself. But what if you discover, through testing, that another one of your ads pulls a 4 percent response rate, you're earning a net profit of $2,000, and, since your advertising is a fixed cost of $500 that means you increased the return on your investment from $500 to $1,500, or from 100 percent to 300 percent!

Online, many programs and scripts are available that enable you to test and track results. For instance, rotator scripts allow you to track the clicks and sales generated by two or more different versions of copy.

Ad-tracking software or services allow you to test and track results without hassles. In a nutshell, here's how these services work: A redirection URL is assigned to each campaign you run, which allows you to count actions such as clicks, sales, and sign-ups to your newsletter or opt-in offer. It allows you to view detailed information and analysis for each campaign: for example, how your Google AdWords pay-per-click campaign is doing, how your ad in the Yahoo! classifieds is doing, how that free report that you're giving away via autoresponder is doing, and so on.

In addition to these basic tracking functions, a tracking service allows you to evaluate all your visitors' click trails so that you can

▶ Know exactly what trail buyers take, and, as a result, streamline your site to get all visitors to follow that proven linear path

- ▶ See what paths nonbuyers take and eliminate the bottlenecks and roadblocks at your site
- ▶ See what visitors who subscribe to your newsletter or opt into your lead generation system really do on your site
- ▶ See which traffic sources create the most sales—or no sales—so you know where to focus your efforts

For those of you who have newsletters or e-zines or who run e-mail marketing campaigns, there are also good direct e-mail marketing services that enable you to easily track and test the results of your e-mail marketing. For example, you can find out who opened your e-mail message, who clicked on which link, what they looked at on your website, how long they stayed on your site, whether they bought something, which item(s) they bought, how much they spent, and who they are, based on demographic and registration data.

Here are four e-mail services that track and test results:

www.emaillabs.com

www.constantcontact.com

www.iContact.com

www.bronto.com

TRAFFIC GENERATION: GETTING THE WORD OUT AND THE VISITORS IN ▼

A website with killer copy but no traffic is like a beautiful store filled with desirable merchandise located in the boondocks—people will never find it. What good are killer copy, opt-in offers, autoresponders that convert website visitors into customers, and all the tracking devices in the world if no one stops by to visit?

Throughout this book, we've focused on the traffic conversion part of the Internet marketing equation, but we can't leave the subject without touching briefly on the traffic generation part of the equation.

The topic of traffic generation is vast, and it would require another volume to do it justice. Therefore, I've limited my discussion to a few strategies that have been effective in my own experience.

Search Engine Positioning

Whenever the subject of traffic generation is discussed, invariably search engine positioning comes up. Some Internet experts contend that an estimated 86 percent of the average website's traffic comes from search engines. No discussion of traffic generation would be complete without the topic of search engine positioning.

I've spent more than 12 years in Internet marketing, and I've learned that a do-it-yourself strategy for getting top search engine rankings is a major undertaking that is best left in the hands of professional search engine positioning and optimization experts. Seeking high search engine rankings in all the major search engines is a complex undertaking that requires diligence and attention because the search engines use different algorithms to rank pages. Even if you succeed in satisfying all the algorithms, those algorithms change constantly, which means if you get the advice that tells you to have your target keyword appear no more than 12 times on your home page, that advice is probably obsolete by the time you hear it. The search engines are always five steps ahead of everyone.

For this reason, I leave search engine positioning to professionals who specialize in that field. Trying to maintain a high search engine ranking is a time-consuming endeavor and requires constant maintenance, so I do what I'm good at and let search engine professionals do what they're good at.

The Internet abounds with search engine professionals who can guarantee that your website listing will appear in the top 10, top 20, or top 30 organic search results in the major search engines under specific keywords or phrases. Do a search on any search engine for the keywords *search engine optimization* or *search engine ranking* and you'll find hundreds, if not thousands, of professionals who can improve the ranking of your website, thereby increasing your website traffic. They don't all have the same way of obtaining high search engine rankings, however. Some specialize in securing one-way links from high-page-rank websites to your site, some specialize in getting links to your website placed in popular blogs, some obtain a large number of inbound links to your site, and so forth. Keep in mind that just because they're able to get high search engine rankings for you doesn't necessarily mean your website will get a lot of traffic. It depends on how compellingly your search engine listing compares with others among the search results and whether people will click through to your website—and in what frame of mind.

The recent online video revolution has opened up a great and relatively low-cost opportunity to gain high search engine rankings in as little as one day. (See the section of the previous chapter titled "Marketing via Online Videos.")

Pay-per-Click Search Engines

Pay-per-click search engines are those that allow you to pay for placement or ranking with them. This is an effective way to attract inexpensive, targeted traffic to your website because you pay only for visitors who actually click through to your website. Google AdWords is the leader of the pack when it comes to pay-per-click search engines As an advertiser, you bid on keywords you predict your target market will use as search terms when they are looking for a product or service like yours. The pay-per-click search engines have different sets of guidelines for writing ads and different algorithms for determining your ad's position among the pay-per-click search results. Google AdWords, for instance, rewards your ad with a high (i.e., more visible) rank if your ad is performing—that is, your ad has a good click-through rate (CTR)—because it considers high-CTR ads more relevant to the people who are searching under those particular keywords.

In the end though, it doesn't matter whether you're ranked number one in the pay-per-click search results or not because if your listing is not compelling, no one will click. AdWords allows you to create your own listing, so when you design it, make sure you follow the guidelines for writing online ads while at the same time abiding by the rules of AdWords (or any other pay-per-click search engine). With a well-constructed listing, you can at least be assured that you will get a good percentage of click-throughs to your website.

Caveat emptor: Do not—I repeat, *do not*—bid to have a high ranking if you do not have killer copy on your website backing you up. All the clicks in the world are worth nothing if your web copy doesn't convert those visitors into customers.

Google AdWords is the top pay-per-click search engine, followed in popularity by Yahoo! Search Marketing (formerly Overture) and MSN adCenter. There are several hundred pay-per-click search engines out there, and if you want to know who they are, as well as get tips and strategies about using pay-per-click search engines, go to www.payperclicksearchengines.com.

Most marketers resort to guesswork when attempting to determine which keywords to use in optimizing their websites for maximum search engine findability or for pay-per-click advertising purposes. Many make the mistake of vying for the most popular and competitive keywords and phrases (also called *short tail keywords*). While it might seem desirable to get a top search engine ranking for highly searched keywords such as *golf* (if you sell a golf-related product or service), *natural cures* (if you sell natural health products), or *weight loss* (if you sell a weight loss product or service), it is a difficult undertaking. Furthermore, even if you did manage to nab a high ranking in those search terms, chances are, the people who typed those terms into a search engine are not looking for the product or service you offer. It's always more advisable to target less-competitive niche markets rather than the highly competitive keywords. An example of a long tail keyword phrase is *small business web design* versus its short tail counterpart *web design*. Another is *weight loss plans for teens* rather than *weight loss*. Online searches have become more specific in recent years; as of the fourth quarter of 2007 the average query on Google consisted of four words, whereas previously three-word searches were the norm. That means surfers are getting more specific in their searches. Landing a high search engine ranking on a long tail keyword may result in less traffic than landing a short tail, but there's much less competition and, therefore, it's much easier to dominate the search engine rankings for those keywords. There are also a lot more long tail keywords to choose from, and dominating a small handful of them has the possibility of bringing more traffic to your website than a single short tail keyword because the search terms are more specific. Two of the resources that I use to find long tail keywords and niche phrases are Hexatracker (www.hexatracker.com) and http://freekeywords. wordtracker.com, the latter of which even displays the number of searches made on each keyword suggestion.

Linking Strategies

Another way to get top rankings in the search engines—without really trying—is by getting other websites to link to your website. The algorithms of the search engines take the number of websites linking to your website into consideration when ranking you. The more websites that link to you, and the higher the page rank of those websites, the higher your search engine ranking will be.

One of the top Internet marketing websites is Ralph Wilson's website, www.Wilsonweb.com, a site that consistently ranks very high on the search engines under frequently searched and extremely competitive keywords such as *web marketing*. Ralph Wilson is one of my business acquaintances, so a couple of years ago I asked him how he achieved such high search engine rankings. He said he just provides solid, bona fide content and gets other websites to link to his website. Last time I checked, Wilsonweb.com had 10,300 websites linked to it. It's no wonder, then, that search engines rank Wilson web.com high in their search results.

The more websites linking to your website, the higher your search engine ranking. Even more important, when you get those websites to link to your site, it will be exposed to all the web visitors of all those websites that link to you, and that means more web traffic and more sales. The key is to get websites with high traffic to link to you. If you get dozens of high-traffic websites funneling their traffic to yours, you'll be amazed how much traffic you can get. Once you get a link from a website, the link will probably stay up forever, paying you dividends in terms of traffic for weeks, months, and years to come.

Of course, websites won't be inclined to link to your site if all you have on it is copy that reeks of advertising, which is yet another reason to aim for an editorial style of writing crafted with hidden selling.

How to Get Websites to Link to Your Site. There's a long, tedious way of doing it, and there's an easy, painless way. I'll tell you about the long, tedious way first so that you'll really appreciate the easy, painless way that I will show you.

The long, tedious way is to scour the web looking for websites that are most likely to link to yours. You'd use a search engine and type in a keyword or phrase that would yield websites that are similar to or related to your website. For example, if you have a website that sells widgets, you'd search for websites catering to widget users, the widget industry, and so on.

When you get your search results, you'll have to scroll through the hundreds, even thousands, of websites and click through to them one by one to find the contact information or the e-mail address of someone to whom you can send your linking proposal. Then you have to type an e-mail to every e-mail address you find, cross your fingers, and hope that after spending countless hours doing this, some of them will say, yes, they'll link to your site.

The easy and painless way is to use a service like LinkMetro (Advanced) that automates the entire link-building process for you. LinkMetro has a network of 19,489 (and counting) websites that are actively looking to exchange links with other websites. In the standard version of LinkMetro, you need to choose websites from LinkMetro's directory and manually add their links to your site, then contact the websites to let them know you've done that so that they can also add your link to their website. The advanced version eliminates the manual adding of links, and all you need do is select websites you want to exchange links with, select the category on your links page that you want to add them to, and click Submit. This makes the process lightning fast.

Traffic to my website, WebCopywritingUniversity.com, significantly increased within two weeks of using LinkMetro's Advanced service. My website's Google page rank went from 3 to 4 that same month, and sales of my Web Copywriting Mastery Course quadrupled in the first two months as a result.

E-Zines and Newsletters

If you've been involved in Internet marketing for any length of time, you've probably heard it said that, dollar for dollar, the best marketing promotion you can do is to run ads in other people's e-zines and newsletters with the same target audience as yours. Even better is to write compelling promotional articles or free reports and offer them as content to websites, newsletters, and e-zines. We've already discussed how to write these articles and reports.

Type the keywords *directory of e-zines* or *e-zine directory* on any search engine, and you'll find resources that list e-zines and online publications in which you can advertise or submit content.

To give you an idea of how powerful an article or report is in generating sales, I once wrote an article on behalf of Joe Sugarman to promote his book entitled *Triggers*. The article told the story of Joe, who almost flunked English and yet went on to become one of the most successful copywriters in the world. A total of 244 website owners posted the article on their websites, and because the article has a resource box at the bottom pointing to the sales page where

Joe's book is sold online, those websites were a viral machine feeding visitors and generating book sales day and night for the past seven years. The interesting part is that articles like that, which have a long shelf life and timeless appeal, could easily be recycled and plugged into the social dynamics of Web 2.0 and probably generate dramatically more buzz and sales. (See Chapter 10.)

Two Degrees of Separation

I'm certain you're familiar with the concept of six degrees of separation, which refers to the idea that if a person is one step (or degree) away from every person he or she knows and two steps away from every person who is known by any of the people he or she knows, then every person is an average of six steps away from any other person on the planet. On the Internet, especially since the advent of Web 2.0 social media, there's an average of two degrees of separation between you and any person on earth—or maybe less. Think about it. If you wanted to establish a connection with any person you can think of, and you're a member of MySpace (which has 242 million members), Facebook (100 million), or LinkedIn (24 million)—or *all* of them—chances are, at least one of those members already knows the person with whom you want to connect. And there's a high probability that the person with whom you want to connect is already on MySpace, Facebook, or LinkedIn, which means you're one step away from that person!

But again, that kind of easy accessibility means nothing unless you know how to communicate on the Web in a way that will get you heard amid those billions of online conversations that are going on at any given time. Only skillful web copywriting will distinguish you from the ocean of sameness and enable you to capture the attention and devotion of those you want to connect with—be they prospects, customers, or possible friends, lovers, or business partners. This brings to mind again the words of author Sidney J. Harris: "The two words 'information' and 'communication' are often used interchangeably, but they signify quite different things. Information is giving out; communication is getting through." I assure you that the principles I've covered in this book will enable you to get through.

Ultimately, the current dynamics of Web 2.0 will cause online entrepreneurs and business enterprises to become better and more honest marketers and motivate companies to develop quality products and services. That's because the online buying population is relying more and more on blogs and social media to get feedback regarding products or services they're considering buying. A simple search on Google for a product's name, for instance, will most likely pull up blog entries—good or bad—about that product. Search engines often crawl blogs, especially if their content is regularly updated. When consumers view blog comments and other entries posted on social networking sites, they are able to obtain a more balanced assessment of your product or service than merely relying on the information you give them at your website, which is obviously skewed in your favor. Good comments travel fast on the Web nowadays, but bad ones travel even faster, able to circle the globe in a matter of minutes. Therefore, if a company's product, service, or way of doing business is substandard or downright unscrupulous, that company won't be able to stay in business for long because its online reputation, thanks to Web 2.0, will be jeopardized, if not completely destroyed by social networks.

I estimate that the majority of Internet users go to search engines to see what other people have said about a product or service they're considering buying before they actually make their buying decision. That's true whether they're buying a software program, an air purifier, a skin care product, a weight loss program, a course, a book, or a widget. In fact, even when buying products or patronizing service businesses in the brick-and-mortar world, people generally rely on reviews of people online before making their buying decisions—whether they're buying a car, thinking of patronizing a local restaurant, choosing videos, or considering that new gadget or gizmo they saw on an infomercial. For a great many people, the Internet has become one gigantic consumer reporting machine, and with the workings of Web 2.0, even more so.

Web 2.0 will also reward those marketers who take the time to learn how to navigate its new terrain and who learn how to communicate effectively within its unique social dynamics. It will also prosper those who make it a priority to serve the best interests of people rather than being the modern counterpart of snake oil salesmen who gave salespeople and marketers a bad name. And one day we'll all learn that marketing is not about viewing people as website visitors, eyeballs, prospects, customers, or means to our own selfish ends—but as human beings who crave emotional connection . . . just as we ourselves do.

Index

success
    components of, 285
    modeling, 31–32, 43
Sugarman, Joe, 12, 154, 299–300
surveys
    for customer feedback, 287–289
    as involvement device, 136
SurviveYourForeclosure.com, 60
syntax, 149, 152, 153, 154

Tailrank, 250
target audience. *See also* customers; sales
        prospects
    for blog posts, 260–261
    in business-to-business marketing, 235–236,
        239–240
    feedback from, 67, 140, 301–302
    focus on, 63
    frame of mind of, 110–112, 124, 125, 129,
        131–133, 137, 146
    headlines tailored to, 16, 22
    identifying, 34, 54
    problem solving for, 35–36, 40
    product/service offer and, 62
    reports written for, 223
    reputation with, 139
    sales propositions tailored to, 177–178,
        286–289
    subject lines tailored to, 122–123
    for video, 263, 265
    web copy tailored to, 14, 205–206, 255–256
Techmeme, 256
Technorati, 242
Tested Advertising Methods (Caples), 80
testimonials
    audio, 275, 280–281
    as bonus ideas, 28
    to build credibility, 50–51, 63
    effectiveness of, 63–69
    sales quotient and, 101
    in web copy, 15, 23, 26
THC method, 186–187, 268
third-party opt-in lists, 142–143
Thomas, Lorne, 185–187, 268
three Ps, 35, 167
thumbnail representations of video, 268–269

traffic conversion
    via opt-in offer, 214
    rate of, 19, 106, 246–247, 292
    web copywriting and, 104
traffic generation
    via blogs, 256, 257, 258
    in e-mail marketing, 106
    importance of, 17
    mechanisms for, 104, 290, 294–300
    via newsletters/e-zines, 224
    via search engines, 196, 294–295
    via videos, 260, 263, 267, 269–271, 274
Traffic Geyser, 272
Trifecta Neuro-Affective Principle
    application of, 183–188
    in audio messages, 283
    in blogs, 248
    components of, 180
    definition of, 173
    examples using, 180–183, 189–191
    five-step blueprint and, 43
    function of, 2, 171, 177
    for short web copy, 97, 192–197
    in videos, 265, 268
Triggers (Sugarman), 299
trust
    audio use and, 275–276
    customer service and, 20
    e-mail marketing and, 109, 110–112
Tube Mogul, 272
Twitter.com, 255

UltimateCareerGuide.com, 167
uniform resource locator (URL)
    placement in videos, 260, 268–269, 270
    redirection, 292
unique selling proposition (USP), 37, 51, 59–61,
        101, 194, 195, 197
unsubscribing from mailing list, 143
user-generated content
    for videos, 260, 265–266
    for websites, 242

video. *See also* YouTube
    creating, 264, 265–268, 274
    for customer registration, 77